Indigenous Peoples and the State

Across the globe, there are numerous examples of treaties, compacts, or other negotiated agreements that mediate relationships between Indigenous peoples and states or settler communities. Perhaps the best known of these, New Zealand's Treaty of Waitangi is a living, and historically rich, illustration of this type of negotiated agreement, and both the symmetries and asymmetries of Indigenous-State relations. This collection refreshes the scholarly and public discourse relating to the Treaty of Waitangi and makes a significant contribution to the international discussion of Indigenous-State relations and reconciliation. The essays in this collection explore the diversity of meanings that have been ascribed to Indigenous-State compacts, such as the Treaty, by different interpretive communities. As such, they enable and illuminate a more dynamic conversation about their meanings and applications, as well as their critical role in processes of reconciliation and transitional justice today. With contributions from historical, legal, political, and indigenous perspectives, that speak to one another across and between traditional disciplinary boundaries, this is a book that promises to generate new conversations about the complexity of Indigenous-State relations.

Mark Hickford, Pro Vice-Chancellor and Dean of Law, Victoria University of Wellington.

Carwyn Jones, Senior Lecturer, Faculty of Law, Victoria University of Wellington.

Indigenous Peoples and the Law

Series editors:

Dr Mark A. Harris
University of British Columbia, Canada

Professor Denise Ferreira da Silva
University of British Columbia, Canada

Dr Claire Charters
University of Auckland, New Zealand

Dr Glen Coulthard
University of British Columbia, Canada

For information about the series and details of previous and forthcoming titles, see https://routledge.com/law/series/INDPPL

The Law Foundation NEWZEALAND

SUPPORTING INDEPENDENT LEGAL THINKING.

The book editors thank the Law Foundation for their assistance in the writing of this book.

A GlassHouse book

Indigenous Peoples and the State

International Perspectives on the Treaty of Waitangi

Edited by Mark Hickford and Carwyn Jones

Routledge
Taylor & Francis Group
LONDON AND NEW YORK

First published 2019 by Routledge

2 Park Square, Milton Park, Abingdon, Oxfordshire OX14 4RN
52 Vanderbilt Avenue, New York, NY 10017

Routledge is an imprint of the Taylor & Francis Group, an informa business

First issued in paperback 2019

British Library Cataloguing-in-Publication Data
A catalogue record for this book is available from the British Library

Library of Congress Cataloging-in-Publication Data
Names: Hickford, Mark, author. | Jones, Carwyn, 1976– author.
Title: Indigenous peoples and the state : international perspectives on the Treaty of Waitangi / Mark Hickford and Carwyn Jones.
Description: Abingdon, Oxon [UK] ; New York, NY : Routledge, 2018. | Series: Indigenous peoples and the law | Includes bibliographical references and index.
Identifiers: LCCN 2018010914 | ISBN 9780815375258 (hardback)
Subjects: LCSH: Treaty of Waitangi (1840 February 6) | Maori (New Zealand people)—Legal status, laws, etc. | Maori (New Zealand people)—Government relations. | Maori (New Zealand people)—Politics and government.
Classification: LCC KUQ353.3 1840 .H53 2018 | DDC 342.9308/72—dc23
LC record available at https://lccn.loc.gov/2018010914

ISBN: 978-0-8153-7525-8 (hbk)
ISBN: 978-0-367-89544-0 (pbk)

Typeset in Galliard
by Apex CoVantage, LLC

Contents

Contributors

Bain Attwood is a professor of History at Monash University. He is the author of several monographs, including *The Making of the Aborigines* (Allen & Unwin, 1989), *Rights for Aborigines* (Allen & Unwin, 2003), *Telling the Truth about Aboriginal History* (Allen & Unwin, 2005), and *Possession: Batman's Treaty and the Matter of History* (Melbourne University Press, 2009), and numerous articles in journals such as the *History Workshop Journal*, the *Journal of Imperial and Commonwealth History*, and the *Journal of Legal History*.

Saliha Belmessous is an associate professor of History at the University of New South Wales. She specialises in European colonial ideologies and the imperial experiences of Indigenous peoples. She is the author of *Assimilation and Empire* (2013), and the editor of *Native Claims* (2012) and *Empire by Treaty* (2015), all published by Oxford University Press.

John Borrows BA, MA, JD, LLM (Toronto), PhD (Osgoode Hall Law School), LLD (Hons, Dalhousie & Law Society of Upper Canada), FRSC, is the Canada Research Chair in Indigenous Law at the University of Victoria Law School in British Columbia. His publications include *Recovering Canada: The Resurgence of Indigenous Law* (Donald Smiley Award for the best book in Canadian Political Science, 2002), *Canada's Indigenous Constitution* (Canadian Law and Society Best Book Award, 2011), *Drawing Out Law: A Spirit's Guide* (2010), *Freedom and Indigenous Constitutionalism* (Donald Smiley Award for the best book in Canadian Political Science, 2016), and *The Right Relationship* (with Michael Coyle, ed.), all from the University of Toronto Press. John is Anishinaabe/Ojibway and a member of the Chippewa of the Nawash First Nation in Ontario, Canada.

Natalie Coates LLM (Harvard), BA (hons), LLB (hons) (University of Otago) is a lecturer at the University of Auckland. Natalie is also a consultant at Kahui Legal, a specialist law firm dealing with issues relating to Māori.

Mark Hickford is Pro Vice-Chancellor and Dean of Law at Victoria University of Wellington. Prior to assuming that role in May 2015, he was advisor to the Prime Minister in the Policy Advisory Group of the Department of the Prime Minister and Cabinet, based in the executive wing. Trained as both a lawyer and historian, he has specialised in Indigenous–State relations, natural resources law, and public law in legal and public policy practice, as well as in his scholarship.

Rawinia Higgins (Tūhoe), is the Deputy Vice-Chancellor (Māori) at Victoria University of Wellington. Previous to this, she was the Professor and Head of School of Te Kawa a Māui, School of Māori Studies. She is a member of the Waitangi Tribunal and has served on a number of Boards, including Te Kotahi a Tūhoe and Tūhoe Fisheries Charitable Trust Board.

Carwyn Jones (Ngāti Kahungunu) is a senior lecturer in the Faculty of Law at Victoria University of Wellington. He is the author of *New Treaty, New Tradition – Reconciling New Zealand and Māori Law* (University of British Columbia Press, 2016) and is the co-editor of the *Māori Law Review*.

Jacinta Ruru (Raukawa, Ngāti Ranginui) is Professor of Law at the University of Otago, Co-Director of Ngā Pae o te Māramatanga New Zealand's Centre of Māori Research Excellence, and a fellow of the Royal Society Te Apārangi. She has published extensively including as co-author of Discovering Indigenous Lands (Oxford University Press, 2010).

Māmari Stephens (Te Rarawa, Ngāti Pākehā) is a senior lecturer at the Faculty of Law at Victoria University of Wellington. She founded the Legal Māori Project (www.legalmaori.net), and her primary research interests are law and language, Māori and the New Zealand legal system, New Zealand legal history and jurisprudence, as well as welfare law. Māmari is married to Maynard Gilgen, has three children, and is an associate minister in the Anglican church.

David V Williams is a Professor of Law at the University of Auckland. He has been engaged with Treaty of Waitangi issues since 1974 as a political activist in the Citizens' Association for Racial Equality (CARE), as an academic, an independent researcher commissioned by numbers of Māori claimant groups, counsel in one Waitangi Tribunal hearing, and a public intellectual offering comments to news media.

Introduction

Carwyn Jones and Mark Hickford

Indigenous–State treaties and the rights of Indigenous peoples

Across the globe, there are examples of treaties, compacts, or other negotiated agreements that mediate relationships between Indigenous peoples and States or settler communities. The Treaty of Waitangi is one living, and historically rich, illustration of these types of negotiated agreements and both the symmetries and asymmetries of Indigenous–State relations across time.

There is a Māori proverb "*Kimihia te kahurangi; ki te piko tōu mātenga, ki te maunga teitei*," which translates as "Seek above all that which is of highest value; if you bow your head, let it be to the highest mountain." The proverb exhorts one to aim for the worthiest of goals and not to be deterred by anything of lesser importance. These high aspirations are to be borne in mind as we continue to give meaning to the compacts between Indigenous peoples and States. The essays in this collection explore the diversity of meanings that have been ascribed to one such Indigenous–State compact, the Treaty of Waitangi, by different interpretive communities. The objective of the collection is to enable and illuminate a more dynamic conversation about the meanings and applications of these sorts of compacts, with the Treaty of Waitangi representing a striking example of how such compacts became critical to processes of reconciliation and transitional justice today. The collection is interdisciplinary, with contributions from historical, legal, political, and Indigenous perspectives that speak to one another across and between traditional disciplinary boundaries. Contributors include both established and emerging scholars, and together, they generate new conversations about Indigenous–State relations.

I. *Te Tiriti o Waitangi* – the Treaty of Waitangi

The Treaty of Waitangi was signed in 1840 by Māori leaders representing their nations/communities and representatives of the British Crown. It was initially signed at Waitangi, and subsequently, copies were signed by Māori leaders in other parts of the country. Not all Māori nations signed the Treaty, and not all were offered the opportunity to do so. The Treaty has three brief written articles and a preamble,[1] and it is written in both English and Māori, which has contributed to significant debate over the meaning of the Treaty. The central exchange in the Treaty is the grant of governmental authority from Māori to the British Crown in return for guarantees of Māori rights. In the English text, the authority that is granted to the Crown is expressed as a cession of sovereignty. However, the Māori text uses the concept of '*kawanatanga*' (government), and the Waitangi Tribunal, a standing commission of inquiry originally established in 1975 to hear Māori claims, has determined that the leaders who signed at Waitangi in 1840 did not cede sovereignty by entering into this agreement. In part, that determination was based on the guarantees made to Māori in the Treaty, in particular, in the Māori text, the guarantee of '*tino rangatiratanga*' (chiefly authority) over all '*taonga*' (those things which are highly valued). The Māori text here is more broadly drafted than the English text, which specifically guarantees 'undisturbed possession' of lands and other natural resources. Both texts include an equal citizenship provision granting Māori "all the rights and privileges of British subjects". In a constitutional sense, the Treaty, therefore, provided for public power to be shared between Māori nations and the Crown, although, as Matthew Palmer has noted, the precise terms on which that power was to be shared were not expressly detailed in the Treaty document.[2]

Today, the Māori population is approximately 600,000, or 15 per cent of the total New Zealand population, and the Treaty of Waitangi is recognised as one aspect of the unwritten constitution of Aotearoa New Zealand.[3] The Treaty has not been recognised as being independently, directly enforceable in the domestic courts. However, a number of pieces of legislation incorporate the 'principles of the Treaty', and the Treaty can be relevant to judicial review of executive action.[4] The Waitangi Tribunal, although primarily limited to making non-binding recommendations to the Crown, provides a forum where claims based on breaches of the principles of the Treaty can be brought for inquiry and report. In the 1990s, the New Zealand Government developed a systematic process for the settlement of claims of historical Treaty breaches. Since that time, settlements have been agreed with many Māori communities across the country. These settlement packages include Crown acknowledgements of Treaty breaches and apologies for those breaches, commercial redress (often cash or properties), and cultural redress (including innovative co-governance and co-management arrangements in respect of natural resources and specific sites).[5] This type of negotiated accommodation or recognition of Māori rights is a distinctive characteristic of the Treaty of Waitangi framework in Aotearoa New Zealand, as illustrated in this collection.

II. The United Nations Declaration on the Rights of Indigenous Peoples

Compacts between Indigenous peoples and States, such as the Treaty of Waitangi, also sit against the backdrop of the international recognition of the rights of Indigenous peoples. Today, a central part of that international framework is the United Nations Declaration on the Rights of Indigenous Peoples (UNDRIP).

Despite the fact that UNDRIP does not take the form of a convention, with binding legal obligations on parties, it nevertheless has the potential to be a genuinely transformative instrument in terms of relationships between Indigenous peoples and States.[6] There are important recent indications that States are beginning to consider more seriously the implementation of UNDRIP.[7]

Treaties and agreements between Indigenous peoples and States are explicitly recognised in UNDRIP. Article 37 of UNDRIP states:[8]

> Indigenous peoples have the right to the recognition, observance and enforcement of treaties, agreements and other constructive arrangements concluded with States or their successors and to have States honour and respect such treaties, agreements and other constructive arrangements.

The UNDRIP's preamble also notes that Indigenous–State compacts, such as the Treaty of Waitangi, "are the basis for a strengthened partnership between indigenous peoples and States".[9]

In the New Zealand context, human rights bodies have recognised the close connection between the Treaty of Waitangi and UNDRIP. In announcing New Zealand's endorsement of UNDRIP in 2010, then Minister for Māori Affairs, Pita Sharples, drew explicit connections between the Treaty of Waitangi and UNDRIP.[10] The New Zealand Human Rights Commission describes the Treaty of Waitangi and UNDRIP as being "strongly aligned and mutually consistent", noting that, therefore, "[t]he Declaration assists with the interpretation and application of the Treaty principles."[11] The Waitangi Tribunal has noted that UNDRIP represents an internationally agreed statement of Indigenous rights and, as such, is relevant to the interpretation and application of the principles of the Treaty of Waitangi.[12] In its report on the Māori Community Development Act, the Waitangi Tribunal explicitly identifies the alignment between particular articles of UNDRIP and recognised Treaty principles.[13]

III. Overview

This collection of essays was developed from a symposium that was held in Wellington in February 2016 on the theme of interpreting the Treaty of Waitangi over 175 years, hosted by the New Zealand Centre for Public Law and supported by the New Zealand Law Foundation and the Ministry for Culture and Heritage. The intention of the symposium was to explore various legal, historical, political, philosophical, and policy dimensions of 'interpreting the Treaty of Waitangi' through time. Leading Canadian, Australian, and New Zealand scholars were invited to address the broad theme of interpreting the Treaty within that frame, the idea being to analyse the Treaty as an example of an Indigenous–State compact and the subject of interpretation in context and the various interpretative communities that have participated in interpreting it.

Alongside the contributors to this collection, Kirsty Gover, Ned Fletcher, and Michael Belgrave also presented papers at the symposium. In addition, we were fortunate to have others attend the symposium and contribute to the discussion, including Justice Joe Williams, Claire Charters, Damen Ward, and Paul Diamond. We would like to acknowledge all these people for their participation in the symposium and their thoughtful engagement in the conversation which has helped to shape the essays collected in this volume. We would also like to thank Madeleine Collinge for her assistance in preparing the manuscript and the team at Routledge for helping to bring this collection to print.

The essays in this collection provide an important platform for re-examining an Indigenous–State compact such as the Treaty of Waitangi and its relationship to imagining legal–political communities. Indigenous and non-Indigenous scholars bring new voices and scholarship to this discussion, wrestling with older accounts and making sense of the new directions evidenced by policy developments and transitional justice processes. The essays have the potential to significantly reframe the discussion of the Treaty of Waitangi and its application to issues of law, policy, and identity. The Indigenous–State relationship embodied in the Treaty is of importance not only to lawyers, judges, policy-makers, and those engaged with the machinery of government, but is relevant also to all New Zealanders in terms of public memory and identity. We hope that this collection will help to re-invigorate the scholarly and public discussion relating to the Treaty of Waitangi and its meaning, and contribute to the international discourse on Indigenous–State compacts.

One of the central aims of this collection is to situate the discussion of the Treaty of Waitangi within an international context, exploring the dynamics of the particular treaty relationship to illustrate important aspects of the nature of compacts between Indigenous peoples and States, the meaning ascribed to such compacts by interpretive communities, and the implications for understanding Indigenous–State relationships more broadly. This collection, therefore, sits against a background of existing scholarship that addresses Indigenous–State relationships,[14] building on this scholarship and examining key themes through the lens of the relationship between Indigenous peoples and the State in Aotearoa New Zealand.

This book is divided into three parts. Part I examines the foundations of relationships between Indigenous peoples and States as mediated by treaties and principles of constitutional interpretation.

In Chapter 1, Carwyn Jones focuses attention on the role of Indigenous constitutional traditions in giving meaning to treaties between Indigenous peoples and States. Jones explains that such treaties sit within the constitutional and legal systems of each of the treaty parties and suggests that the appropriate interpretive frame for these agreements is to be derived from both Indigenous and State constitutional traditions. Jones identifies key principles that can be drawn from the Māori constitutional tradition and considers the ways in which those principles frame the interpretation of the Treaty of Waitangi as a Māori legal instrument. Fundamentally, Jones contends that “the Treaty should be seen as one component of an ongoing and developing relationship between distinct constitutional traditions.” This suggests an interpretive approach to the Treaty of Waitangi that is predicated on the creation of spaces for continuing interaction between Māori and State constitutional traditions.

John Borrows, in Chapter 2, further problematises interpretive approaches which ignore the complexities of the different sources of authority that underpin treaties between Indigenous peoples and States. Drawing analogies between law and religion, Borrows uses the concept of 'treaty metaphysics' and teleological questions to tease out the features of treaty interpretation in Canada and Aotearoa New Zealand. Borrows describes the way in which law creates its own 'origin stories', which, if not properly recognised, can conceal the nature and sources of legal authority. Borrows notes, "Law's exile of moral, philosophical, and religious insight about the nature of its own meaning-making metaphysics sustains a dangerous lack of self-reflexivity." In the context of treaty interpretation, this lack of self-reflexivity and transparency constrains the ability to challenge the assumption of the supremacy of State law and the applicability of State law's interpretive processes. However, Borrows suggests that the work of treaty interpretation is best undertaken with more deliberate attention to the fundamental principles that structure the interpretive process and free it from unquestioned assumptions about the priority of either State or Indigenous law.

In Chapter 3, David V Williams draws on Borrows' perspective on constitutional discourse in Canada, particularly as it applies to Indigenous rights, to reassess the constitutional canon in Aotearoa New Zealand. Williams challenges the assumption that the doctrine of *terra nullius* never applied in New Zealand, identifying that both the foundational cases of *R v Symonds* (1847) and *Wi Parata v Bishop of Wellington* (1877) determined, as Williams notes, "the Crown held underlying or radical title to all land in New Zealand from 1840." Williams goes on to point out that "This is very similar to the reasoning now embraced by the Canadian courts, as in *Tsilhqot'in Nation*, on the origins of the doctrine of aboriginal title." Williams suggests that not only does this approach ignore Māori understandings of land and constitutional authority, but it also obscures the meaning of the English text intended by its drafters. Williams contends that greater attention to the intention of the English text of the Treaty might suggest that it is consistent with the Māori text insofar as it supports the ongoing application of Māori law.

Part II of the book considers meaning that has been given to the Treaty of Waitangi over and through time. The chapters in this part grapple with providing historical contexts and perspectives to the dynamic legal relationships between Indigenous peoples and States that are often framed by instruments such as the Treaty of Waitangi.

In Chapter 4, Saliha Belmessous contextualises the Treaty of Waitangi by locating it within a framework of European expansion and treaty-making with non-European populations. In particular, Belmessous examines the colonial practices of the British Empire in the nineteenth century. Significantly, Belmessous identifies that there was not a single, uniform view among the political class of nineteenth-century Britain as to how Indigenous rights ought to be addressed. Belmessous notes that treaty-making practices were consequently very dependent on each treaty's particular circumstances and objectives, pointing out that although treaties, conceptually, appear to be deployed as a non-violent means of imperial expansion, they often remained linked to colonial coercion, force, and war. Belmessous considers the place of the Treaty of Waitangi against this background and how that particular treaty was perceived outside of New Zealand. Belmessous concludes that contextual studies assist us to give meaning to treaties such as the Treaty of Waitangi, commenting that "[i]f we seek to examine the continuing value of colonial treaties that still have a bearing on their post-colonial societies, we need to understand their past, that is, the various contexts in which they were concluded."

In Chapter 5, Bain Attwood argues for developing post-foundational histories of the Treaty of Waitangi. Attwood contends that a significant amount of historical work done on the Treaty could be described as 'foundational history' in which "historians try to discern in a particular historical event, in this case the Treaty of Waitangi, some norm or another that they believe created, or should have created, or could still create, the foundations of the nation." However, Attwood contends that understanding of the Treaty would be assisted by undertaking a post-foundational approach, which

> historicises the past in such a way that it unsettles any notion of the past being comprised of self-same essences over time and instead reveals that forms of knowledge are contingent and therefore unstable as they are constructed by historical processes and relationships, especially relationships of power.

In Chapter 6, Jacinta Ruru surveys the recent history of Treaty of Waitangi jurisprudence, particularly examining the way in which Treaty interests have been addressed in cases relating to water under the Resource Management Act 1991. The issues relating to water provide a powerful case study, in part because of the fundamental importance of water to the life of all communities. As Ruru notes, Māori water rights have also been central to some of the most innovative co-management/co-governance regimes that have developed through the Treaty of Waitangi settlement process, such as the settlements in relation to the Te Arawa Lakes, the Waikato River, and Te Awa Tupua (the Whanganui River system). However, Ruru argues, judicial decisions relating to water use and management under the Resource Management Act appear to be still rooted in colonial assumptions and are failing to deliver on the potential provided by the Treaty of Waitangi.

Part III of this book turns to examine the diverse sites of Indigenous–State relationships and the role of instruments such as the Treaty of Waitangi in framing those relationships into the future.

In Chapter 7, Rawinia Higgins provides a perspective on the Treaty of Waitangi from her own community, the Tūhoe nation. Tūhoe has a complex relationship with both the Treaty of Waitangi and the Crown. Tūhoe never signed the Treaty of Waitangi and have always asserted their *mana motuhake* (self-determination/self-government). Tūhoe have nevertheless used the Treaty of

Waitangi framework to achieve a negotiated redress package to settle their historical claims against the Crown and to establish a platform to further advance their *mana motuhake*. Higgins explores the relationship between the Treaty of Waitangi and Tūhoe expressions of their autonomy, reflecting on Tūhoe's history of interactions with the Crown and their journey through the settlement of their historical claims. Higgins illustrates the challenges of creating governance and co-governance structures that appropriately reflect *te mana motuhake* of Tūhoe (Tūhoe self-determination). However, these challenges are responded to with innovation and determination to realise that autonomy, that *mana motuhake*, which remains fundamental to the lives and identity of the people of Tūhoe.

In Chapter 8, Mark Hickford reflects on the ways in which interpretive communities engage with the Treaty of Waitangi as a feature of a historical-political constitution. Hickford considers the meaning of the Treaty in the context of a range of activity that constructs constitutional relationships between Māori nations and the Crown. In this chapter, Hickford contends "that the Treaty of Waitangi ought to be seen as a set of texts – English and Māori – instantiating contested and contestable, negotiated and negotiating communities of practice and interpretation." Hickford is careful to pay attention to the varied and contingent nature of meaning attributed to the Treaty. The result is an account which draws on the contested and negotiated life of the Treaty of Waitangi to create space for pluralist understandings of interaction between legal systems and sources of authority. This chapter describes an approach to 'legal association' that is grounded in the distinctive histories of Aotearoa New Zealand, yet also speaks to the experiences of Indigenous–State relations in other parts of the world.

Natalie Coates explores, in Chapter 9, the future contexts in which the Treaty of Waitangi may be further interpreted and given meaning. In particular, Coates examines the settlement of historical claims that are based on breaches of the Treaty of Waitangi and suggests ways in which these settlements might affect understanding of the Treaty. Coates identifies the range of relationship instruments that are common features of Treaty settlements and notes that these instruments establish new and ongoing relationships between settling groups and government agencies. This has the potential to transform the Māori–Crown relationship and will undoubtedly have implications for how the Treaty relationship is understood. Coates also considers some of the key issues that are on the horizon for Māori communities and suggests that the traditional collectivism of Māori society will be an important dimension of how those issues are addressed within the context of a re-shaped Treaty relationship.

In the final chapter in this collection, Māmari Stephens looks forward to the bicentenary of the signing of the Treaty of Waitangi in 2040. Stephens frames this chapter with 'an instrumental question', in essence asking, what is the best mechanism for giving effect to the relationship and recognising the rights for which the Treaty of Waitangi provides? Stephens draws together strands of the political, constitutional, legal, academic, and public discussions of the Treaty of Waitangi to examine the ways in which we might try to answer that question. Constitutional issues, never far from discussion of the Treaty, remain central to the path to 2040 that Stephens outlines. However, this is perhaps not the same kind of constitutionalism that we have seen in the past. The kind of constitutionalism that Stephens articulates is one that includes Māori constitutional principles at its core, that is grounded in the lived realities of individuals, institutions, and communities of Aotearoa New Zealand. And it is a constitutionalism that takes for granted the place of the Treaty of Waitangi and looks to how the Treaty's various interpretive communities might give shape to the Treaty partnership as we approach its 200th year.

Across the essays in this collection, three interconnected themes tend to emerge or come to the fore, relevant to Indigenous–State relations in a variety of colonial settlement jurisdictions. First, a number of the contributors, whether directly or obliquely, address the ongoing question of 'hinge propositions', as James Tully refers to them, specifically the contestable assumptions that the introduced political–legal regime's claim to exclusive jurisdiction is both efficacious and legitimate; and, second, that no other viable or plausible alternatives are available.[15] There is another complication implicated in these claims, and one which scholars such as Noel Pearson are alive to as well; that is, those assumptions underlying the colonial framing are everywhere or effectively endemic and always speaking. Questions invariably emerge – or at least ought to – as to how well-adapted discourses centred upon a Treaty compact (or comparable instrument) admitting the presence of colonial actors is to problematising an imperial-colonial framing, perhaps radically critiquing and challenging it. To varying degrees, these questions and complexities lurk within the chapters of Māmari Stephens, Mark Hickford, and Rawinia Higgins, although the methodological stances might differ, such as with Stephens adumbrating an indigenous legal analytical approach and Hickford assuming one that is informed by contested histories. As well explored in the earlier work of Ranginui Walker and Andrew Sharp, the Treaty compact in 1840 has enjoyed a late twentieth-century resurgence as a centrepiece in legal–political vocabularies coursing through policies on Indigenous–State reconciliation, as well as in modalities of 'legitimacy' and 'justice'-talk.[16] There is a live question as to whether one can and should endeavour to 'get outside of this' solipsistic colonial omnipresence, this everywhere, to look upon it, to radically criticise it, or at least refine and modify it over time so that, step by step, it becomes something different (this is observed as a focal point in Hickford's chapter, but it also seems implicit, if we are reading them correctly, in a range of the other essays such as those of Coates, Jones, Ruru, and Stephens). Higgins's essay concerning Tūhoe perspectives on the Treaty of Waitangi is an important cautionary analysis as to the contingent place of a treaty with strangers in circumstances where it is the ancestral communities cleaving to Tūhoetanga in which spiritual and practical political authority resides.

A second recurring theme is the role that history or histories might play. Here, some of the essays offer cautions (expressly at least in Attwood's and in Hickford's) – the care to avoid originalist or foundational histories predicated on a treaty are brought to the fore in these pieces, although the functional legal–political significance of the Treaty of Waitangi is certainly recognised.

Contrastingly, David Williams is consciously wishing to deploy history as a resource for jurisprudential development and legal interventions but that crashes into observations above quite quickly in a variety of ways. For instance, can the colonists' courts decolonise? What would that look like in terms of institutional, discursive and behavioural change? Is not the real effect of reciting so-called originalist interpretive understandings of a treaty merely to replicate at least aspects of a colonial framework that accompanied the negotiations in 1840 and to do some form of violence to the histories as lived with all their imperfections and frailties? Does not a foundational version comfort the colonial projects through setting out palliative and palatable accommodations of indigenous authority? These sorts of inquiry get us back into contested matters of institutional transformation across time and other constitutional issues, which we are not certain legal scholars are well cut out to address. Indeed, Stephens and Hickford raise points about this, again from differing intellectual inheritances, but the vital point made in this collection is to be acutely conscious of these contexts – to be aware, in short, of what one is purporting to do in recovering histories. To that end, a number of the insights developed by contributors to the edited collection *Histories, Power and Loss: Uses of the Past – A New Zealand Commentary* remain apposite.[17] A treaty-centred history or set of histories, while performatively useful in the twenty-first century, can nevertheless obscure the significance, indeed centrality, of *hapū* (tribes) and other indigenous polities in time.

The foregoing also raises difficult questions around how we think about legitimacy and what counts as legitimate in thought and action in jurisdictions where the *demos* (the politically relevant population) is considered relevant to governance. These are big questions lurking in a range of jurisdictions, including Canada, Australia, the United States, and a host of communities engaging with difference. None of the chapters can resolve these issues. If anything, they present the incomplete, work-in-progress nature of these challenging points.

Notes

1 The Treaty agreement is often said to also include an oral agreement, sometimes described as the 'fourth article', which protects religious freedom. See C. Orange *The Treaty of Waitangi* (2nd ed, Bridget Williams Books, Wellington, 2011) at 58.

2 See M. Palmer *The Treaty of Waitangi in New Zealand's Law and Constitution* (Victoria University Press, Wellington, 2008).

3 See Cabinet Office *Cabinet Manuel 2017* at 1 https://www.dpmc.govt.nz/our-business-units/cabinet-office/supporting-work-cabinet/cabinet-manual.

4 See, for example, State Owned Enterprises Act 1986, s 9; *New Zealand Māori Council v Attorney-General* [1987] 1 NZLR 641.

5 See Office of Treaty Settlements *Ka tika ā muri, ka tika ā mua – Healing the Past, Building a Future: A Guide to Treaty of Waitangi Claims and Negotiations With the Crown* (2nd ed., Ministry of Justice: Office of Treaty Settlements, Wellington, 2002). See also, Te Urewera Act 2014 and Te Awa Tupua (Whanganui River Claims Settlement) Act 2017.

6 See S. Lightfoot *Global Indigenous Politics: A Subtle Revolution* (Routledge, Oxford, 2016); C. Charters "The Legitimacy of the UN Declaration on the Rights of Indigenous Peoples" in C. Charters and R. Stavenhagen (eds) *Making*

the Declaration Work: The United Nations Declaration on the Rights of Indigenous Peoples (International Work Group for Indigenous Affairs, Copenhagen, 2009) at 280.

7 See, for example, the establishment by the Government of Canada in 2017 of a Ministerial Working Group to review all relevant federal laws, policies, and operational practices to help ensure the Crown is meeting its obligations to Indigenous peoples by, among other things, adhering to UNDRIP.

8 UNDRIP, art 37.

9 UNDRIP, Preamble.

10 Pita Sharples "Statement to the United Nations Permanent Forum on Indigenous Issues" 19 April 2010.

11 New Zealand Human Rights Commission "The Rights of Indigenous Peoples: What You Need to Know" <www.hrc.co.nz/files/5814/5618/4456/NZHR_Booklet_12_WEB.pdf>.

12 Waitangi Tribunal *Whaia Te Mana Motuhake – In Pursuit of Mana Motuhake: Report on the Māori Community Development Act Claim* (Wai 2417, 2014) at 55.

13 At 56–63.

14 See, for example, Saliha Belmessous (ed) *Native Claims: Indigenous Law Against Empire, 1500–1920* (Oxford University Press, New York, NY, 2011); Federico Lenzerini (ed) *Reparations for Indigenous People: International and Comparative Perspectives* (Oxford University Press, New York, NY, 2009); Laura Benton and Richard Ross (eds) *Legal Pluralism and Empires, 1500–1850* (New York University Press, New York, NY, 2013), which provide broad geographical and historical coverage of specific dimensions of Indigenous–State relationships; and Lisa Ford and Tim Rowse (eds) *Between Indigenous and Settler Governance* (Routledge, Oxford and New York, NY, 2013) also draw out themes from multiple jurisdictions to examine the ways in which Indigenous peoples and settler States have interacted.

15 Refer to James Tully *Public Philosophy in a New Key: Volume I – Democracy and Civic Freedom* (Cambridge University Press, Cambridge, 2008) at 276–277.

16 Ranginui Walker *Ka Whawhai Tonu Motu; Struggle Without End* (Penguin, Auckland, 2004); Andrew Sharp *Justice and the Māori: The Philosophy and Practice of Māori Claims in New Zealand Since the 1970s* (2nd ed, Oxford University Press, Auckland, 1997).

17 Andrew Sharp and Paul McHugh (eds) *Histories, Power and Loss: Uses of the Past – A New Zealand Commentary* (Bridget Williams Books, Wellington, 2001).

Part I

Foundations of Indigenous–State relationships

1 Māori and State visions of law and peace

Carwyn Jones

The legal interpretation of te Tiriti o Waitangi has, at least in recent years, been dominated by a Western law, and in particular, a common law approach to understanding a treaty of this nature. Māori perspectives have, of course, been taken into account, but the interpretive approach has nonetheless been framed by State institutions – the courts, the Waitangi Tribunal, Parliament, and the executive branch of government. This chapter aims to sketch out a different kind of legal interpretation of te Tiriti – one that considers te Tiriti as a Māori legal mechanism, which protects Māori rights, sourced in Māori legal traditions. The Waitangi Tribunal's 2014 report *He Whakaputanga me te Tiriti – The Declaration and the Treaty* provides a thorough analysis of Māori perspectives of te Tiriti in the North in 1840.[1] This analysis is a useful foundation for a Māori law analysis, but the Tribunal necessarily remains focused on defining Treaty principles in accordance with its statute and the existing constitutional traditions of the New Zealand state.

The assertion of Crown sovereignty over New Zealand did not arrive in a landscape devoid of constitutional thought and practice. A Māori constitutional tradition was already in operation, revolving around a set of key underlying values and principles. These principles, discussed in more detail later in this chapter, are the drivers of Māori constitutional and legal traditions and give rise to a diverse range of strategies in the development of Māori law and the institutions of Māori legal and constitutional systems. This is the context into which British constitutional and legal traditions arrived. It is also the context in which British officials engaged with Māori communities in the North around adopting some of the governmental apparatus of European states and making a formal statement of the collective sovereignty held by the chiefs. And it is the context in which the Treaty of Waitangi was signed and in which later contestations of sovereignty played out. Māori constitutional thought and practice is therefore an important part of the constitutional foundations of the modern New Zealand state. Although there has been significant discussion, debate, and scholarship about the validity and impact of the Treaty from the perspective of the common law and international law,[2] there has been very little discussion of how the Treaty fits within patterns of Māori constitutional thought and practice.

In this chapter, I first consider the importance of exploring the meaning of treaties such as the Treaty of Waitangi from the perspective of Indigenous constitutional traditions. Here, I draw particularly on Robert Williams study of treaties in the North American Encounter era, *Linking Arms Together – American Indian Treaty Visions of Law and Peace, 1600–1800.*[3] Williams's study identifies the role of treaties in establishing and maintaining relationships within the context of Indigenous constitutional traditions. This then provides the framework for my examination of the Treaty of Waitangi within the Māori constitutional tradition. In the second part of this chapter, I describe central principles from the Māori constitutional tradition and consider the ways in which these central principles give meaning to the Treaty of Waitangi within the context of the Māori constitutional tradition. Ultimately, understanding the Treaty of Waitangi in the context of Māori law suggests that the Treaty ought to be seen as an instrument that connects, rather than amalgamates, State and Māori visions of law and peace.[4]

I. Understanding the Indigenous context

The title of this chapter references the subtitle of Robert Williams's *Linking Arms Together*. Williams's work is important because it examines treaties and treaty-making as features of Indigenous diplomacy within Indigenous constitutional traditions.[5] This chapter adapts Williams's approach to the circumstances of Aotearoa, the Treaty of Waitangi and Māori visions of law and peace. Ultimately, Williams suggests that treaties can be understood as a means of connecting diverse communities with common aspirations. This forms links between distinct constitutional traditions but does not require an amalgamation of those traditions. Treaties provide bridges between those traditions but are premised on a continuing diversity of thought and practice of law and peace.

Later in this chapter, I outline some key strands of a Māori constitutional tradition that are crucial to understanding the Treaty of Waitangi as a Māori legal instrument, promoting Māori visions of law and peace. First, it is helpful to set out the framework for this analysis. This includes a description of the concept of constitutional traditions and an explanation of how this concept is deployed in this chapter. I also set out here some of the key strands of Robert Williams's work on Indigenous treaty-making that can contribute to shifting the conversation about the Treaty of Waitangi, its interpretation, and its application to New Zealand's law and constitution.

In this chapter, I use the term 'constitutional tradition' to describe the collection of rules, principles, and practices that shape the way in which public power is exercised within a political community.[6] Like all traditions, constitutional traditions carry core values of a community, but do not necessarily remain static and unchanging. Traditions can be understood as packages of information that transmit important messages across the community and across time, and they only survive as long as they are relevant to the community. In some instances, traditions may constrain the range of choices available to a community, but, in other cases, traditions may act as a 'legitimating agent' for ideas or developments which might not otherwise have any 'social resonance'.[7]

The Māori constitutional tradition can be found in the system of '*tikanga*'. *Tikanga* literally describes the right or correct way of doing things. It could also be interpreted as the just way of doing things. In essence, it reflects the appropriate way of behaving in the Māori world. *Tikanga* applies to all aspects of Māori life, from the everyday to the very pinnacle of human endeavour.[8] *Tikanga* includes the Māori legal system as well as incorporating knowledge, principles, and practices that apply to other social, political, and spiritual/religious activity. I outline some basic principles of this system of *tikanga* below and suggest ways in which the Treaty of Waitangi can be understood in the context of those principles. As a general proposition, the Māori constitutional tradition is shaped by the aspects of *tikanga* that speak to the exercise of public power and the relationships between the institutions of public power and the interaction between those institutions and members of the community.[9]

I should note that my reference to a single Māori constitutional tradition is not intended to suggest that Māori communities all operate under a uniform set of constitutional mechanisms. That is not the case. There is great diversity among Māori communities in their *tikanga*, including their constitutional practice. However, it is possible to identify the high-level dimensions of a constitutional tradition which guide the application of particular practices across Māori communities. This may be understood in the same way that countries such as Canada, Australia, New Zealand, and the United Kingdom each have distinct constitutional structures. Nonetheless, they can all be seen to come under the umbrella of a Westminster constitutional tradition. This guides and shapes the priorities and objectives of constitutional design and development in each of those jurisdictions, but they are applied to the particular circumstances and needs of each state.

In *Linking Arms Together*, Robert Williams explores the way in which treaties can be understood within Indigenous constitutional traditions.[10] Not only does this suggest a different way of interpreting and giving meaning to treaties than the approach derived from the Western tradition of international law, but it draws attention to the intention to connect and sustain distinctive constitutional communities.[11] Viewed in this way, treaties become instruments of connection and association, not assimilation or amalgamation.

One way in which the treaties examined by Williams can be understood is by approaching them as sacred texts.[12] Williams suggests that, for the Indigenous communities in his study "peace was a matter of achieving 'good thoughts' between different peoples according to a scared tradition prescribed long ago."[13] According to this view, treaties were sustained by a pre-existing sacred narrative and acted as the means of renewing and re-inscribing "the connections of peace and goodwill that had bound the different peoples of the world together since time immemorial".[14]

Understood in this way, treaties are not merely negotiated political settlements, but instead reflect higher purposes that the parties are bound to pursue. As discussed in greater detail below, the Māori constitutional tradition also constructs agreements as sacred covenants and the Treaty of Waitangi is clearly an agreement formed within the context of that constitutional tradition.

Williams also notes that the worldview of the Indigenous communities that he considers in his study inform their constitutional traditions and locate treaty agreements against a background of interconnected relationships.[15] Williams points to the way in which kin relationships provide an important frame of reference for these communities, and the way in which "the very meaning of a treaty relationship was contained in the language of a tribal life spoken through kinship terms, name-titles, and the performance of sacred ceremonies and gifting rituals."[16] The use of this language of relationships allows for visions of law and peace to be shared. As Williams notes, "[i]n a world of human diversity and conflict, connection to others was a prerequisite for survival."[17]

This constitutional tradition and worldview has rights and identity inherently bound up with relationships. This includes an important emphasis on kin relations, but also recognises the significance of the relationships between people and the natural world and the power of mechanisms, like treaties, that make new, enduring relationships possible.

One of the ways in which Native American nations sought to forge constructive relationships across different communities was by using various forms of storytelling. In fact, treaties themselves can be seen as a form of creating a story of relationship and mutual benefit between the parties.[18] Richard Delgado has noted that storytelling and narrative devices can be an "effective means of overcoming otherness, of forming a new collectivity based on a shared story".[19] In the context of Indigenous treaty-making, that meant telling "a special kind of story, a story that imagined a world of human solidarity achieved according to an American Indian treaty vision of law and peace".[20]

It is notable that these mechanisms were about making relationships between distinctive and diverse communities that might be able to be comprehended by each other's vision of law and peace. These are not mechanisms of assimilation, but rather co-existence, interaction, and interdependence. Diversity and difference are not necessarily obstacles to forming and maintaining valuable relationships. Again, there are parallels here from the Māori constitutional tradition applicable to the Treaty of Waitangi.

Williams also contends that treaties can be seen as part of the constitutional obligation for people to recognise their common humanity and so to engage in relationships on that basis. Williams identifies this obligation as evidenced by the "multicultural constitutionalism" of the Native American nations in his study:[21]

> [D]ifferent peoples in a relationship of close connection were expected to embrace the sacredly revealed truth of their shared humanity as a basis of normative action toward each other.

Agreements such as treaties are, therefore, just one component of the set of instruments that construct and maintain relationships across a broad network of interconnections. These instruments reinforce the basic obligation of peoples who are living together to strive to live under law and peace. At the heart of this worldview and these relationship instruments is the central element of trust.[22]

Williams's study of treaties in the North American Encounter era demonstrates the importance of considering treaties within the context of Indigenous constitutional traditions. Treaties between Indigenous peoples and colonising nations are not simply the legal instruments of the colonising states themselves. Treaties, by their very nature, reach across jurisdictions, across legal systems, and across constitutional traditions. It is, therefore, important when interpreting such treaties, to consider how they are given meaning within Indigenous constitutional traditions.[23] This requires an exploration that goes beyond simply identifying Indigenous understandings of particular terms or concepts, but necessitates an examination of how Indigenous constitutional traditions understand the kinds of relationships that are given effect in treaties with states. In the remainder of this chapter, I turn to consider the meaning of the Treaty of Waitangi in the context of the Māori constitutional tradition.

II. Key values of the Māori constitutional tradition

There are key values or principles that are central to the Māori constitutional tradition. I consider four such key principles in this chapter: ***whanaungatanga*** (the centrality of relationships), ***mana*** (spiritually sanctioned authority), ***tapu/noa*** (recognition of the spiritual dimension), and ***utu*** (reciprocity).

i) Whanaungatanga

Whanaungatanga can be understood, at a basic level, as 'relationships'. On a deeper level, the principle of *whanaungatanga* reflects the centrality of relationships within the Māori world-view. This principle exhorts individuals to always think carefully about one's place within a complex network of kin relations and the connections that link people to each other, to the gods, to lands, rivers, and mountains, and to all aspects of the natural world.

There are a number of implications of this emphasis on relationships. For example, it means that Māori legal and constitutional systems tend to emphasise the maintenance of relationships and foster mechanisms and processes that provide for this. Relationships are generally prioritised in decision-making and legal and constitutional practice. An individual's rights and obligations are always understood in the context of his or her network of relationships and are, effectively, defined by those relationships. This leads to legal and constitutional systems that are primarily collective in their orientation.[24]

At first blush, this might suggest a relatively rigid system of hereditary rights, but there is, in fact, a significant amount of flexibility built into this approach. Even though one's place within the network of relationships is fixed, there are always multiple relationships that need to be considered and there will be good reasons to prioritise particular ones over others in different situations. Furthermore, the principle of *whanaungatanga* allows one to draw other types of relationships into the kinship framework. As alluded to above, this extends to relationships with the gods and with the natural world. Viewing those relationships as kin relationships, encompassing all the rights and obligations that go along with kin relationships, influences the way in which people engage with the world around them.

Mead suggests that this is manifested in the obligations associated with *whanaungatanga*:[25]

> The whanaungatanga principle reached beyond actual whakapapa [genealogy] relationships and included relationships to non-kin persons who became like kin through shared experiences and to the ancestral house at the marae, because it is usually named after an ancestor. Although a high value is placed upon whanaungatanga and its obligations, the ideal is difficult to achieve. All *tikanga* are underpinned by the high value placed upon manaakitanga – nurturing relationships, looking after people, and being very careful about how others are treated.

Understanding the Treaty of Waitangi as a Māori legal instrument, framed by the Māori legal system, necessitates understanding the ways in which the Treaty engages the principle of *whanaungatanga*. How does the Treaty invoke this principle? How does the Treaty influence the application of *whanaungatanga*? And how does the principle of *whanaungantanga* frame the way in which the Treaty is to be read?

First, the principle of *whanaungatanga* has fundamental implications for the way in which rights and obligations and the exercise of political power operates in the Māori world. As noted above, there is an emphasis on collective rights and obligations, and the rights of individuals are always understood in relation to the rights of the wider kinship group. Anne Salmond has noted that a "world based on *whakapapa* and one based on individual rights were grounded upon very different assumptions about humanity and the relations between people and other forms of life – and thus, very different understandings of mutual rights and responsibilities."[26]

Whanaungatanga even influences the way in which one approaches the text and terms of the Treaty. The Māori world is understood as a vast system of relationships. This gives rise to a generally holistic outlook, where interconnectedness is assumed, and all phenomena are analysed within the context of their own particular network of connections. Within this framework, phenomena cannot be understood in isolation or by separating them from that network of connections. Evidence given in the Waitangi Tribunal illustrates how this affects the interpretation of the Treaty. Dame Joan Metge gave evidence that, within a Māori worldview, the Treaty ought to be understood as an "undivided whole".[27] This is also evident in Dr Patu Hohepa's response to written questions posed by Crown counsel in the inquiry:[28]

> While I have tried to answer the string of questions posed by the Crown in the way in which they were asked, I think it is important to highlight the concerns

> I have with the dissective way in which they seek to have Te Tiriti interpreted. Essentially these questions have separated out certain strands from the covenant in an effort to place them in conflict with each other. In this way, the exercise of tino rangatiratanga [sovereignty or self-determination] is conceptualised as separate and in opposition to the exercise of kawanatanga [government]. The Crown's search for conflict within the document negates its overall context which was the desire to create a relationship.

Of central importance is the way in which the principle of *whanaungatanga* facilitated diplomatic relations. The Māori who signed the Treaty at Waitangi were used to developing relationships across and between independent political communities, using the principle of *whanaungatanga* as the foundation for those relationships. The Waitangi Tribunal's report described the nature of these relationships as follows:[29]

> Though hapū [tribes] were autonomous, kinship ties with other hapū created mutual obligations. Related hapū had long traditions of meeting regularly and acting together as circumstances demanded. At times they shared resources, worked together in communal gardens, and formed alliances to fight alongside each other against people who were unrelated or more distantly related. To some of the claimants, it was this combination of hapū authority and autonomy, close kinship ties, and the ability to act in concert with others where that served hapū interests, that defined the Bay of Islands and Hokianga system of political authority.

The particular form of a written treaty may have been relatively novel for Māori in 1840, but the concept of establishing diplomatic relationships for mutual benefit was very familiar. *Whanaungatanga* would traditionally have provided the framework for these relationships and understanding the obligations that underpin them. Establishing such a relationship with an entity like the British Crown would necessarily have added a distinctive gloss to the agreement. The Crown did not have pre-existing kinship ties that could be drawn on. However, one of the fundamental aspects of the principle of *whanaungatanga* is the way in which it can be deployed to reach across *whakapapa* lines. The principle effectively demands that all relationships be seen through a kinship lens. Although the Treaty of Waitangi signalled a new type of relationship in its written form and in the nature of the parties involved, it nevertheless sat within a Māori legal tradition that structured rights and obligations around the principle of *whanaungatanga*.

Whanaungatanga shapes the way in which political authority and public power operate within the Māori world. The principle of mana is the central concept relating to the exercise of public power in Māori society. I discuss the concept of *mana* in more detail in the following section of this chapter. However, the concept of *mana* is itself understood within the framework of *whanaungatanga*, and *whanaungatanga* provides some important constraints and limitations on the exercise of public power. The importance of understanding the exercise of public power in this context is illustrated by claimant counsel in the Waitangi Tribunal's *He Whakaputanga me Te Tiriti* report:[30]

> Counsel have no submissions to make about the Crown's lengthy discussion of Blackstone on this legal point apart from submitting that it is irrelevant to Ngapuhi as they knew nothing of it. Their framework was mana and Rangatiratanga within the tribal structure.

In the same report, Moana Jackson describes the constraints that *whanaungatanga* imposes on the exercise of public power as follows:[31]

> (a) Firstly, the power was bound by law and could only be exercised in ways consistent with tikanga and thus the maintenance of relationships and responsibilities.
>
> (b) Secondly, the power was held by and for the people, that is, it was a taonga [treasure] handed down from the tipuna [ancestors] to be exercised by the living for the benefit of the mokopuna [descendants].
>
> The ramification of those prescriptions was that mana was absolutely inalienable. No matter how powerful rangatira [chiefs or people of high rank] might presume to be, they never possessed the authority nor had the right to subordinate the mana of the collective because to do so would have been to give away the whakapapa and the responsibilities bequeathed by the tipuna. The fact that there is no word in Te Reo Māori for 'cede' is not a linguistic shortcoming but an indication that to even contemplate giving away mana would have been legally impossible, politically untenable, and culturally incomprehensible.

ii) Mana

Mana is the central principle that sets the parameters of Māori leadership. *Te Mātāpunenga* describes *mana* as "A key philosophical concept combining notions of psychic and spiritual force and vitality, recognised authority, influence and prestige, and thus also power and the ability to control people and events".[32] Mead reflects the important role that the principle of *mana* plays within *tikanga* and Māori law, noting "Personal and group relationships are always mediated and guided by the high value placed upon mana."[33] Part of the reason that *mana* can be said to be a driving force within the Māori world is that one's *mana*, one's influence, prestige, and the ability to exercise authority is never fixed. Rather, *mana* is dynamic.

The dynamism of *mana* is related to the different sources of *mana*. *Mana* comes from the gods, one's ancestors, and one's own actions. Every person is born with *mana*. Mead has noted:[34]

> People of mana draw their prestige and power from their ancestors (mana tipuna). This power is socially founded upon the kinship group, the parents,

the whānau, hapū and iwi [tribal federation]. There is also a personal increment based on the proven works, skills and/or contributions to the group made over time by an individual that provide human authority (mana tangata). The element of psychic power relates also to whakapapa and connections with the Gods of the Māori world (mana Atua).

Eddie Taihakurei Durie has pointed out that, in this way, *mana* should be understood as being both ascribed and achieved:[35]

> Mana tupuna expressed the basic ideology that all things came from ancestors, land rights, status, authority, kinship, knowledge, ability, etc. Mana was usually presented as ascribed but ascription was usually retrospective to validate achievement ('he is brave, caring, etc for he is the descendant of so and so') so that in practice, mana was both ascribed and achieved.

The different strands of *mana* described above provide inherent limitations to the authority of *rangatira* or leaders. Māori politician Shane Jones has noted:[36]

> Inherent in the Māori conception of power is the notion that the agent who uses it in an unprincipled manner will lose it. Authority which is exercised beyond the value framework is not rangatiratanga.

'*Rangatiratanga*', the powers and authority of leaders, then can be seen to reflect the autonomy and self-determination of the community itself, rather than the absolute authority of an individual leader.[37] This captures both the grant of public power and the limitations that the exercise of such power is subject to within a Māori constitutional tradition.

There has been significant commentary on the way in which concepts relating to political authority are addressed in the Treaty of Waitangi. However, when examined through the lens of the Māori legal system, one thing becomes clear: whatever authority was granted to the British Crown by way of the Treaty, Māori did not give up their *mana*. As noted above, Māori political authority, expressed as *mana*, was embedded in a kinship framework. It is inextricably connected to the principle of *whanaungatanga* and sits within a network of relationships. This *mana* is, at least in part, inherited from the ancestors, and tied to the collective self-determination of a community. Salmond points out,

> No-one with any knowledge of Māori life in 1840 . . . would have asked the *rangatira* to surrender their *mana*, which came from the ancestors, and was not theirs to cede. Its loss would have meant death and disaster to themselves and their people.[38]

The Treaty does not refer to the concept of *mana*. Instead, the term *kawanatanga* is used as a translation of sovereignty, and is ceded to the British Crown in Article 1, while *tino rangatiratanga* is guaranteed in Article 2. Over the past

40 years, there has been significant scholarly historical and legal debate about the correct interpretation of these key terms in the Treaty.[39] There is no need to rehearse that debate here. My aim is not to examine whether *mana* would have been a more appropriate translation of sovereignty or to argue about the relative strength and scope of *kawanatanga* and *tino rangatiratanga*. Rather, I am interested in the overarching question: how does the principle of *mana* shape our understanding of the Treaty as a Māori legal instrument?

To understand how *mana* might frame the discussion of forms of political authority in the Treaty (sovereignty, *kawanatanga*, and *tino rangatiratanga*), it is instructive to consider the way in which political authority had previously been addressed by the chiefs in the 1835 Declaration of Independence – *He Whakaputanga o te Rangatiratanga o Nu Tireni*. The Waitangi Tribunal directly addressed the relationship between the Declaration/*He Whakaputanga* and the Treaty of Waitangi. One aspect that was drawn out in the Waitangi Tribunal inquiry related to the nature of authority that would be exercised collectively by the chiefs. In the Declaration/*He Whakaputanga*, Māori leaders agreed to meet annually in congress to pass laws for the good government of the country. The British official, James Busby, who encouraged the chiefs to make this declaration of independence, might well have intended that this congress was to be a supreme legislature, but the chiefs, operating from the context of a Māori legal system and constitutional tradition grounded in *whanaungatanga* and *mana*, would have seen things differently. Evidence given to the Waitangi Tribunal was that the annual congress would have been understood as "a gathering of the leaders of autonomous hapū"[40] and essentially "an extension of the traditional practice of gathering when there were important matters to discuss".[41] Moreover, this would not have been understood as transferring *mana* or authority from one body to another, or subordinating the authority of either the *rangatira* or the *hapū* to the 'congress'.[42] Evidence given to the Waitangi Tribunal also stated that the chiefs involved had agreed to meet as a congress to frame '*ture*', which they would have understood "as a European form of rules, distinct from tikanga".[43] This also suggests that the intention was not to create a supreme legislature that would override the independence of *hapū*.

This is reinforced in the Treaty of Waitangi itself. The protection of *tino rangatiratanga* in Article 2 would have given the chiefs confidence that the intention of the Treaty was not to undermine their own authority.[44] Signatories to the Treaty would have understood its meaning within the context of *te ao Māori* (the Māori world) and the Māori legal system. As evidence given in the Waitangi Tribunal notes:[45]

> the issue for the rangatira was not whether they understood sovereignty[,] it was whether they understood mana, and clearly they did, and so in that sense the English text was effectively irrelevant to the discussions that our people had.

Viewed as a Māori legal instrument, the Treaty simply could not have purported to transfer the kind of political authority encapsulated in the concept of *mana*. To do so would have been inconsistent with the way *mana* operates within the Māori constitutional tradition.

iii) Tapu/Noa

Closely connected to *mana* is the concept of *tapu*. This principle is about recognising the spiritual dimension of all things. As Mead has noted:[46]

> Tapu is everywhere in our world. It is present in people, in places, in buildings, in things, words, and in all tikanga. Tapu is inseparable from mana, from our identity as Māori and from our cultural practices.

Recognising the spiritual dimension means engaging appropriately with the *tapu* nature of all things. It can often require setting aside things that are very *tapu* or keeping them separate from the more everyday aspects of life. Life in the Māori world involves a constant management of *tapu* and in particular the interaction of the *tapu* of different things.

One example of the management of *tapu* can be seen in the Māori welcome ceremony or *pōwhiri*. The *pōwhiri* is a common process which takes place whenever Māori groups meet in a formal setting, often at a *marae* (the physical space which is a central community space on which these rituals of encounter occur). It is not necessary for the purposes of this chapter to describe the *pōwhiri* process in detail. It is sufficient to outline the principles at play and the key objective. The *pōwhiri* ceremony has a number of recognised and well-established components, though there is some regional variation across the country. The process is all about *tapu* and the management of *tapu*. It is a process which carefully and deliberately brings a visiting group into the community space of the home people. The *tapu* nature of the visitors and the *tapu* nature of the space they are coming into are both recognised in this process. To create an environment which is safe for ordinary interactions to occur in this space, the interaction of *tapu* needs to be carefully managed. This is done through various ceremonial practices to get to a state where those normal interactions between hosts and visitors can occur. It is, however, important to recognise that this does not mean that the *tapu* of hosts, visitors, or the *marae* itself is removed. People have an intrinsic *tapu*, as does the *marae*. The *pōwhiri* process is about managing the interaction of that *tapu*, not removing it.

The principle of *tapu* invokes a spiritual dimension but often has very practical purposes. In the *pōwhiri* process, visitors are dealt with cautiously until it can be established that they do not represent a threat to the home community and any interactions are made safe. The *tapu* nature of sites where blood has been spilt in battle or where there have been deaths has a public health aspect. These places are dangerous, and people ought not to go to such places without recognising that and taking appropriate precautions. If *tapu* is not recognised, respected, and carefully managed, there are consequences.

The importance of the concept of *noa* in relation to *tapu* is explained by Professor Hirini Moko Mead:[47]

> Noa is often paired with tapu indicating that often noa refers to restoring a balance. A high level of tapu is regarded as dangerous. Here the role of tikanga and tohunga [skilled spiritual leaders or experts] is to reduce the level of dangerous tapu until it is noa or safe. It is not useful to think of noa as being the opposite of tapu or as the absence of tapu. This is plainly not the case. For example a person can be very tapu if one is very ill or there is bleeding and shedding of blood. Once these tapu-increasing symptoms have passed the person returns to a safe state, but still has personal tapu. The state of noa indicates that a balance has been reached, a crisis is over, health is restored and life is normal again.

Similarly, Ani Mikaere has also emphasised the role of *noa* in transitioning through different spaces and activities and maintaining balance.[48] These concepts provide a key motivation for obedience to laws and the perceived consequences of breaching *tapu* act as an enforcement mechanism.[49]

The Treaty of Waitangi is often talked about as a *tapu* document or a sacred covenant and, when examined through a Māori legal lens, it is clear that the intention of the chiefs who signed was that the *tapu* character of the agreement would be explicit. This is consistent with the way in which Robert Williams identified that treaties in North America can be understood as sacred compacts.[50] In addition to the particular features of the Treaty and its signing that emphasise its *tapu* character, the Treaty also sits within a Māori legal system in which all agreements are *tapu*.

In the Māori world, agreements are understood to be *tapu*. Obligations to keep one's word are taken very seriously and there are serious consequences for breaching an agreement. Because of the *tapu* nature of agreements, consequences for breaching an agreement are ultimately backed by spiritual sanction. There are likely to be relationship/social costs to breaching an agreement, but a breach of *tapu* will always result in some spiritual cost as well. Evidence given in the Waitangi Tribunal's Te Paparahi o Te Raki inquiry told how the chiefs believed that the death of William Hobson (the representative of the British Crown who proposed the Treaty and became the first Governor of New Zealand) was connected to his failure to understand the *tapu* nature of the agreement and act accordingly.[51] It is important to note that this is unavoidable in the sense that it is not something that the other party to the agreement has control over or can forgive. A breach of *tapu* is an offence against a spiritual order, and those consequences follow inexorably.

When the *rangatira* signed the Treaty of Waitangi, most did so by recreating part of their facial tattoo or *ta moko*. Something so intimately connected with the person and the identity of the *rangatira* imbued the Treaty with an especially *tapu* character. In evidence to the Waitangi Tribunal, claimants noted that these '*tohu tapu*' or 'sacred signs' were placed on the Māori language text in particular, indicating that the emphasis for the *rangatira* was, unsurprisingly, focused on the Māori text.[52] The significance of the way in which the *rangatira* deployed these very personal symbols of identity is further explored in the Waitangi Tribunal's report:[53]

> It is significant that when signing Te Tiriti the Rangatira used only a small part of their ta moko. When we look at ta moko, we can read the entire universe represented there, but in signing He Whakaputanga and Te Tiriti, the Rangatira only chose to use a small part of their moko which signified a humble acknowledgement that the meaning of their actions in signing, was insignificant to the meaning of the universe that was held and represented in the total ta moko.

iv) Utu

The principle of *utu* is a driving force in the maintenance of relationships within the Māori legal system. It drives actions which seek to restore balance and to provide for reciprocity. The principle operates in both negative and positive contexts. That is, in gift exchange it requires that a gift of value is responded to by providing something desirable in return. However, the principle also demands that actions which cause damage or harm must be responded to in order to provide compensation or restitution. *Utu* addresses physical and material balance as well as spiritual balance.[54] As identified above, a breach of *tapu* will result in consequences. Ahu and others have noted:[55]

> In terms of Māori custom, "utu" defines the process of compensation for breaches of tikanga Māori. According to tikanga Māori, disputes that arise from a breach of tikanga Māori require some form of utu to be paid to a wronged party. The utu itself can take many forms depending on the circumstances; however, "utu" has a compensatory role in restoring a breach of tikanga.

The principle of *utu* is also central to the operation of authority within the Māori world and is a motivating force in the context of the *mana* of an individual or a community.[56]

Hirini Mead suggests that *utu* is part of an analytical framework that motivates actions within the Māori legal system. Mead describes this framework as a process of '*take-utu-ea*'.[57] '*Take*', in this context, refers to the reason that imbalance has been created, the breach of *tikanga*/law, or the cause of action. '*Utu*' is the response required to restore balance. '*Ea*' is the state of resolution or equilibrium that is achieved once the appropriate action has been taken to address the breach and restore balance. This framework of *take-utu-ea* captures the underlying objective of Māori law to achieve balance. Joan Metge has noted the key role in which the striving for balance can maintain relationships within both positive and negative cycles of actions and responses, or the principle of *utu* can be deployed to disrupt those cycles.[58] For example, if two parties have been locked in a cycle of a negative relationship, perhaps involving escalating acts of retaliation, a positive act, such as a strategic marriage or the unilateral gifting of land could act as a circuit-breaker, requiring positive and constructive reciprocation and transforming the cycle of action and response at the heart of the relationship.[59]

The principle of *utu* suggests that the Treaty of Waitangi, when viewed through the lens of the Māori legal system, represents a set of agreements within ongoing reciprocal relationships. According to this view, the specific exchanges set out in the text of the Treaty do not encompass the entire relationship between Māori and the Crown. In this instance, the concept of *utu* gives expression to the need to maintain and perpetuate relationships through ongoing reciprocal exchanges.

Anne Salmond gave evidence in the Waitangi Tribunal that the Treaty would have been understood in this way: a series of reciprocal exchanges that set the foundation for an ongoing personal relationship.[60] Salmond also notes the way in which the *rangatira* engaged in the signing process at Waitangi was another indication that their understanding would have been that this was to be just the beginning of a relationship of reciprocity.[61] The relationship does not begin and end with the specific articles of the Treaty, rather there are enduring obligations on the Treaty partners to continually respond to exchanges within the relationship. This intention and expectation is illustrated by the way in which the *rangatira* who signed the Treaty set about planning for further engagements with the Crown:[62]

> immediately after the signing of Te Tiriti, the rangatira planned an agenda for a meeting they hoped would take place with Hobson and Queen Victoria one year later, on 6 February 1841. Issues they planned to discuss included trade, the application of English law in cases of murder, the rights of rangatira in land matters, the application of hapū custom law and Bible law to land transactions, and the limited value the rangatira thought should be placed on money. The rangatira presented this agenda to the missionaries and entrusted them to convey the message to Hobson and the Queen. Edwards did not say how the missionaries may have responded or if they relayed the information to Hobson, but we interpret this tradition as evidence that, at the time of its signing, the claimants tūpuna considered te Tiriti as subject to ongoing discussion and reassessment.

Salmond also points to "instances in Muriwhenua of rangatira repudiating signed agreements where their understanding of them had been dishonoured",[63] suggesting that the chiefs would likely see the Treaty agreement as void if the continuing reciprocity required by the principle of *utu* was not maintained by the Treaty partners.

The principle of *utu* provides a lens through which the Treaty of Waitangi can be understood as the maintenance of a continuing relationship across distinctive communities through reciprocal and ongoing exchanges. And when this principle is placed alongside the principles of *whanaungatanga*, *mana*, *tapu*, and *noa*, we can begin to construct a framework for interpreting the Treaty as part of a Māori constitutional tradition.

Conclusion

This chapter has argued for the need to consider treaties between Indigenous peoples and States, such as the Treaty of Waitangi, against the backdrop of Indigenous constitutional traditions. The work of Robert Williams and others illustrates the importance of understanding the meaning of these treaties by viewing them as instruments within the Indigenous world and not only as a legal mechanism of the colonising State. This opens up different possibilities of interpretation but, most importantly, taking this approach demonstrates the need to recognise treaties as instruments that connect diverse and distinctive constitutional traditions and polities. This moves us away from an assimilationist approach or seeing the role of these treaties as amalgamating Indigenous and State law and government. Instead, recognising different visions of law and peace becomes a possibility, and, arguably, the most appropriate framework for these treaties.

The second main part of this chapter explored what this approach would mean for our understanding of the Treaty of Waitangi. The objective was to move the discussion about the Treaty beyond a debate about meaning that takes place entirely within the State's constitutional traditions and instead frames the Treaty's meaning by the parameters of the Māori constitutional tradition. Considering the Treaty of Waitangi in the context of the Māori constitutional tradition provides a distinctive interpretive frame. Key Māori legal principles such as *whanaungatanga*, *mana*, *tapu* and *noa*, and *utu* can be seen at work in the way in which Māori have engaged with the Crown as a Treaty partner since the initial signing of the Treaty in 1840. The overarching point that can be drawn from examining the Treaty of Waitangi as part of the Māori constitutional tradition is that the Treaty should be seen as one component of an ongoing and developing relationship between distinct constitutional traditions. The ongoing relationship recognises ongoing diversity and so directs us to focus on mechanisms for interaction and connection between communities with distinctive constitutional traditions. This does not require one party being subsumed by the other or the legal traditions of one party smothering the other's. Rather, on this view, the Treaty provides a framework for contemplating how we might best give effect to both Māori and State visions of law and peace.

Notes

1 Waitangi Tribunal *He Whakaputanga me te Tiriti – The Declaration and the Treaty: The Report on Stage 1 of the Te Paparahi o Te Raki Inquiry* (Wai 1040) (Waitangi Tribunal, Wellington, 2014).

2 See, for example, Matthew Palmer *The Treaty of Waitangi in New Zealand's Law and Constitution* (Victoria University Press, Wellington, 2008); Paul McHugh

The Māori Magna Carta: New Zealand Law and the Treaty of Waitangi (Oxford University Press, Auckland, 1991); Claudia Orange *The Treaty of Waitangi* (2nd ed, Bridget Williams Books, Wellington, 2011).

3 Robert A. Williams Jr *Linking Arms Together: American Treaty Visions of Law and Peace, 1600–1800* (Routledge, New York, NY, 1999).

4 For a theoretical framework of this type of legal association, see Nicole Roughan *Authorities: Conflicts, Cooperation, and Transnational Legal Theory* (Oxford University Press, Oxford, 2013).

5 For a consideration of different perspectives to interpreting treaties with Indigenous peoples, see also Alexandra Harmon (ed) *The Power of Promises: Rethinking Indian Treaties in the Pacific Northwest* (University of Washington Press, Seattle, WA, 2008); and Jeremy Webber and Colin M. Macleod (eds) *Between Consenting Peoples: Political Community and the Meaning of Consent* (University of British Columbia Press, Vancouver, 2010).

6 Carwyn Jones "A Māori Constitutional Tradition" (2014) 12 *New Zealand Journal of Public and International Law* 187 at 188.

7 H. Patrick Glenn *Legal Traditions of the World* (4th ed, Oxford University Press, Oxford, 2010) at 24.

8 Joe Williams "He Aha Te Tikanga Māori" (unpublished paper for the New Zealand Law Commission, 1998) at 2.

9 Jones, above n 6, at 189.

10 Williams, above n 3.

11 See Glen Coulthard *Red Skin, White Masks: Rejecting the Colonial Politics of Recognition* (University of Minnesota Press, Minneapolis, MN, 2014) at 60–62; Vine Deloria Jr *God Is Red: A Native View of Religion* (Fulcrum Publishing, Golden, CO, 1992) at 61–76.

12 Williams, above n 3, at 40–61.

13 At 61.

14 At 61.

15 At 82.

16 At 82.

17 At 82.

18 At 97.

19 Richard Delgado "Storytelling for Oppositionists and Others: A Plea for Narrative" (1989) 87 *Michigan Law Review* 2411 at 2438.

20 Williams, above n 3, at 97.

21 At 123.

22 At 136.

23 See *Report of the United Nations Expert Seminar on Strengthening Partnership Between Indigenous Peoples and States: Treaties, Agreements and Other Constructive Arrangements* United Nations Office of the High Commissioner for Human Rights (Geneva, July 2012).

24 Hirini Moko Mead *Tikanga Māori: Living by Māori Values* (2nd ed, Huia, Wellington, 2013) at 32.

25 At 33.

26 Tribunal, above n 1, at 471.

27 At 452.

28 At 452. See also, the application of a kin relationship framework applied to the Treaty of Waitangi and the Declaration of Independence to explain the nature of authority and sovereignty as understood by Ngāpuhi: Hone Sadler *Ko Tautoro Te Pito o Tōku Ao – A Ngāpuhi Narrative* (Auckland University Press, Auckland, 2014) at 11–13.

29 Tribunal, above n 1, at 499.

30 At 489.

31 At 454.

32 R. Benton, A. Frame, and P. Meredith (eds) *Te Mātāpunenga: A Compendium of References to the Concepts and Institutions of Māori Customary Law* (Victoria University Press, Wellington, 2013) at 154.
33 Mead, above n 24, at 33.
34 At 34.
35 E. T. Durie "Custom Law" (unpublished, paper prepared for Waitangi Tribunal Members and Later Referred to the Law Commission, 1994) at 8.
36 S. Jones "Consultation With Tangata Whenua" (1992) (unpublished) at 6, cited in Nin Tomas *Key Concepts of Tikanga Māori (Māori Custom Law) in Tai Tokerau Past and Present* (PhD Thesis, University of Auckland, 2006) at 95.
37 See, for example, the comments of missionary Octavius Hadfield in *Native Tenure: Opinions of Various Authorities* (1861) AJHR, E No 1, Appendix A at 9: "The Chief of the tribe, since he has no absolute right over the territory of the various *hapu*, nor over the lands of individual freemen of his own *hapu*, cannot sell any lands but his own . . . nor can he do so in opposition to the opinion of the Chiefs of the *hapu* of the tribe, if they consider the territory, and thus the independence of the tribe impaired by doing so."
38 Tribunal, above n 1, at 461.
39 See, for example, R. M. Ross "Te Tiriti o Waitangi: Texts and Translations" (1972) 6 *New Zealand Journal of History* 129; M. Mutu "Constitutional Intentions: The Treaty of Waitangi Texts" in M. Mulholland and V. Tawhai (eds) *Weeping Waters: The Treaty of Waitangi and Constitutional Change* (Huia, Wellington, 2010) at 13.
40 Tribunal, above n 1, at 500.
41 At 501.
42 At 500.
43 At 501.
44 At 452.
45 At 453.
46 Mead, above n 24, at 34.
47 At 31–32.
48 Ani Mikaere *He Rukuruku Whakaaro – Colonising Myths, Māori Realities* (Huia, Wellington, 2011) at 212.
49 McCully Matiu and Margaret Mutu *Te Whānau Moana: Ngā Kaupapa me ngā Tikanga – Customs and Protocols* (Reed, Auckland, 2003) at 159.
50 Williams, above n 3, at 40–61.
51 Tribunal, above n 1, at 451.
52 At 453.
53 At 457.
54 Tai Ahu, Rachael Hoare, and Māmari Stephens "Utu: Finding a Balance for the Legal Māori Dictionary" (2011) 42 *Victoria University of Wellington Law Review* 201 at 203. See also Māmari Stephens and Mary Boyce (eds) *He Papakupu Reo Ture: A Dictionary of Māori Legal Terms* (LexisNexis, Wellington, 2013) at 98.
55 Ahu, Hoare, and Stephens, above n 54, at 204.
56 At 204.
57 Mead, above n 24, at 31.
58 Joan Metge "Returning the Gift – *Utu* in Intergroup Relations" (2002) 111 *Journal of the Polynesian Society* 311.
59 Metge, above n 58.
60 Tribunal, above n 1, at 461.
61 At 461.
62 At 460.
63 At 470.

2 Origin stories and the law

Treaty metaphysics in Canada and New Zealand

John Borrows

This chapter explores the scope of interpretive frameworks for understanding treaties in Canada and New Zealand. It questions the value, uses, and limits of both history and abstract principles in implementing treaties in both countries. Treaties between the Crown and Indigenous peoples occurred in multiple sites in both lands. They were developed through different eras and have been interpreted across diverse periods of time. As such, the importance of both space and time are live considerations when interpreting treaties. Furthermore, both the Crown and Indigenous peoples have different sources of authority which they bring to the interpretative process. Moreover, these sources of laws interact. These interactions influence the broader contours of constitutional thought and practice in both countries. These complexities have pushed courts and legislatures to impose some semblance of order on these otherwise messy processes. Thus, despite the untidy circumstances surrounding the formation of treaties, legal actors have attempted to create a coherent framework for their interpretation.

Unfortunately, this background search for consistency has generated some troubling consequences. By and large, non-Indigenous law has been made supreme. Despite the treaties' bijural formation, Parliaments and legislatures have the upper hand. Parties engaged in treaty interpretation often act as if post-hoc national structures mirror historical circumstances. In my view, this has generated dubious metaphysical approaches. It has encouraged the growth of questionable origin stories in both countries. National origin stories and the false visions they conjure are the subject of this chapter's critique.

I examine these issues through the lens of treaty metaphysics, teleological inquiries, and the analogies of law to religion.

I. Treaty metaphysics

Treaty law in New Zealand and Canada has problematically come to rely on first principles, including abstract concepts related to knowledge, causation, identity, time, and space. This metaphysical turn propels our national origins stories. It drives legal actors to search for foundational first causes. Kit Fine, a leading philosopher of metaphysics, has characterised metaphysics in the following terms.

His description channels legal approaches to treaty interpretation in Canada and New Zealand. Professor Fine writes:[1]

> There are, I believe, five main features that serve to distinguish traditional metaphysics from other forms of enquiry. These are: the aprioricity of its methods; the generality of its subject-matter; the transparency or 'non-opacity' of its concepts; its eidicity or concern with the nature of things; and its role as a foundation for what there is.

Treaty interpretation in Canada and New Zealand may be considered a metaphysical inquiry because it seemingly mirrors these five qualities.

First, a priori reasoning about the nature of treaties in our constitutional frameworks suggests that they are generally subordinate to Parliamentary authority. This a priori assumption conditions the entire field. In New Zealand, the Treaty of Waitangi has no direct force without Parliamentary enactment,[2] and in Canada, treaties can be infringed if Parliament meets a justificatory standard.[3] Crown law is broadly considered the first-and-last mover in generating and enforcing constitutional frameworks.[4] Notions of terra nullius and the doctrine of discovery,[5] continue to set the stage for subsequent action,[6] despite words to the contrary.[7] Parliament's authority is placed before a treaty's power even though the Crown's authority chronologically follows pre-existing Indigenous legal orders.[8] Questionable jurisdictional claims reverse time's linear order in the law's metaphysics. This occurs despite compelling arguments that treaties are necessary to grant the Crown governance rights in an Indigenous territory.[9]

Second, treaty interpretation operates at a high level of generality when it comes to elucidating principles governing the content of these agreements. In New Zealand, so-called high-level treaty principles govern Parliament's implementation of the agreement.[10] In Canada, section 35(1) of the Constitution sets the parameters of inquiry and likewise defers to Parliament. This high level of generality, disconnected from historically relevant experience, is evident in section 35(1)'s leading case, *R v Sparrow*.[11] In *Sparrow* the Court wrote "there was from the outset never any doubt that sovereignty and legislative power, and indeed the underlying title, to such lands vested in the Crown."[12] The judges arrived at this conclusion despite significant questions about the veracity of these propositions when the Crown asserted sovereignty in North America.[13] Nevertheless high-level generalisations problematically prevail. Artificial premises reinforce the fabricated nature of treaty metaphysics. Reasoning is premised on abstract propositions. Inquiries into 'the actual state of things',[14] are manipulated or subordinated to high-level primary assertions.[15]

Third, treaty interpretation deceptively illustrates another feature of Fine's metaphysics – transparency concerning the field's nature and scope.[16] By transparency, Professor Fine means that "the field of enquiry comes with a built-in restriction not only on its propositions but also on how those propositions may properly be expressed."[17] Both New Zealand and Canadian jurisprudence contain built-in propositional restrictions concerning their non-international and domestic character.[18] Under current practice, they are clearly subordinate to Crown-centric sources. Propositions related to treaty interpretation can only be expressed and enforced through legislatures and courts. Parliamentary supremacy and jurisprudential support for domestic power defines the Indigenous treaty field. Such deference makes it clear that there are built-in restrictions concerning their meaning and *how* this meaning should be expressed. In both countries, treaties are disciplined by a priori foundational views concerning their non-international and domestic character.

Fourth, treaty interpretation in each country is eidetic. Domesticated primary laws not only purport to resolve specific issues, but, additionally, such resolutions seemingly reveal something more about the general nature of 'reality'. Treaty interpretations propound universalised conceptions of law. They propagate views about the essential nature of knowledge, causation, identity, time, and space. In New Zealand, institutional players express the purpose of treaty interpretation in both specific and general terms. Here is one example:[19]

> The Waitangi Tribunal's vision is that, having reconciled ourselves with the past and possessing a full understanding of the Treaty of Waitangi, Māori and non-Māori New Zealanders will be equipped to create a future for two peoples as one nation.

Likewise, Canadian treaty interpretation is also eidetic. The Supreme Court of Canada writes about Indigenous–Crown treaties in both specific and general terms: "The fundamental objective of the modern law of aboriginal and treaty rights is the reconciliation of aboriginal peoples and non-aboriginal peoples and their respective claims, interests and ambitions."[20] In understanding this point, it must be remembered that so-called reconciliation allows for the Crown's ultimate override.[21] This is part of our law's dubious metaphysics. Treaty interpretation keeps us focused on specific disputes, yet it simultaneously fosters broader worldviews. State-dominated relationality – directed toward the fusion of knowledge – seems to reveal both specific and general purposes for life in each country.[22]

Finally, Professor Fine says metaphysical reasoning is "capable of providing some kind of basis or underpinning for other forms of enquiry". This ostensibly occurs through treaty interpretation in both New Zealand and Canada because it rests on foundational reasoning. Origin-ism or originalism animates treaty interpretation in both countries,[23] although it goes much further.[24] Law works on multiple scales; when answering specific questions, it also layers 'deeper' coded meanings through foundational hypothesis. Treaty interpretation is never solely about an agreement's meaning; it also channels (erroneous) assumptions about the nature of life itself.

Despite appearances to the contrary, treaty interpretation is ultimately structured by deductive, inferred, postulated, and suppositional reasoning about our origins and purposes. This approach supports the paramountcy of law and the Crown's ultimate control of the legal system. While courts and tribunals gather and evaluate detailed historic treaty evidence, law metaphysically subordinates empirical data to 'fit' underlying foundational principles. Propositional assumptions about the nature of law ultimately undergird reasons for decision – historic details are merely arranged, ignored, or overturned to support a supposed broader 'reality'.

Thus, our countries' feigned originalism goes much deeper than merely searching for first treaty principles. Law's narrative invents a prologue; it starts with a metaphysical genesis. 'In the beginning' tales create origin stories which superficially address broader questions such as where we came from, why we are here, and where we are going. The explicit message in treaty interpretation is that the Crown is supreme. The implicit message more broadly conveyed is that 'higher' centralised legal control creates the conditions for human flourishing. Thus, Professor Fine's criteria are seemingly realised: enquiries related to treaties "form the basis or underpin other forms of enquiry". Enquires about treaties apparently reveal that law is considered to be the ultimate source and arbiter of meaning for directing our lives. The remainder of this chapter discusses how treaty interpretation implicitly channels foundational messages about life's meaning through its placement of law as both 'prior to' and 'above us' in structuring reality.

At the same time, this chapter also sharply critiques this approach. Treaty interpretation is not best premised on Crown dominance. Reality is not necessarily revealed by the law mediating our relationships. While it seems obvious to say so, it is not likely that law ultimately enlightens us about the meaning of life in our respective countries. Nevertheless, our system generates and reproduces meanings which disclose its actors' (specious) assumptions about the point of life itself. New Zealand and Canada's origin stories are unconvincing. They preach a false religion. They promulgate faulty philosophical lines of reasoning. As such, they should be rejected. Invalidation not only requires rejecting particular interpretive doctrines related to treaty interpretation. Retraction also necessitates the quashing of a priori propositions which imply that the Crown-dominated law is supreme.

II. Law's teleologies: where did we come from? Why are we here? Where are we going?

Law grapples with the broadest questions of our day. It claims pre-eminent authority in relation to issues which in past ages were almost exclusively within the purview of religion and philosophy. Law considers questions such as where do we come from, why are we here, and where are we going? Our legal systems are called upon to decide where and when life begins,[25] how we should live during our years on earth,[26] and what might happen after death.[27] Moral, social, economic, emotional, scientific, religious, spiritual, and philosophical questions are framed as justiciable issues.

These are the grand questions of life. Yet legal discourse treats them in a pedestrian manner. It prohibits explicit discussion of 'extra-legal' factors. Lawyers are forbidden from making open and candid arguments on moral, social, economic, scientific, spiritual, and philosophical grounds. As every first-year law student learns, you cannot bring an unvarnished moral or religious argument to court. They must be framed as legal issues. Legal argumentation must be deployed.

This is how judges and lawyers can pretend they are not moral philosophers, religious figures, or social activists when they make decisions. However, the authority they exercise, and the weight of questions considered, propel them into the realm of metaphysics. Their inquiries animate questions which implicate our broader search for life's meaning and purpose. The transformation of moral, spiritual, scientific, and philosophical questions into legal issues can deceive us. We can be lulled into believing that metaphysics is not in play when courts and legislatures consider questions related to choice, life, death, security, and liberty of the person.

i) Where do we come from?

Indigenous issues in Canada and New Zealand also raise metaphysical questions. 'Where do we come from?' is a fundamental inquiry in the treaty field. The answer to this question structures subsequent legal analysis. Law's origin is a big deal. If we believe our primary laws come from Britain, this will produce different normative obligations from those laws which originate on Indigenous shores. Thus, we should not overlook law's 'in the beginning' inquiries. When we identify law's source, we can learn more about in whose image it was created. Origins matter. Or to use a scientific analogy: origins *are* matter; they spawn the elements from which legal worlds are subsequently formed.

Judge Joseph Williams explored the role of law's origins in his groundbreaking article "Lex Aotearoa".[28] In this work, he discussed what he called Aotearoa's First Law, Second Law, and Third Law. He wrote that Aotearoa's First Law originated in tropical Pacific Islands and was transplanted in Aotearoa over 800 years ago when ancestral Māori arrived on its shores. This First Law became Tikanga Māori, an "old system built around kinship that was adapted to the new circumstance of this place".[29] Judge Williams wrote that the Second Law of Aotearoa formed from the collision between the First Law and laws originating from Great Britain. Through time, norms originating overseas were transplanted in Aotrearoa's soil. They came to enjoy a pride of place. As this Second Law developed, Justice Williams wrote that it[30]

> rejected the legal relevance of the Treaty, reduced native title to its statutory boxes and acknowledged tikanga Māori only as a temporary expedient in the wider project of title extinction and cultural assimilation.

In this instance, the British legal answer to 'where do we come from' subordinated Māori norms. Finally, Judge Williams described the Third Law of Aotearoa. He regarded it as the First Law's revitalization and its impact on the Second Law to create a new kind of law – a Third Law. In his words: "This third law is predicated on perpetuating the first law, and in so perpetuating, it has come to change both the nature and culture of the second law."[31] Judge Williams' legal description of 'where we came from' is generally similar to Canadian law's origin story narrated by the Royal Commission on Aboriginal Peoples.[32] It is a powerful story which shows the dominance of Crown sovereignty despite challenges to this power throughout the years.

ii) Why are we here?

The next grand question 'Why are we here' can also be found when interpreting treaties in New Zealand and Canada. As discussed above, the 'why' of treaties produces answers which have significance beyond Crown–Indigenous relations. It supports a centralised view of authority. It is Crown-centric. In the Canadian context, treaties seem to exist to preserve a relatively narrow band of traditional activities for Aboriginal peoples, while simultaneously opening up the country for settlement and economic development for non-Indigenous peoples. As the Court observed in relation to numbered treaties which cover most of Canada's prairies and Ontario's north:[33]

> The post-Confederation numbered treaties were designed to open up the Canadian west and northwest to settlement and development. Treaty 8 itself recites that "the said Indians have been notified and informed by Her Majesty's said Commission that it is Her desire to open for settlement, immigration, trade, travel, mining, lumbering and such other purposes as to Her Majesty may seem meet". This stated purpose is reflected in a corresponding limitation on the Treaty 8 hunting, fishing and trapping rights to exclude such "tracts as may be required or taken up from time to time for settlement, mining, lumbering, trading or other purposes".

The general pattern of dispossession and assimilation when interpreting treaties has been hotly contested by Indigenous peoples for generations.[34] The idea that 'we are here' to make way for non-native economic development is the subject of constant challenge.[35] Despite such resistance, Crown domination in the treaty sphere continues to eclipse other visions concerning life's purpose.[36] Economic exploitation of lands and resources seems to be what we live for – particularly if we regard our actions as evidence of what we believe. While New Zealand treaty interpretation recognises broader Māori purposes,[37] struggles with assimilatory issues as to 'why we are here' also form a significant part of their experience.[38]

iii) Where are we going?

Finally, 'where are we going' is a key question when interpreting treaties in New Zealand and Canada. It shows law's strained metaphysics. Again, the issue of assimilation looms large. In contemplating the future, we enter the prophetic sphere. No one can predict it, although lawyers try all the time. Aside from judging the past and making decisions about present action, law often deals with future states. A legal opinion is a prediction about how the courts might rule on a question posed by a client. A legal judgment is expected to guide resolutions of similar future issues. A statute is intended to prescribe and/or empower future action, and regulations particularise these possibilities.

When it comes to treaties however, their future orientation is contested. At least two lines of thought prevail. Some see treaties as only being about the past. They can be seen as settling certain messy relational issues before moving on to the real work of law through legislation and judicial decision-making. Others, however, see treaties as future-oriented agreements.[39] In this light, treaties can be seen as creating frameworks for future action.[40] Issues related to 'where we are going' in the treaty context oscillated along a spectrum between these two visions. Choosing between these views has metaphysical dimensions. Beliefs about whether our future should be 'free from' or 'full of' treaty considerations reveals our faith concerning future states.

The Canadian Supreme Court places reconciliation of Crown sovereignty with the pre-existence of Indigenous peoples at the centre of the country's future goals in this sphere.[41] Reconciliation seems to exist to create 'one nation'. For example, in the *Mikisew Cree* the Supreme Court wrote that "Treatymaking is an important stage in the long process of reconciliation, but it is only a stage."[42] Treaties are a means to other ends. 'Where we are going' is seemingly beyond treaties to a rule of law which is dominated by Crown frameworks. The New Zealand drive to finally settle by 2020 in the New Zealand context dictates a similar purpose.[43]

In thinking about Aboriginal and treaty rights, my own work highlights how the resurgence of Indigenous peoples' own law should guide future regulation and dispute resolution.[44] Like Justice Williams,[45] I argue that Indigenous law will continue to influence the development of broader non-Indigenous law in significant ways.[46] However, I must pause to be self-reflective. In arguing for this result, I am really saying that I submit, contend, declare, and assert that this should occur. Making this prediction about a future state is merely just another way of saying 'I believe'. However, like most predictions, or expressions of faith – I could be wrong. This may be particularly likely if we also believe that treaty interpretation does not merely address the resolution of particular agreements, but simultaneously and necessarily reinforces the Crown's pre-eminence.[47]

I am not deterministic when addressing the future of treaty interpretation.[48] Those who argue that 'where we are going' in treaty interpretation is 'more of the same' (in terms of Crown dominance) are likewise expressing their faith.[49] An aspect of prophecy can be detected in both our calls to reflection and repentance. If we analogise from Professor Fine's description of metaphysics, we both stand accused. For those who see the future as inexorably replicating past Crown dominance, I have outlined a plausible argument (which I nevertheless dispute) that field of treaty interpretation "comes with a built-in restriction not only on its propositions but also on how those propositions may properly be expressed".[50] To recap, these restrictions are *first* said to prevent Indigenous peoples from challenging fundamental assumptions about law's source. *Second*, they are also thought to prevent Indigenous peoples from challenging the very institutions and language through which treaty propositions are expressed. It is very possible that these conditions might mean 'where we are going' does not differ significantly from our Crown-dominated past – although I have raised questions about inevitability of this view.

My bigger target in this chapter, however, is not to choose the better argument when it comes to describing the future of treaty interpretation. Of course, I am deeply interested in this particular inquiry. I have expressed my views here and elsewhere. To restate my position: I believe that Indigenous law's resurgence could overturn essential arguments about the inevitability of Crown dominance, even as Indigenous law struggles against colonialism's contemporary subordination.

Despite my argument, the airing of my preferences is not this chapter's sole or even wider purpose. My broader project is to make clear that, whatever position is advanced, law seems unable to escape from metaphysics. Faith, belief, speculation, and reason (which always involves emotional calibration of how we perceive the world)[51] are omnipresent in legal reasoning. The mere presentation of agonistic legal genealogies and social contingencies does not release metaphysics' grip, at least in the legal field. For legal theorists, practices of the self are also metaphysical practices. Anti-essentialism generates another kind of (ironically) foundational a priori worldview.[52] It is a world where law is everywhere yet nowhere – invisible yet incarnate – without body, parts of passions.[53] Genesis in this account says the legal world is without form, and void, until legal agents move across its waters, and contingently shed their subjective lights on particular interpretive subjects. Even anti-essentialist legal practitioners who may claim that law can be practised without metaphysics risk the danger of creating origins stories that reify propositional first-order principles.

The fact that we often act without often acknowledging law's metaphysical turns makes my project even more pressing. Our lack of transparency concerning how law transports us into the metaphysical realm is deeply troubling. It blinds us. This approach banishes wisdom from other fields by failing to acknowledge law's own relationship with and manipulation of metaphysics. It can make us complicit in labelling ourselves as post-something societies (as if we are not always entangled with event activities we want to place in the past).[54] Legal theorists and practitioners are not beyond the hand-wringing which goes on in moral, religious, and philosophical spheres. Legal actors should not believe that the problems we attribute to religious, philosophical, cultural, and other social systems need not concern us. *We* (speaking as a legal academic and practitioner) are *them*: we are a species of 'prophets, priests, and philosopher kings'. Law is just as metaphysically oriented – and disoriented – as 'those' systems of thought and practice which we try to keep at a distance.

Law merely replicates metaphysical debates in its own sphere. Of course, it deploys its own language and structure to do so, but law is also a meaning-making system. Origin narratives abound. Law is not impervious to metaphysical turns.[55] The reason for making metaphysics the target of this chapter is to highlight the stakes involved in concealing a priori assumptions through legal argumentation.[56] Such concealment leads to domination because legal argumentation expels self-reflexivity about the sources of itself from its realm.[57] Law becomes enforceable because we believe this to be the case. Authority is easier to exercise if its deeper sources are concealed from question and dispute.

Law's exile of moral, philosophical, and religious insight about the nature of its own meaning-making metaphysics sustains a dangerous lack of self-reflexivity. This allows us to be dominated by unexamined fictitious limits regarding the scope of legal inquiry. This in turn leads to domination by those who patrol law's so-called limits. We need legal processes which are more transparent about their nature and sources, so that they can be questioned and placed in the realm of contestation.[58]

III. Law as religion

Law's metaphysics may become more visible if we compare and contrast it with religion. Law can operate like religion.[59] Both are cultural activities which draw on doctrinal and ideological premises to guide thought and action.[60] Both are prescriptive. Law and religion claim allegiance and obedience. Authority, text, and interpretive hermeneutics play a large role in both systems. Both generally claim independence in their spheres, although law has eclipsed religion in its ability to monopolise power over the last 150 years (in New Zealand and Canada at least). Both law and religion are picked up by practitioners with different ideological and social commitments. Different worldviews abound within each system. Contestation about which worldview should prevail is a sectarian activity. Practitioners organise themselves in different ways to advance their causes and teleological commitments in both law and religion.

Treaty interpretation engages many of the same metaphysical meaning-making moves which are present in religion.[61] Treaty interpretation is a cultural activity which draws on underlying doctrinal and ideological premises. Treaty interpretation is prescriptive, as it guides the conduct of the Crown, Indigenous communities, and the public more generally. It demands obedience. Treaty interpretation relies on appeals to authority, text, and hermeneutics. It monopolises power and has eclipsed other competitors for interpretive supremacy. Morality, war, diplomacy, and religion are not as dominant or relevant as they once were in this realm. Furthermore, treaty interpretation, like religion, can also be sectarian. The Crown and Indigenous peoples organise themselves differently to achieve their varied ends. Governments who represent the Crown can wear different political stripes; moreover, iwi (tribal federation), First Nations, Metis, and Inuit groups can be internally diverse in addition to exhibiting differences across communities.

The issues of authority, text, and differentiation deserve further attention to highlight similarities between law and religion to demonstrate the metaphysical nature of treaty interpretation.

i) Authority

Many religious traditions organise the world hierarchically. They rest on essential, fundamental, or foundational bases. God, gods, or other divine forms create, structure, command, rule, organise, guide, or direct human affairs. The universal nature of this control is said to structure everything else. God or the gods are the first-movers. His, Her, their, or its existence is thought to be the source of life and wisdom. Meaning is calibrated by their actions and/or teachings. In many religious traditions, God takes an a priori form: existence flows from and is given value and significance by this belief.

As a metaphysical activity, treaty interpretation mirrors religion's authoritative turns. It attempts to draw on a priori forms. Treaty interpretation is organised hierarchically in New Zealand and Canada. The Crown is considered to be supreme. As noted earlier, the Crown's placement at the pinnacle of authority draws on a set of deeper norms related to why we are here. The exploitation of resources to build broader economic systems is like a national (if not international) religion. Crown supremacy to facilitate, centralise, and sustain access to development draws on assumptions which see hierarchy and human-held God-like oversight as vital to human flourishing.[62] Law's metaphysical propensities pay great attention to authority, and the need to secure deference to its rule. The search for meaning is framed by reference to first principles and first principals.

My colleague Noel Lyon brought this observation into sharp relief when we worked with treaty elders in Saskatchewan over a decade ago. Professor Lyon was struck by how positivism and Parliamentary Supremacy were very different from First Nations' ideas concerning the basis for treaties. At the same time, he perceptively identified parallel similarities in worldviews. He said:[63]

> As I've listened to the Elders, I have begun to understand that what I've learned about Aboriginal peoples and their situation in Canada has largely come from written sources, from books, and there are a lot of things that were embedded in me in my legal education that I haven't overcome. The most important one, I think, is that law school indoctrinated me with the belief that the Crown is all powerful, and I think that's a real problem, because I think legal education, it may not be that bad today, but I think there is a tendency to regard the Crown almost in the way that the First Nations people regard the Creator, as being the source of all things. And from that flows the proposition that the treaties are seen by the non-Aboriginal community as just another body of laws that define the status and rights of Aboriginal peoples, rather than seeing the treaties as a nation-to-nation partnership, inter-societal law. . . . It had never occurred to me until Elder Crowe said this yesterday or the day before: that the right of the white people to be on this land is founded in the treaty.

Despite their differences, Professor Lyon observed that the Crown's view of its authority has parallels with First Nations' views about the Creator as the source of authority in treaty interpretation. The Crown acts as if rights flow from its own a priori authority, whereas Indigenous peoples on Canada's prairies regard another pre-existing force as being the source of law – the Creator. Both rest on foundational arguments, though their polarities are reversed. I have been arguing that both views are metaphysical. They depend on presuppositions rooted in abstract concepts related to knowledge, causation, identity, time, and space.

In addition to law and religion's attentiveness to ultimate authority, both systems also focus on tracing and delegating that authority through the human realm. Each system raises the question of leadership and to whom should we defer in channelling ultimate authority. In the past, societies like New Zealand and Canada would have looked to priests, shamans, ceremonial leaders, elders, and other spiritual figures to interpret supreme law. These hierarchies are now replaced by judges, parliamentarians, lawyers, professors, historians, lawyers, and other ceremonial 'keepers of the tradition' who work with common law and constitutional forms in each country.

In Canada and New Zealand an established 'priestly class' of lawyers, judges, and legislators discerns and conjures the Crown's supreme will. Law societies are given self-governing monopolies to accredit and supervise law practitioners. Law Schools introduce students to customs, rituals, and doctrines to guide their future service. Deference to the Crown's supreme authority by judges and lawyers in treaty interpretation is ever present in Canada and New Zealand. While law schools and law societies are doing a better job of introducing Indigenous perspectives in their work, most lawyers practise with the Crown in their mind as the first moving legal principle/principal. Law's seminaries have long preached and maintained this orthodoxy. Courts are filled with curates who preside over this view.

For example, in Canada, the cases of *R v Marhsall I & II*, judges make it very clear that the Crown is supreme in when it comes to treaty matters. Justice Binnie writes the following statements to indicate this 'fact':

- This right was always subject to regulation.[64]
- The treaty right is a regulated right and can be contained by regulation within its proper limits.[65]
- Such regulations would *not* constitute an infringement that would have to be justified under the *Badger* standard.[66]
- In a series of important decisions commencing with *R v Sparrow*, [1990] 1 SCR 1075 . . . this Court affirmed that s 35 aboriginal and treaty rights *are* subject to regulation, provided such regulation is shown by the Crown to be justified on conservation or other grounds of public importance.[67]
- In other words, regulations that do no more than reasonably *define* the Mi'kmaq treaty right in terms that can be administered by the regulator and understood by the Mi'kmaq community that holds the treaty rights do not impair the exercise of the treaty right and therefore do not have to meet the *Badger* standard of justification.[68]

Like God, the Crown is supreme when it comes to regulating treaties. Human agents (judges and lawyers) have taught and upheld this canon in high institutional contexts. This power is not necessarily drawn from the treaties but exists because of an a priori supposition that matters of public importance are best controlled, managed and regulated by a higher power.[69] This view supports Professor Ben Berger's astute observation that law acts like religion when it "sits above and is separate from particular claims".[70] He observes that Law regards itself as a "means of managing and adjudicating cultural difference" and "enjoys a strong form of autonomy from culture" and religion.[71] The assumption of supreme authority demonstrates the questionable metaphysical firstness (presumed to lie with the Crown) when it comes to interpreting treaties in Canada and the United States.

ii) Texts

I have consistently repeated the central point in this chapter: law manipulates principles in an a priori fashion. Text is an important referent in this process. In examining the metaphysics of treaty interpretation, we can ask: What are our sacred texts? Where do we look to understand our rights, obligations, and commitments? In the past, societies looked to scriptures, songs, sagas, and psalms to govern themselves. Traditions, customs, and rituals, recited through chronicles, codes, and conventions, regularised conduct for many people. In more explicitly metaphysical times, these were our sacred texts. They were sacred because we gave them deference. While there were always dissenters, societies regarded them as necessary to live fulfilling, meaningful lives.

In contemporary affairs, societies turn to constitutions, statutes, and regulations to guide our collective lives. They are our touchstones. Customs and underlying normative assumptions play a significant role in giving these formal written sources meaning.[72] At the same time, constitutions have a special identity and meaning in directing our collective affairs. They form our countries' highest laws. While the analogy can be stretched too far, they are to us what the Bible and Indigenous creation stories were to many people when the treaties were signed. Alongside Indigenous spiritual forms, treaties were influenced by biblical language and metaphors.[73] Missionaries, priests, and Indigenous spiritual leaders played a vital role in securing agreements.[74] However, our society has largely moved on in its deference to these sources when giving treaties meaning. While Indigenous spiritual teachings with legal dimensions might find a small place in treaty interpretation in the present day, it would be very usual to regard the Bible as possessing this authority in today's courtrooms. Religious and spiritual metaphysics have been replaced with other sanctified 'secular' texts. Constitutions are set apart for the guidance of society in an era when we largely pretend there are no foundational metaphysical commitments concerning life's order and meaning.

Interpreting the contemporary canon in relation to treaties reinforces the Crown's pre-eminence. In the Canadian context, canons of construction reinforce a search for original meanings,[75] modified by the Crown primary supremacy.[76] While treaties are to be given a large, liberal, and general construction,[77] interpreting them as the Indians would understand them,[78] and resolving ambiguities in their favour,[79] the court selectively applies,[80] ignores,[81] or subordinates these principles to the Crown's overriding placement in the constitutional order.[82] Likewise, in the New Zealand context, canons of construction have considered the Treaty of Waitangi to be without effect unless implemented through legislation.[83] Thus, while the Waitangi Tribunal pleads for the adoption of canons of construction which are similar to those found in the North American context, it too recognises the challenge in accomplishing this goal. Nevertheless, it is helpful to reproduce the Tribunal's preferred approach to treaty interpretation to demonstrate that[84]

> The Treaty was also more than an affirmation of existing rights. It was not intended to merely fossilise a status quo, but to provide a direction for future growth and development. The broad and general nature of its words indicates that it was not intended as a finite contract but as the foundation for a developing social contract.
>
> We consider then that the Treaty is capable of a measure of adaptation to meet new and changing circumstances provided there is a measure of consent and an adherence to its broad principles.

While I am in agreement with the Waitangi Tribunal's interpretative approach towards the Treaty of Waitangi, I wish to also highlight that it wishes to replace one foundational principle (Crown-*aprioricity*) with another ('the foundation for a developing social contract'). In either version, metaphysical appeals to first principles/principals lives on. Parties each appeal to the text for their own fundamental (fundamentalist?) narrative to prevail.

iii) Confessions

The point just made, that parties appeal to different origin stories to support their preferred approach to treaty interpretation, highlights law's sectarian nature. Law is practised along differential devotional lines. There are multiple confessional-like legal traditions in Canada and New Zealand. Varied schools of thought vie for attention in the field. Law's theology is organised along competing metaphysical lines.

To understand law's metaphysics, it might be helpful to identify catholic, protestant, agonistic, ecumenical, agnostic, or non-believer-traditions when it comes to treaty interpretation. I am not referring to religious denominations or movements in this list. I am attempting to identify broader interpretive traditions. Perspicuous contrast between religious classifications and legal approaches might assist us in identifying gaps, blind-spots, and incongruities in our legal practices.[85] Religiously labelled analogies in this section are for the pedagogical purpose of inquiry and further scrutiny. These rough categorisations are entry points for examining commitments which may be based on a priori assumptions animating views. They must be nuanced or abandoned once their utility as entry points have been established. No person is ever unified in his or her thoughts, and no approach to life is ever fully pure. "Beware the danger of a single story" is an appropriate reminder when it comes to working with interpretive complexity.[86]

Unfortunately, as I have been arguing, when it comes to treaty interpretation, single-source explanations seem to prevail. Crown sovereignty, while constitutionally circumscribed in important ways, is ultimately supreme when dealing with Indigenous peoples. Of course, I also worry about the Crown's replacement in these frameworks with equally abstract Indigenous or inter-societal origin stories. It is the lack of transparency involved in our legal commitments which greatly troubles me. There may be no escape from metaphysics in legal circles: I confess I am not sure. However, the failure to self-reflexively interrogate law's own subjectivity can lead people and institutions to claim authority in ways which appear neutral, natural, and beyond question. This is the metaphysical mischief I am trying to uncover in this work.

To turn to law's devotional sects: some lawyers, judges, and professors are catholic, meaning they interpret the legal world through a holistic lens. Katholikos is a Greek word derived from two roots: *kata* or *kath* (meaning "in respect of") and *holos* (meaning "whole").[87] Some legal practitioners are catholic – meaning they see their field in universal terms. Adherents with this view of treaties do not encourage boundaries or line-drawing in demarcating those who are 'in' and those who are 'out'; they attempt to unify and reconcile shared power under Crown frameworks.[88] A catholic (*not* Catholic) view is demonstrated when Governor Hobson signed the Treaty of Waitangi. He shook the hand of each of the original 43 Māori signatories and said "*He iwi tahi tatou* – We are now all one people."[89] Others who write about treaties are protestant (*not* Protestant) – they protest the unity of legal authority as flowing from and being vested in the Crown.[90] They critique the view that treaties must be backstopped and controlled by the Crown. They argue for revitalised processes "driven by the principles underpinning *tikanga*, a process which Pākehā do not control".[91] They are not fans of reconciliation without our past institutional wrongs and our inherently corrupt nature being acknowledged. Yet, other interpretative practitioners perceive the field as agonistic. They regard political conflict and perpetual renegotiation as social realities.[92] Ecumenical schools of thought also find place in the field. People who approach treaty interpretation in this light champion coordinated activity. They believe differences should not be sublimated, and yet they express hope that reconciliation can work across difference.[93] Finally, others who work in the field are either agnostic or do not believe in the value of legal interpretation before legislatures and the courts. Others are non-believers, like atheists in a religious sphere; they reject or even seek to actively overturn State authority and its God-like hold on our social imaginations.[94] They seek to exit law's metaphysics (though as I have argued they may unwittingly replicate another kind of *aprioricity* in their work).

Constitutional faiths might also be expressed through interpretive traditions. Two of the most prominent devotions are originalism and living constitutionalism. Originalism is a mode of argumentation which roots constitutional rights and principles in historic argumentation.[95] Originalists believe a law's meaning must be the same today as when it was first drafted or ratified.[96] Many prominent expressions of originalism can be found in both Canada and New Zealand.[97]

Like Biblical or Koranic literalism, originalism seeks to give the same meaning to texts that they possessed at the time they were written down.[98] Literal historicism is rife in the field of treaty interpretation, as history is equated with law in many cases.[99] This seems to be another metaphysical turn in the field. Historians' disciplinary convictions and judges' reproduction of their origin stories represent another form of *aprioricity* in the law.[100] It can be practised with evangelical zeal, as witnessed in the United States where strict historicism and originalism has become the constitutional gospel for many devotees.[101]

While history should be an important aid when interpreting treaties, it is easy to forget that law and history have different disciplinary touchstones.[102] Historians search for evidence of past events without adding to these interpretations' subsequent 'downstream' understandings which developed through passage of time.[103] "History and judging operate in different fields; they belong to different disciplines. Historians and judges are not just people with different titles; they are people with different jobs."[104] This is consistent with FW Maitland's observations: "What the lawyer wants is authority and the newer the better; what the historian wants is evidence and the older the better."[105]

I worry when the metaphysics of law attempts to make history determinative, particularly when Canada and New Zealand's histories are rife with colonial subordination and discrimination in the so-called age of contact, discovery, and assertion of Crown sovereignty. Originalism attempts to banish competing interpretive choices which do not comport with its own fundamental, foundational first principles. Both the Crown and Indigenous peoples problematically practise this interpretive form, highlighting different 'facts' from our national origin stories to try to establish their views.[106]

By way of contrast, another pervasive interpretive tradition is called living constitutionalism. In the Canadian context the courts have long compared Canada's highest law to a 'living tree'.[107] This interpretive mode seeks to incorporate developing insights and interpretations of law as it travels through time.[108] In this respect, living interpretation is said to reject frozen and static forms of reasoning.[109] As the Canadian Supreme Court wrote in the *Reference Re Provincial Electoral Boundaries (Sask.)*, "The doctrine of the constitution as a living tree mandates that narrow technical approaches are to be eschewed," which means that "the past plays a critical but non-exclusive role" in interpreting fundamental rights.[110]

Like originalism, living constitutionalism can also reproduce the kind of metaphysical claims identified by Professor Fine's frameworks outlined earlier in the chapter. Like scriptural hermeneutics, living interpretive traditions place faith in contemporary judges' and parliamentarians' capacities to experience continuing revelation. Living constitutionalists argue that law can be reproduced in each generation in ways which address the "realities of modern life."[111]

To apply Professor Fine's framework to living traditionalism: *aprioricity* is still present in this story because overarching control continues to be vested in the institutions and actors of the State, mediated by law. The Crown is still privileged in this view because high-level principles/principals structure the field. The field of inquiry contains built-in restrictions about which living traditions have value, and there is control over how they are expressed. Living constitutionalism can be eidetic because it operates at both particular and generalised levels. Finally, this mode of interpretation also rests on foundational reasoning.

As Indigenous peoples have been repeatedly cautioned, living constitutionalism has its limits. Living constitutionalism cannot "fracture the skeleton of principle which gives the body of our law its shape and internal consistency".[112] Living constitutionalism insists that Indigenous perspectives "must be framed in terms cognizable to the Canadian legal and constitutional structure".[113] Living constitutionalism demands that this approach must not "strain the Canadian legal and constitutional structure",[114] "beyond the weight they can reasonably hold".[115] Thus, when it comes to living constitutionalism, Indigenous expansion can be easily contained by first principles/principals. As the Supreme Court of Canada noted when rejecting living tree reasoning when it departed from foundational Crown-centric premises: "[g]enerous rules of interpretation should not be confused with a vague sense of after-the-fact largesse."[116]

Conclusion

In 1989 Chief Judge Eddie Durie gave the Waitangi Day speech. He said:[117]

> We [Māori] must not forget that the Treaty is not just a Bill of Rights for Māori. It is a Bill of Rights for Pakeha too. It is the Treaty that gives Pakeha the right to be here. Without the Treaty there would be no lawful authority for the Pakeha presence in this part of the South Pacific. The Pakeha here are not like the Indians of Fiji, or the French in New Caledonia. Our Prime Minister can stand proud in Pacific forums and in international forums too, not in spite of the Treaty but because of it. We must remember that if we are the Tangata Whenua, the original people, then the Pakeha are the Tangata Tiriti, those who belong to the land by right of that Treaty.

This is an alternative origin story. On the surface, it significantly differs from one that places the Crown in control of treaty interpretation. Justice Durie's origin story is one I am generally inclined to support. I am in favour of decentring Crown supremacy in both Canada and New Zealand. But my support is qualified. I worry when surface acceptance implicates deeper metaphysical commitments to supreme authority. This chapter has highlighted the dangerous metaphysics found in the politics of 'firstness' practised in both countries. Justice Durie's speech potentially replaces one a priori assumption with another. Crown-*aprioricity* may simply be substituted for Māori firstness under the Treaty as the foundation of legal order in New Zealand.

If this is the case, Justice Durie's potential placement of the Treaty of Waitangi as the moving cause of the country's genesis has metaphysical implications. If accepted by Parliament and the courts, it will become more difficult to contest particular visions which would be contrary to this view. This is perhaps not a bad thing. It may even lead to positive results. This is particularly the case if Indigenous peoples are empowered to live with greater dignity in their lands because their views have greater weight.[118] However, Justice Durie's approach can also replicate underlying assumptions about State-centric law as the grand mediating force in human affairs. Origin-story replacement should not represent the outer edges of reform.[119] Transubtantiation has its limits; changing forms have less value if we are not conscious of our ongoing metaphysical error – of placing the State above us in our interpretive decision-making processes. Changing something from one form into another does not change us for better without this acknowledgement.

A range of non-state-first choices may be available to help us understand and implement treaties. This requires us to question a fundamental article of faith concerning the essentially fallen and corrupt nature of the human condition, which requires a Leviathan or supreme authority to protect us from ourselves.[120] This chapter does not argue that nation-states like New Zealand and Canada have no place in our facilitating treaty interpretation. My target in this work relates to first-order assumptions which we have not sufficiently scrutinised. This must change. Neither the Crown nor Indigenous Peoples need to be considered absolutely supreme. Right relationships among peoples and the earth deserve greater attention in our quest to honour the treaties.[121] Deference to absolute authority can be dangerous in many contexts.

I anticipate some readers will have difficulty with the 'practicality' of my conclusion. They may wonder whether it is 'realistic' to decentre the State as the ultimate arbiter of Crown/Indigenous relationships. If we believe we have no alternatives to State-first 'realities', this may be the ultimate signal that legal metaphysics has a deeper hold on our societies than we care to admit.[122] My approach and conclusions may thus present a challenge to State-centric believers who (pre)suppose that life is given its highest possibility for making-meaning if we are guided under a supreme State's principles and principals.

In reply, it might be said that faith, devotion, and consecration to a higher worthy cause may be a good thing – if such beliefs are deliberately chosen.[123] We need to explicitly 'own' our metaphysics and more fully interrogate the implications of our beliefs. Problems often arise when we are blind to how faith structures our lives.[124] Creeds which operate through silent compulsion do not develop human capabilities.[125] Convictions which manipulate our choices repress human agency and stint our social growth.[126] Without critical inquiry, Law can make its practitioners intellectually idle and vulnerable to oppression. Idleness can lead to idolness. When this occurs, Law can force us to submit to lifeless forms. Idolatry has long been decried in Abrahamic religious traditions; submission to empty forms should also be rejected when it comes to legal interpretation.

Notes

1 Kit Fine "What Is Metaphysics" in Tuomas E. Tahko (ed) *Contemporary Aristotelian Metaphysics* (Cambridge University Press, Cambridge, 2011) 8–25 at 8.

2 *Te Heuheu Tukino v Aotea District Māori Land Board* [1941] NZLR 590, 596–597, AC 308, 324 (PC 1941) (holding that the Treaty was not enforceable in domestic law).
3 *R v Badger* [1996] 1 SCR 771.
4 For example, the British assumed they had sovereignty in New Zealand before the creation of the Treaty of Waitangi. Governor Hobson's letter of instructions allowed claim to the South Island by right of discovery, and Letters Patent of 1839 "provided for the attachment to New South Wales of any territory annexed to New Zealand". See Alan Ward *An Unsettled History: Treaty Claims in New Zealand Today* (Bridget Williams Books, Wellington, 1999) at 13.
5 See *Report of the Royal Commission on Aboriginal Peoples: Looking Forward and Looking Back* Vol 1 (Supply and Services Canada, Ottawa, 1996) at recommendation 1.16.2 at page 696:

> Federal, provincial and territorial government further the process of renewal by:
>
> (a) acknowledging that concepts such as *terra nullius* and the doctrine of discovery are factually, legally and morally wrong

6 See Robert J. Miller and others *Discovering Indigenous Lands: The Doctrine of Discovery in the English Colonies* (Oxford University Press, Oxford, 2010); Lindsay G. Robertson *Conquest by Law: How the Discovery of America Dispossessed Indigenous Peoples of Their Lands* (Oxford University Press, New York, NY, 2007); John Borrows "The Durability of Terra Nullius" (2015) *UBC Law Review* 701. See also John Borrows "Aboriginal Title in Tsilhqot'in v British Columbia" (2014) *Māori Law Review* <http://maorilawreview.co.nz/2014/08/aboriginal-title-in-tsilhqotin-v-british-columbia-2014-scc-44/>.
7 The New Zealand Court of Appeal has observed: "New Zealand was never thought to be terra nullius (an important point of distinction from Australia)": *Ngati Apa v Attorney General* [2003] NZCA 117 at para. 37. The Supreme Court of Canada has written: "At the time of the assertion of British sovereignty, North America was not treated by the Crown as *res nullius*": *R v Marshall, R v Bernard* [2005] 2 SCR 220 at para 132.
8 See *Calder v Attorney-General of British Columbia* [1973] SCR 313, at 328: "the fact is that when the settlers came, the Indians were there, organized in societies and occupying the land as their forefathers had done for centuries."
9 *United States v Winans* (1905) 198 US 371 at 381, 25 S Ct 662. The US Supreme Court stated: "In other words, the treaty was not a grant of rights to the Indians, but a grant of rights from them – a reservation of those not granted."
10 Janine Hayward "Appendix, the Principles of the Treaty of Waitangi" in *Rangahau Whanui Series, National Overview* Vol II (Waitangi Tribunal, Wellington, 1997) at 475. See also *New Zealand Māori Council v Attorney-General* [1987] 1 NZLR 641.
11 *R v Sparrow* [1990] 1 SCR 1075. For critical commentary on the *Sparrow* case, related to its foundational choices, see Michael Asch and Patrick Macklem "Aboriginal Rights and Canadian Sovereignty: An Essay on *R v Sparrow*" (1991) 29 *Alberta Law Journal* 498.
12 *R v Sparrow*, above n 11, at 1103.
13 John Borrows, "Constitutional Law From a First Nation Perspective: Self-Government and the Royal Proclamation" (1994) 28 *UBC Law Review* 1.
14 The actual state of things as a high-level general assertion justifying the doctrine of discovery is found in the first North American cases dealing with Indigenous issues, see *Worcester v Georgia*, 31 US 515, 560 (1832). For critique of

this approach, see Robert A. Williams Jr *The American Indian in Western Legal Thought: The Discourses of Conquest* (Oxford University Press, New York, NY, 1990).

15 For a critique of a prior, general reasoning in Aboriginal rights cases, see John Borrows "Sovereignty's Alchemy: An Analysis of Delgamuukw v British Columbia" (1999) 37 *Osgoode Hall Law Journal* 537.

16 The nature and scope of treaties is often central in their interpretation, see *Simon v The Queen* [1985] 2 SCR 387 at para 25; *R v Sioui* [1990] 1 SCR 1025; *R v Badger*, above n 3, at paras. 61, 76.

17 Fine, above n 1, at 22.

18 "An Indian treaty is unique; it is an agreement *sui generis* which is neither created nor terminated according to the rules of international law." *R v Simon* (185) 24 DLR (4th) 390 at para 34; *R v Symonds* (1847) NZPCC 387 at 395.

19 Waitangi Tribunal "Mihi" <www.justice.govt.nz/tribunals/waitangi-tribunal/about>.

20 *Mikisew Cree First Nation v Canada (Minister of Canadian Heritage)* [2005] 3 SCR 388 at para 1. See also Justice Binne in *Mitchell v MNR* [2001] 1 SCR 911: "The constitutional objective is reconciliation not mutual isolation."

21 *Tsilhqot'in Nation v British Columbia*, 2014 SCC 44 [2014] 2 SCR 256:

> The Court in *Delgamuukw* confirmed that infringements of Aboriginal title can be justified under s. 35 of the *Constitution Act, 1982* pursuant to the *Sparrow* test and described this as a "necessary part of the reconciliation of [A]boriginal societies with the broader political community of which they are part" (at para. 161), quoting *R. v Gladstone*, [1996] 2 S.C.R. 723, at para. 73.

22 The grand purpose of s 35 is "[t]he reconciliation of Aboriginal and non-Aboriginal Canadians in a mutually respectful long-term relationship": *Beckman v Little Salmon/Carmacks First Nation* [2010] 3 SCR 103, at para. 10.

23 John Borrows "Ground Rules: Indigenous Treaties in Canada and New Zealand" (2006) 22 *New Zealand Universities Law Review* 188; John Borrows "(Ab)Originalism and Canada's Constitution" (2012) 58 *Supreme Court Law Review* 351.

24 For further discussion of origin-ism, see Benedict Anderson *Imagined Communities: Reflections on the Origin and Spread of Nationalism* (Rev ed, Verso, London, 2006).

25 For discussions about when life begins and whether the foetus can be terminated, see *Borowski v Canada (AG)* [1989] 1 SCR 342; *R v Morgentaler* [1988] 1 SCR 30; *Right to Life New Zealand Inc v The Abortion Supervisory Committee* [2012] NZSC 68 (9 August 2012).

26 For discussions about issues related to the meaning of life, liberty, and security see *Carter v Canada (Attorney General)*, 2015 SCC 5, [2015] 1 SCR 331; *Canada (Attorney General) v PHS Community Services Society*, 2011 SCC 44, [2011] 3 SCR 134; *Seales v Attorney-General* [2015] NZHC 1239.

27 Differences of views concerning death and preparation for an afterlife was the issue for many Māori in *Josephine Takamore v Denise Clarke and Others* [2012] NZSC 116 (18 December 2012).

28 Justice Joseph Williams "Lex Aotearoa: An Heroic Attempt to Map the Māori Dimension in Modern New Zealand Law" (2013) 21 *Waikato Law Review* 1.

29 At 5.

30 At 10.

31 At 12.

32 Royal Commission on Aboriginal Peoples *Partners in Confederation: Aboriginal Peoples, Self-Government and the Constitution* (Supply and Services, Ottawa, 1993).

33 *Mikisew Cree First Nation v Canada (Minister of Canadian Heritage)* [2005] 3 SCR 388 at para 24.

34 Harold Cardinal and Walter Hildebrandt *Treaty Elders of Saskatchewan: Our Dream Is that Our Peoples Will One Day Be Clearly Recognized as Nations* (University of Calgary Press, Calgary, 2000); Walter Hildebrandt and others *The True Spirit and Original Intent of Treaty 7* (McGill-Queen's University Press, Montreal and Kingston, 1996) at 133; René Fumoleau *As Long as This Land Shall Last: A History of Treaty 8 and Treaty 11* (University of Calgary Press, Calgary, 2004) at 74, 133, 240, 257, 314, 340, 502; Arthur J. Ray, J. R. Miller, and Frank Tough *Bounty and Benevolence: A History of Saskatchewan Treaties* (McGill-Queen's University Press, Montreal and Kingston, 2000) at 116–117; William C. Wicken *Mi'kmaq Treaties on Trial: History, Land and Donald Marshall Junior* (University of Toronto Press, Toronto, 2002).

35 Yale Belanger and P. Whitney Lackenbauer (eds) *Blockades of Breakthroughs: Aboriginal Peoples Confront the Canadian State* (McGill-Queen's University Press, Montreal, 2014); John Borrows *Freedom and Indigenous Constitutionalism* (University of Toronto Press, Toronto, 2016).

36 For the subordination of Indigenous concerns in favour of non-Indigenous development, see *Grassy Narrows First Nation v Ontario (Natural Resources)* [2014] SCC 48 at para 40.

37 Andrew McIndoe "A Pluralistic Imperialism – Britain's Understanding of Sovereignty at the Signing of the Treaty of Waitangi" (2015) 21 *Auckland University Law Review* 60.

38 See, generally, James Anaya "Report of the Special Rapporteur on the Rights of Indigenous Peoples in the Situation of Māori People in New Zealand" (2015) 32 *Arizona Journal of International and Comparative Law* 1; Claire Charters "Responding to Waldron's Defence of Legislatures: Why New Zealand's Parliament Does Not Protect Rights in Hard Cases" (2006) 40 *New Zealand Law Review* 621.

39 Saskatchewan Office of the Treaty Commissioner *Treaties: The Road of Reconciliation, Interim Report* (Saskatchewan Office of the Treaty Commissioner, Saskatoon, 2006) at 105–108.

40 Rt Hon Dame Sian Elias, GNZM, Chief Justice of New Zealand "The Meaning and Purpose of the Treaty of Waitangi" (2015) *Māori Law Review* <http://maorilawreview.co.nz/2015/10/the-meaning-and-purpose-of-the-treaty-of-waitangi-dame-sian-elias/>:

> In looking into the future, I think we can expect to see change in the status of the Treaty as domestic law and perhaps as an acknowledged part of the New Zealand constitution. It is possible that we will see increasing pluralism within the New Zealand domestic legal order in fulfilment of the Treaty guarantees. The role of law in Treaty recognition may well evolve.

41 *Beckman v Little Salmon/Carmacks First Nation* [2010] 3 SCR 103 at para 10.

> The reconciliation of Aboriginal and non-Aboriginal Canadians in a mutually respectful long-term relationship is the grand purpose of s. 35 of the Constitution Act, 1982. The modern treaties, including those at issue here, attempt to further the objective of reconciliation not only by addressing grievances over the land claims but by creating the legal basis to foster a positive long-term relationship between Aboriginal and non-Aboriginal communities. . . .

> The treaty is as much about building relationships as it is about the settlement of ancient grievances. The future is more important than the past. A canoeist who hopes to make progress faces forwards, not backwards.

42 *Mikisew Cree First Nation v Canada (Minister of Canadian Heritage)* [2005] 3 SCR 388 at para 54.

43 Te Puni Kōkiri "Legislative Reform Treaty of Waitangi 1975" <www.tpk.govt.nz/en/consultation/reform/treatyofwaitangi>.

44 For a discussion of the resurgence of Indigenous law in the Canadian context, see John Borrows *Recovering Canada: The Resurgence of Indigenous Law* (University of Toronto Press, Toronto, 2002); John Borrows *Canada's Indigenous Constitution* (University of Toronto Press, Toronto, 2010).

45 Ani Mikaere argues that Tikanga Māori should be the starting point of human relationships in Aotearoa, see "Are We all New Zealanders Now? A Māori Response to the Pākehā Quest for Indigeneity" (Lecture Delivered at Maidment Theatre, Auckland, 15 November 2004) <http://twm.co.nz/nov15_Mikaere.html>:

> For Pākehā to gain legitimacy here, it is they who must place their trust in Māori, not the other way around. *They must accept that it is for the tangata whenua to determine their status in this land, and to do so in accordance with tikanga Māori. This will involve sorting out a process of negotiation which is driven by the principles underpinning tikanga, a process which Pākehā do not control. There is no doubt that many Pākehā will find this challenging: their obsession with control over the Māori-Pākehā relationship to date could almost be categorised as a form of compulsive disorder. Giving up such control requires a leap of faith on the part of Pākehā. In my view, however, nothing less will suffice if they truly want to gain the sense of belonging they so crave, the sense of identity that until now has proven so elusive.*

Under this view, treaties may a necessary but certainly not sufficient condition for undermining colonialism in Canada and New Zealand.

46 Thus, in my view where we are going seems to involve judgments about the intermingling of legal sources and the displacement of Crown dominance when we are interpreting treaties.

47 While I have argued this is an enticing yet deceiving metaphysics, many legal actors continue to act and believe in ways consistent with this view.

48 My position is outlined in John Borrows *Freedom and Indigenous Constitutionalism*, above n 35.

49 See Neil Peart, lyrics, "Freewill", with Geddy Lee and Alex Lifeson, from the album by Rush, *Spirit of the Radio* (Mercury Records, Toronto, 1979) <www.youtube.com/watch?v=OnxkfLe4G74>:

> You can choose a ready guide in some celestial voice
> If you choose not to decide, you still have made a choice
> You can choose from phantom fears and kindness that can kill
> I will choose a path that's clear
> I will choose freewill

50 Fine, above n 1, at 22.

51 Jennifer Nedelsky "Embodied Diversity and the Challenges to Law" (1997) 42 *McGill Law Journal* 91; Antonio Domasio *Descartes' Error: Emotion, Reason and the Human Brain* (Quill, New York, NY, 2000); Antonio Domasio *The Feeling of What Happens: Body and Emotion in the Making of Consciousness* (Harcourt, New York, NY, 1999); Antonio Domasio *Looking for Spinoza: Joy, Sorrow and the*

Feeling Brain (Harcourt, New York, NY, 2003); Martha Nussbaum *Upheavals of Thought: The Intelligence of Emotions* (Cambridge University Press, Cambridge, 2001); Peter Goldie *The Emotions: A Philosophical Exploration* (Oxford University Press, Oxford, 2000); Richard Wollheim *On the Emotions* (Yale University Press, New Haven, CT, 2000); Julien Deonna and Fabrice Teroni *The Emotions: A Philosophical Introduction* (Routledge, New York, NY, 2012).

52 Practices of the self are "those reflective and voluntary practices by which men not only set themselves rules of conduct, but seek to transform themselves, to change themselves in their singular being, and to make of their life into an oeuvre that carries certain aesthetic values and meets certain stylistic criteria". Michel Foucault *The Use of Pleasure. The History of Sexuality: Volume Two* (Penguin, New York, NY, 1992) at 10–11.

53 In this respect, law is somewhat like the God of the Nicene Creed and the Westminster Confession of 1647 <http://carm.org/westminster-confession>:

> There is but one only living and true God, who is infinite in being and perfection, a most pure spirit, invisible, without body, parts, or passions, immutable, immense, eternal, incomprehensible, almighty, most wise, most holy, most free, most absolute, working all things according to the counsel of his own immutable and most righteous will, for his own glory, most loving, gracious, merciful, long-suffering, abundant in goodness and truth, forgiving iniquity, transgression, and sin; the rewarder of them that diligently seek him; and withal most just and terrible in his judgments; hating all sin; and who will by no means clear the guilty.

54 John Borrows "Foreword: Entanglement" in Sylvie Poirier and Françoise Dussart (eds) *Entangled Territorialities: Negotiating Indigenous Lands in Canada and Australia* (University of Toronto Press, Toronto, 2016).

55 Even avowed anti-metaphysicians like Michel Foucault seem to have had difficulty escaping its grasp, see Ian Burkitt "Overcoming Metaphysics: Elias and Foucault on Power and Freedom" (1993) 23 *Philosophy of the Social Sciences* 50.

56 This is demonstrated in another context, where seeing power as being linked to war, Foucault wrote:

> [P]ower is war, a war continued by other means. This reversal of Clausewitz's assertion that war is politics continued by other means . . . implies that the relations of power that function in a society such as ours essentially rest upon a definite relation of forces that is established at a determinate, historically specifiable moment, in war and by war. Furthermore, if it is true that political power puts an end to war, that it installs, or tries to install, the reign of peace in civil society, this by no means implies that it suspends the effects of war or neutralizes the disequilibrium revealed in the final battle. The role of political power, on this hypothesis, is perpetually to reinscribe this relation through a form of unspoken warfare; to reinscribe it in social institutions, in economic inequalities, in language, in the bodies themselves of each and everyone of us.

Michel Foucault *Two Lectures in Power/Knowledge* (Pantheon Books, New York, NY, 1980) at 90–91. If we substituted the word 'law' for 'power' in the above quote, we might see how metaphysics persists even in practitioners who try to replace it with typologies and genealogies of practice. For a discussion of Foucault's metaphysics, see James Miller *The Passion of Michel Foucault* (Harvard University Press, Cambridge, MA, 2010) at 119.

57 For extended arguments which examine "the inescapable yet often unarticulated, or unseen, moral frameworks within which contemporary moral values

exist", see Charles Taylor *Sources of the Self: The Making of Modern Identity* (Harvard University Press, Cambridge, MA, 1989).

58 Michel Foucault has written: "The problem . . . [of politics] is to give oneself the rules of law, the techniques of management, and also the ethics, the *ethos*, the practice of the self, which would allow these games of power to be played with a minimum of domination." Michel Foucault *The Final Foucault* (MIT Press, Cambridge, MA, 1988) (eds James Bernauer and David Rasmussen) at 18, cited in James Tully *Public Philosophy in a New Key: Volume 1, Democracy and Civic Freedom* (Cambridge University Press, Cambridge, 2008) at 121.

59 Ben Berger *Law's Religion: Religious Difference and the Claims of Constitutionalism* (University of Toronto Press, Toronto, 2015).

60 Sanford Levinson *Constitutional Faith* (Princeton University Press, Princeton, NJ, 1988).

61 Many of these examples are visible in Robert Williams Jr *Linking Arms Together: American Indian Treaty Visions of Law and Peace, 1600–1800* (Oxford University Press, New York, NY, 1997).

62 Thomas Hobbes *Leviathan* (G. Routledge and Sons, London, 1887); Jean Jacques Rousseau *The Social Contract* (Dent, London, 1973); John Locke *Two Treatises on Government* (New American Library, New York, NY, 1965); James Tully *An Approach to Political Philosophy: Locke in Contexts* (Cambridge University Press, Cambridge, 1993).

63 Noel Lyon, Elder Jacob Bill, Saskatchewan Office of the Treaty Commissioner Symposium [on file with the author].

64 *R v Marshall* [1999] 3 SCR (SCC) 456 at para 4.

65 At para 58. For a history, see generally Wicken, above n 34; Thomas Issac *Aboriginal and Treaty Rights in the Maritimes: The Marshall Decision and Beyond* (Purich Publishing, Saskatoon, 2001).

66 *R v Marshall*, above n 64, at para 61.

67 *R v Marshall (No 2)* [1999] 3 SCR 533 at para 6.

68 At para 37.

69 For example, see *R v Badger*, above n 3, at 11 where the Court observed that Crown regulatory power preceded treaties:

> At the time the treaties that preceded the *NRTA* [Natural Resources Transfer Agreement] were signed, there was already in place legislation enacted for conservation purposes which affected the Indians' rights.

70 Ben Berger *Law's Religion: Religious Difference and the Claims of Constitutionalism* (University of Toronto Press, Toronto, 2015) at 12.

71 At 12.

72 Jeremy Webber "The Grammar of Customary Law" (2009) 54 *McGill Law Journal* 579; Jeremy Webber "Legal Pluralism and Human Agency" (2006) 44 *Osgoode Hall Law Journal* 167.

73 Claudia Orange *The Treaty of Waitangi* (Allen and Unwin, Wellington, 1987).

74 Keith Newman *Bible & Treaty: Missionaries Among the Māori – A New Perspective* (Penguin, Auckland, 2010); Jill St Germain *Indian Treaty-making Policy in the United States and Canada, 1867–1877* (University of Toronto Press, Toronto, 2001) at 67–72.

75 *R v White and Bob* (BCCA) at 648–49 cited in *R v Sioui*, above n 16, at para 16; *R v Taylor and Williams* [1981] 34 OR (2d) 360 at 367; *R v Horseman* [1990] 1 SCR 901 at 907; *R v Badger*, above n 3, at paras 4 and 41; *R v Sundown* [1999] 1 SCR 393 (SCC) at paras 24–25; *R v Marshall*, above n 64, at paras 9–14; *R v Marshall* [1999] 3 SCR 533 at para 19; *R v Marshall, R v Bernard*, above n 7, at para 26; *R v Morris* [2006] 2 SCR 915 at para 19. See, more

generally, Leonard Rotman "Taking Aim at the Canons of Treaty Interpretation in Canadian Aboriginal Rights Jurisprudence" (1997) 46 *UNBLJ* 1.

76 Borrows, above n 23, 351; John Borrows "Aboriginal and Treaty Rights and Violence Against Women" (2013) 50 *Osgoode Hall Law Journal* 699.

77 *R v Badger*, above n 3, at paras 76–78; *R v Sundown*, above n 77.

78 *R v Marshall*, above n 64, at para 78.

79 Len Rotman "Taking Aim at the Canons of Treaty Interpretation in Canadian Aboriginal Rights Jurisprudence" (1997) 46 *UNBLJ* 11.

80 The canons of treaty construction were selectively applied in *R v Horseman*, above n 75.

81 The canons of treaty construction were not cited in *Grassy Narrows First Nation v Ontario (Natural Resources)* [2014] 2 SCR 447.

82 The canons of treaty interpretation were subordinated to the Crown's overriding interests in *Quebec (Attorney General) v Moses* [2010] 1 SCR 557; *McDiarmid Lumber Ltd v God's Lake First Nation* [2006] 2 SCR 846.

83 Waitangi Tribunal *Motunui Waitara Report* 10 Interpretation of The Treaty of Waitangi <www.justice.govt.nz/tribunals/waitangi-tribunal/Reports/wai0006/06ch10>:

> [T]he Māori people have persistently pleaded the Treaty in the Courts but without success, and refer to – *R. v Symonds* (1847) N.Z.P.C.C. 387; *Wi Parata v Bishop of Wellington* (1877) 3 N.Z. Jur (N.S.) S.C. 72; *Mangakahia v New Zealand Timber Company* (1881–82) 2 N.Z.L.R. 345; *Nireaha Tamaki v Baker* (1901) N.Z.P.C.C. 371 (1902) A.C. 561; *Hohepa Wi Neera v Bishop of Wellington* (1902) 21 N.Z.L.R. 655 (C.A.); *Baldick v Jackson* (1911) 13 G.L.R. 398; *Tamihana Korokai v Solicitor-General* (1912) 32 N.Z.L.R. 321; *Waipapakura v Hempton* (1914) 33 N.Z.L.R. 1065; *Hoani Te Heuheu Tukino v Aotea District Māori Land Court* (1941) A.C. 308; *Inspector of Fisheries v Ihaia Weepu and anor* (1956) N.Z.L.R. 920l *In re the Bed of the Wanganui River* (1962) N.Z.L.R. 600; *In re the Ninety Mile Beach* (1963) N.Z.L.R. 46; *Keepa v Inspector of Fisheries* (1965) N.Z.L.R. 322: *R. Hita v H. D. Chisholm, Inspector of Fisheries* (Supreme Court 8 February 1977). While the Treaty may have a dubious status in international and municipal law it is interesting to note that in the cases in which the Treaty of Waitangi has been referred to, no argument has been adduced to question the existence of the Treaty as such or to deny the moral obligation it imposed.

84 Tribunal, above n 83.

85 Charles Taylor *Sources of the Self: The Making of the Modern Identity* (Harvard University Press, Cambridge, MA, 1989).

86 Chimamanda Ngozi Adichie (2009) "The Danger of a Single Story" <www.ted.com/talks/chimamanda_adichie_the_danger_of_a_single_story?language=en>.

87 Oxford Dictionary "Catholic" <www.oxforddictionaries.com/definition/english/catholic>.

88 Justice Binnie of the Supreme Court of Canada expressed this view as follows:

> "Merged sovereignty" asserts that First Nations were not wholly subordinated to non-aboriginal sovereignty, but over time became merger partners. The final *Report of the Royal Commission on Aboriginal Peoples, vol. 2* (Restructuring the Relationship, 1996) at 214, says that "Aboriginal governments give the constitution [of Canada] its deepest and most resilient roots in the Canadian soil." This updated concept of Crown sovereignty is of importance. Whereas historically the Crown may have been portrayed

as an entity across the seas with which aboriginal people could scarcely be expected to identify, this was no longer the case in 1982 when the s. 35(1) reconciliation process was established. The Constitution was patriated and all aspects of our sovereignty became firmly located within our borders. If the principle of "merged sovereignty" articulated by the *Royal Commission on Aboriginal Peoples* is to have any true meaning, it must include at least the idea that aboriginal and non-aboriginal Canadians together form a sovereign entity with a measure of common purpose and united effort. It is this new entity, as inheritor of the historical attributes of sovereignty, with which existing aboriginal and treaty rights must be reconciled.

Mitchell v MNR [2001] 1 SCR 911 at para 129.

89 For a discussion of the relationship of history to law in the Treaty of Waitangi, see J. Pocock "Law, Sovereignty and History in a Divided Culture: The Case of New Zealand and the Treaty of Waitangi" (1998) 43 *McGill Law Journal* 481.

90 Authors who protest Crown sovereignty as a basis for treaty interpretation include Ani Mikaere "The Treaty of Waitangi and Recognition of Tikanga Māori" in Michael Belgrave, Merata Kawharu, and David Williams (eds) *Waitangi Revisited: Perspectives on the Treaty of Waitangi* (Oxford University Press, Melbourne, 2005) 330 at 341; Andrew Erueti "The International Labour Organization and the Internationalisation of the Concept of Indigenous Peoples" in S. Allen and A. Xanthaki (eds) *Reflections on the UN Declaration on the Rights of Indigenous Peoples* (Hart Publishing, Oxford, 2011) at 93–120; Claire Charters "Indigenous Peoples' Rights and International Law and Policy" in B. J. Richardson, S. Imai and K. McNeil (eds) *Indigenous Peoples and the Law: Comparative and Critical Perspectives* (Hart Publishing, Oxford, 2009); Sharon Venne "Understanding Treaty Six: An Indigenous Perspective" in Michael Asch (ed) *Aboriginal and Treaty Rights in Canada: Essays on Law, Equality, and Respect for Difference* (University of British Columbia Press, Vancouver, 1997) 173 at 194.

91 Mikaere, above n 45.

92 Agonistic accounts of treaty and legal interpretation are found in Mark Hickford *Lords of the Land: Indigenous Property Rights and the Jurisprudence of Empire* (Oxford University Press, Oxford, 2012); Jeremy Webber *The Constitution of Canada: A Contextual Analysis* (Hart Publishing, Oxford, 2015); James Tully *Strange Multiplicity: Constitutionalism in an Age of Diversity* (Cambridge University Press, Cambridge, 1995); Aaron Mills "Constitutional Stories: Pride, Violence and Citizenship in Canada" (2015) 17 *Cairo Review of Global Affairs* 115; Aaron Mills "Aki, Anishinaabek, Kaye Tahsh Crown" (2010) 9(1) *Indigenous Law Journal* 107; Aaron Mills "Rooted Constitutionalism: Growing Political Community" in Michael Asch, John Borrows and James Tully (eds) *Resurgence and Reconciliation* (University of Toronto Press, Toronto, 2018) [under consideration]; Aaron Mills "What Is a Treaty? On Contract and Mutual Aid" in John Borrows and Michael Coyle (eds) *The Right(s) Relationship: Reimagining the Implementation of Historical Treaties* (University of Toronto Press, Toronto, 2018) [forthcoming].

93 Ecumenical type approaches in a secular context seem to saturate much of the work of the Indian Truth and Reconciliation Commission *Honouring the Truth, Reconciling for the Future: Summary of the Final Report of the Truth and Reconciliation Commission of Canada* (2015) <www.trc.ca/websites/trcinstitution/File/2015/Findings/Exec_Summary_2015_05_31_web_o.pdf>.

94 Glen Coulthard *Red Skin, White Masks: Rejecting the Colonial Politics of Recognition* (University of Minnesota Press, Minneapolis, MN, 2014); Taiaiake Alfred *Wasase: Indigenous Pathways to Action* (Broadview Press, Peterborough, 2005).

95 Robert Bork *The Tempting of America* (Free Press, New York, NY, 1990). New originalism is represented by Randy Barnett *Restoring the Lost Constitution: The*

Presumption of Liberty (Princeton University Press, Princeton, NJ, 2004); Keith E. Whittington "The New Originalism" (2004) 2 *Georgetown Journal of Law and Public Policy* 599.

96 Randy E. Barnett "An Originalism for Non-originalists" (1999) 45 *Loyola Law Review* 611.

97 Paul McHugh *Aboriginal Title: The Modern Jurisprudence of Tribal Land Rights* (Oxford University Press, Oxford, 2011); Paul McHugh *Aboriginal Societies and the Common Law* (Oxford University Press, Oxford, 2004); Alex Cameron *Power Without Law: The Supreme Court of Canada, the Marshall Decisions and the Failure of Judicial Activism* (McGill-Queen's University Press, Montreal, 2009).

98 Peter Smith and Robert Tuttle "Biblical Literalism and Constitutional Interpretation" (2011) 86 *Notre Dame Law Review* 693 at 695.

99 Borrows, above n 23.

100 For critique and discussion of these views, see Paul Brest "The Misconceived Quest for the Original Understanding" (1980) 60 *Boston University Law Review* 204; Mitchell N. Berman "Originalism Is Bunk" (2009) 84 *New York Law Review* 1; David A. Straus *The Living Constitution* (Oxford University Press, New York, NY, 2010); Robert W. Bennett and Lawrence B. Solum *Constitutional Originalism: A Debate* (Cornell University Press, Ithaca, NY, 2011); Thomas Colby "The Sacrifice of the New Originalism" (2011) 99 *Georgetown Law Journal* 713.

101 Steven G. Calabresi (ed) *Originalism: A Quarter-Century of Debate* (Regnery, Washington DC, 2007); Keith Whittington *Constitutional Construction: Divided Powers and Constitutional and Meaning* (Harvard University Press, Cambridge, MA, 1999). Canada also has few originalists too, see Bradley Miller "Origin Myth: The Persons Case, The Living Tree, and the New Originalism" in Grant Huscroft and Bradley Miller (eds) *The Challenge of Originalism: Theories of Constitutional Interpretation* (Cambridge University Press, Cambridge, 2011) at 120; Bradley Miller "Beguiled by Metaphors: The 'Living Tree' and Originalist Constitutional Interpretation in Canada" (2009) 22 *Canadian Journal of Law and Jurisprudence* 331.

102 However, it is important to note the challenge in creating too sharp a distinction between the disciplines of history and law, see Alan Carr *What Is History?* (2nd ed, Penguin Books, New York, NY, 1987) at 30: History "is a continuous process of interaction between the historian and his facts, an unending dialogue between the past and the present".

103 The challenge of understanding history without reference to an historian's own social positioning is discussed in Daniel Woolf *The Social Circulation of the Past* (Oxford University Press, Oxford, 2003).

104 For further discussion, see Helen Irving "Outsourcing the Law: History and the Disciplinary Limits of Constitutional Reasoning" (2015) 84 *Fordham Law Review* 957 at 958: "History and judging operate in different fields; they belong to different disciplines. Historians and judges are not just people with different titles; they are people with different jobs."

105 F. W. Maitland *Why the History of English Law Is Not Written: An Inaugural Lecture 14 (Oct 13, 1888)* (Cambridge University Press, Cambridge, 1888).

106 Borrows, above n 23.

107 *Edwards v Attorney-General for Canada* [1930] AC 124 at 136 (JCPC). A comparative analysis of this metaphor in other constitutional contexts is found in Vicki Jackson "Constitutions as 'Living Trees'? Comparative Constitutional Law and Interpretive Metaphors" (2006) 75 *Fordham Law Review* 921.

108 Cases which apply living-tree interpretation in a Canadian context include: *Reference re Same-Sex Marriage* [2004] 3 SCR 698 at para 22; *Attorney General of British Columbia v Canada Trust Co et al* [1980] 2 SCR 466 at 478–479; *Canada (Attorney General) v Hislop* [2007] 1 SCR 429 at para 94; *Re Residential*

Tenancies Act, 1979 [1981] 1 SCR 714 at 723; *Re BC Motor Vehicle Act* [1985] 2 SCR 486 at para 53; Reference re *Employment Insurance Act* (Can.) *ss 22 and 23* [2005] 2 SCR 669 at para 9; *Reference Re Provincial Electoral Boundaries (Sask)* [1991] 2 SCR 158 at p 180; *R v Demers* [2004] 2 SCR 489 at para 78; *Canadian Western Bank v Alberta* [2007] 2 SCR 3 at para 23; *Ontario Home Builders' Association v York Region Board of Education* [1996] 2 SCR 929 at para 145.

109 *Attorney General of British Columbia v Canada Trust Co et al*, above n 108, at 478–479: "[t]here is nothing static or frozen, narrow or technical, about the Constitution of Canada."

110 *Reference Re Provincial Electoral Boundaries (Sask)*, above n 108, at p 180.

111 *Reference re Same-Sex Marriage*, above n 108, at para 22.

112 *Mabo v Queensland No 2* (1992) (1992) 175 CLR 1 at 29–30.

113 *R v Van der Peet* [1996] 2 SCR 507 at para 49.

114 *Delgamuukw v British Columbia* [1997] 3 SCR 1010.

115 *Mitchell v MNR* [2001] 1 SCR 911 at para 51.

116 *R v Marshall*, above n 64, at para 14, cited in *R v Blais* [2003] 2 SCR 236 at paras 39–40.

117 Eddie Durie (1990) "New Zealand Church Leaders' Statement" at page 10.

118 The role of agency and choice are the focus of at least two of my books, John Borrows *Drawing Out Law: A Spirit's Guide* (University of Toronto Press, Toronto, 2010); Borrows, above n 35. I also believe this is a central theme of my other published books.

119 James Tully expresses the idea in this way:

> A 'limit' can mean either the characteristic forms of thought and action that are taken for granted and not questioned or contested by participants in a practice of subjectivity, thereby functioning as the implicit background or horizon of their questions and contests, or it can mean that a form of subjectivity (its form of reason, norms of conduct and so forth) is explicitly claimed to be a limit that cannot be otherwise because it is universal, necessary or obligatory (the standard form of legitimization since the Enlightenment). . . . [H]umans can develop the capacities of thought and action to question and contest both types of limit.

Tully, above n 58, at 75.

120 Hobbes, above n 62.

121 Aaron Mills "Driving the Gift Home" (2016) 33(1) *Windsor Yearbook of Access to Justice* 167; Aaron Mills "The Lifeworlds of Law: On Revitalizing Indigenous Legal Orders Today" (2016) 61(4) *McGill Law Journal* 847.

122 The process of internalising the commands of a hegemonic power has been labelled imperialism, see Tully, above n 58, at 264–267.

123 For a critical discussion of the metaphysics of free will and moral agency, see Derk Pereboom *Living Without Free Will* (Cambridge University Press, Cambridge, 2001); Galen Strawson *Freedom and Belief* (Clarendon Press, Oxford, 1986); Saul Smilansky *Free Will and Illusion* (Oxford University Press, Oxford, 2000); Daniel Wegner *The Illusion of Conscious Will* (MIT Press, Cambridge, MA, 2002).

124 Richard Dawkins *The Blind Watchmaker: Why the Evidence of Evolution Reveals a Universe Without Design* (Norton, New York, NY, 1986); Rabbi Sachs "Faith Lectures: Revelation – Torah From Heaven" (23 March 2001) <www.rabbisacks.org/faith-lectures-revelation-torah-heaven/>.

125 For the development of ideas which connect freedom and choice with capabilities, see Amartya Sen *The Idea of Justice* (Harvard University Press, Cambridge, MA, 2009).

126 Tully, above n 58, at 196–197, citing John Rawls *The Law of Peoples With the Idea of Public Reason Revisited* (Harvard University Press, Cambridge, MA, 1999) at 140–143.

3 Originalism and the constitutional canon of Aotearoa New Zealand

David V Williams[1]

This chapter draws on my presentation at the symposium on "175 Years of Interpreting the Treaty of Waitangi" held in the Legislative Council Chamber at Parliament in February 2016 and revised in the light of the stimulating conversations at that event. It has four component parts. First, I will highlight arguments presented at the symposium by John Borrows on "(Ab)Originalism and Canada's Constitution"[2] and reflect on their relevance for the constitutional canon in New Zealand. I will suggest that neither Canadian nor New Zealand jurisprudence is as free as we might hope and assume of the taint of *terra nullius* conceptions said to have been applicable in Australia prior to *Mabo (No2)*.[3] Second, while embracing the desirability of the 'living tree' approach to constitutional interpretation in Canada derived from the advice of the Privy Council in the *Persons case*,[4] as Borrows does, I will urge that it is important to reconsider some generally accepted historical orthodoxies about the original meanings of the Treaty of Waitangi. In the decades since 1972, most interpretations of the Treaty of Waitangi have accepted unquestioningly the propositions put forward by Ruth Ross in her seminal *New Zealand Journal of History* paper of that year.[5] As a consequence, the English drafts and the English text of the Treaty have been sidelined as irrelevant to the meaning of the true primary text – te Tiriti o Waitangi – and as suspiciously inconsistent with a proper understanding of the Māori text's guarantees of *te tino rangatiratanga* (sovereignty or self-determination) to *rangatira* (chiefs or people of high rank) and *hapū* (tribes).[6] Third, I will highlight the contributions of an English scholar, Trevor Williams, to an understanding of the aims and purposes of those who drafted the English text of the Treaty. His papers published in 1940 and 1941 have been generally neglected in New Zealand historical scholarship.[7] I will suggest that they remain highly pertinent to a reappraisal of the Treaty and its interpretations as we move beyond the 175th anniversary. Fourth, I will note the important reassessment of Treaty interpretations to be found in a PhD thesis completed by Ned Fletcher in 2014.[8] In conclusion, I will suggest that an assessment of the English text in line with the analyses of Trevor Williams and Fletcher may provide a historical justification for the innovative co-governance regimes incorporated in recent Treaty Settlements of historical claims negotiated by the Crown and Māori claimants. In this respect, an element of originalist argumentation may support (rather than frustrate) a 'living tree' development of the status of the Treaty of Waitangi as a founding document in the constitutional canon of New Zealand today.[9]

I. Borrows on (ab)originalism

The holder of the Canada Research Chair in Indigenous Law at the University of Victoria and the Nexen Chair in Indigenous Leadership at the Banff Centre, John Borrows is an eloquent advocate for his own Anishinabe/Ojibway people, for the advancement of self-governing First Nations following their own pathways and for the greater recognition of Indigenous perspectives within all the various jurisdictions that operate within the federal nation of Canada.[10] His contribution to our symposium focused on an important but little discussed disjuncture between the usual norms of constitutional discourse in Canada and the assumptions applied to the "existing aboriginal and treaty rights of the aboriginal peoples of Canada" that are "recognized and affirmed" by section 35(1) of the Constitution Act 1982. Canadian jurisprudence and case law tend to look askance at various forms of 'originalism' found in the reasoning of some United States Supreme Court judges and academic commentators when interpreting and applying their constitution to contemporary disputes.[11] In Borrows' words:[12]

> A living constitution allows people with different interests to prune and graft it in accordance with its broader context. The Constitution is not just a dead piece of historical writing: it "facilitates – indeed makes possible – a democratic political system by creating an orderly framework within which people may make political decisions", as the Supreme Court wrote in the *Quebec Secession Reference.*

Yet there is a completely different approach to Indigenous claims:[13]

> The Supreme Court's abnormal originalism, or (ab)originalism, measures the constitutionality of Aboriginal claims by attributing public meaning to events that are regarded as being foundational to constitutional relations between Aboriginal peoples and the Crown at some point in the past. For example, Aboriginal rights can only be claimed if they flow from Aboriginal practices that were "integral to their distinctive culture" prior to European contact. Similarly, Aboriginal title can only be recognized and affirmed if a group occupied land prior to the assertion of settler sovereignty. Likewise, treaty rights must be proved by reference to the common intention between the parties at the time the agreement was made. In each instance, constitutional rights are contingent upon the Court creating an original public meaning for a past event, when such rights were first recognized, "crystallized", or contemplated by the parties (in the case of treaties).

Particularly galling for Borrows is the fact that leading cases in Canada on the establishment of enforceable duties owed by the Crown to Indigenous peoples – usually perceived by mainstream scholars as positive for First Nations – are still based on the eighteenth- and nineteenth-century ethnocentric assumptions of European superiority. The laws and political arrangements of Indigenous social formations prior to contact with Europeans count for nothing. The doctrine of "discovery", as articulated by judges of the Supreme Court of Canada in the late twentieth century, "gave the ultimate title in the land" to the Crown, insisted that "underlying title" was vested in the Crown, and stated that "Because it does not make sense to speak of a burden on the underlying title before that title existed, aboriginal title crystallized at the time the sovereignty was asserted."[14]

II. *Terra nullius* 'never applied' in Canada?

Gordon Christie is an Indigenous scholar from Canada who has criticised the underlying reasoning of the Supreme Court when it finally made its first aboriginal title to land declaration in the *Tsilhqot'in Nation* decision in 2014 – more than 40 years after the possibility of such declarations was mooted in 1973.[15] Christie writes about the 'fictional legal history' put forward by the Supreme Court in support of its analysis of the doctrine of aboriginal title.[16] The court explicitly stated that *terra nullius* "never applied" in Canada:[17]

> At the time of assertion of European sovereignty, the Crown acquired radical or underlying title to all the land in the province. This Crown title, however, was burdened by the pre-existing legal rights of Aboriginal people who occupied and used the land prior to European arrival. The doctrine of *terra nullius* (that no one owned the land prior to European assertion of sovereignty) never applied in Canada, as confirmed by the *Royal Proclamation* of 1763. The Aboriginal interest in land that burdens the Crown's underlying title is an independent legal interest, which gives rise to a fiduciary duty on the part of the Crown.

Christie describes this as "disingenuous" because it reveals that "Aboriginal title is *only* about ownership, with no tinge of Indigenous authority in the background."[18] He observes, correctly in my view, that aboriginal title is a legal instrument of Canadian law "developed unilaterally over time, with no dialogue whatsoever with pre-existing Indigenous sources of power, authority, and meaning".[19]

Borrows, likewise, was deeply disturbed by the court's claim in *Tsilhqot'in Nation* that *terra nullius* never applied:[20]

> Canadian law still has *terra nullius* written all over it. . . . If that land was owned by Indigenous peoples prior to the assertion of European sovereignty, one wonders how the Crown acquired title in the same land by merely asserting sovereignty, without a version of *terra nullius* being deployed. The Crown's claim to underlying title on this basis "does not make sense." Some kind of legal vacuum must be imagined in order to create the Crown's radical title. The emptiness at the heart of the Court's decision is disturbing.

Prior to the Royal Proclamation 1763, there must have been a 'legal vacuum', because after the Proclamation, the British Crown by its own unilateral act had 'acquired' radical or underlying title to all land. From whom had the Crown 'acquired' that title? From no-one, it seems. Is that not what is meant when we use the term *terra nullius*?

III. *Terra nullius* did apply in Australia

Those two words – *terra nullius* – were powerful dynamite in the 'history wars' in Australia concerning frontier violence when Europeans settled (or invaded) the continent from 1788. It was said to be "black armband" history to denigrate the great achievements of Australians in building their country by dwelling on difficult questions as to how precisely the nation's origins might be legitimated.[21] There were court decisions on the point, though. The Judicial Committee of the Privy Council in 1889 described New South Wales in 1788 as "practically unoccupied without settled inhabitants" and on that basis, it should be treated as a "settled colony" to which English law applied.[22] Justice Blackburn in 1971 used the words "desert and uncultivated", which included territory in which resided "uncivilized inhabitants in a primitive state of society" before European settlement, and, therefore, by the law that applied at the time, the entire continent was open to be claimed by right of occupancy, and there was no such thing as native title in Australian law.[23]

When the doctrine of aboriginal title or native title was upheld by the High Court of Australia in 1992, the judgments in *Mabo (No 2)* recognised that the *terra nullius* doctrine had informed the reasoning in earlier precedents but should now be rejected. In doing so, the judges cited and relied on the writings of an historian Henry Reynolds. One of his books – *The Law of the Land* – was cited by four of the judges.[24] His writings featured again in a second leading case on native title – *Wik Peoples v Queensland* (1996).[25] The volatility of the 'history wars' debates can be illustrated by the public furore that followed when Bain Attwood wrote in 2004 that Reynolds's use of the *terrra nullius* concept in Australian law "can be regarded as a lie" by an academic historian. *Terra nullius* was not a term in use in the late eighteenth century when the first British settlements were established, but only came to be used later in time.[26] This reference to 'a lie' appeared in a theoretical discussion on the difference between academic history and history as myth. Nevertheless, conservative commentators, always on the lookout to attack Reynolds for his "black armband" view of Australian history, pounced on Attwood's phrase.[27]

Be that as it may, legal historians are very familiar with the influential writings of William Blackstone that were first published in 1765 a couple of decades before the Botany Bay landings. Blackstone did not use the term *terra nullius*, but he was largely responsible for the important legal distinction between conquered or ceded colonies, and colonies of settlement:[28]

> [Our] more distant plantations in America, and elsewhere, are also in some respects subject to English laws. Plantations, or colonies in distant countries,

> are either such where the lands are claimed by right of occupancy only, by finding them desart [sic] and uncultivated, and peopling them from the mother country; or where, when already cultivated, they have been gained by conquest or ceded to us by treaties.

In writing of English laws as "the birthright of every subject" applying in "desart and uncultivated" lands, Blackstone also referred to plantations in "an uninhabited country". It was the cultivated/uncultivated distinction, though, rather than inhabited or otherwise, that appeared paramount for him in legitimating colonies of settlement. His reasoning as understood by British officials, colonists, and lawyers (but, of course, without reference to Indigenous peoples) resulted in the immediate application of English law in a "settled colony". That reasoning is what in the next century and since then came to be called the doctrine of *terra nullius*. It was a legal doctrine that was applied in New South Wales and later recognised in Australian law until rejected in *Mabo (No 2)*.

IV. *Terra nullius* 'never applied' in New Zealand?

It has been argued that, unlike Australia and Canada, the doctrine of *terra nullius* has not been part of New Zealand law. For example, the Chief Justice proclaimed in the 2003 Court of Appeal *Ngati Apa* decision on customary rights to the foreshore and seabed of the Marlborough Sounds that:[29]

> New Zealand was never thought to be terra nullius (an important point of distinction with Australia). From the beginning of Crown colony government, it was accepted that the entire country was owned by Māori according to their customs and that until sold land continued to belong to them.

That conclusion has been supported by scholars who suggest that "this finding is not to rewrite or skew history, but to justify overriding a historic case that enabled subsequent courts to cling inappropriately to *terra nullius*."[30] As a result, the court in *Ngati Apa* overruled that historic case – *Wi Parata v Bishop of Wellington*.[31] I profoundly disagree. Elsewhere I have critiqued at some length the Chief Justice's claim that the reasoning of the court in *Ngati Apa* was not a "modern revision".[32] The main difficulty lies in the incorrect assumption that the law laid down in the *R v Symonds* case[33] in 1847 differed in any crucial respects from the conclusions of the *Parata* judgment in 1877. On the contrary, the basic point of both decisions was that the Crown held underlying or radical title to all land in New Zealand from 1840. This is very similar to the reasoning now embraced by the Canadian courts, as in *Tsilhqot'in Nation*, on the origins of the doctrine of aboriginal title. Both the 19th century New Zealand cases indicated that there were indeed obligations binding on the Crown to recognise aboriginal title as a burden on the Crown's underlying title. Both cases relied on the doctrine of discovery to legitimate and justify European domination of Indigenous peoples – expounded by the United States Supreme Court in *Johnson v M'Intosh*[34] – as the source of native title rights. What *Parata* also made clear was that this obligation was a moral and political obligation binding on the Crown, but not enforceable in the courts:[35]

> [The] supreme executive Government must acquit itself as best it may, of its obligation to respect native proprietary rights, and of necessity must be the sole arbiter of its own justice.

This is what Chief Justice Elias in her *Paki* judgment in 2014 has now accurately labelled the "political trust" doctrine.[36]

Those scholars who praise the *Symonds* case for its dictum on aboriginal title fail to note that the decision was deliberately intended (both by the judges and by Governor Grey who instigated the litigation) to marginalise the Treaty of Waitangi. Far from being "the Magna Charta of New Zealand" – which was the view of Grey's dismissed predecessor, Governor Robert FitzRoy[37] – the Treaty was now construed narrowly as nothing more than a declaration of the principles of imperial common law. The crucially important element of the decision was to uphold the Crown's radical title.[38] Radical title in New Zealand, as in Canada, was a legal fiction that assumed a legal vacuum prior to 1840 and did not base native proprietary rights on how they might have been understood in *tikanga Māori* (protocol). New Zealand statute and case law on these matters in the nineteenth century was codified by John Salmond and enacted in the Native Land Act 1909. Section 2 definitions include the following: " 'Customary land' means land *vested in the Crown* and held by Natives under the customs and usages of the Māori people."[39] This remained New Zealand law until 1993.[40] Prior to 1993, I would submit, *Symonds* was the leading New Zealand case assuming *terra nullius* in our legal system. The judgments in *Symonds* upheld the Crown grant in dispute in that case by invoking the doctrine of the radical title of the Crown. They did so without reference to Māori and without regard to the pre-existing conceptual regulators of *tikanga Māori*. I have been on record since 1989 dissenting from the general view that *Symonds* was a praiseworthy decision.[41]

I find it heartening, therefore, that Indigenous scholars such as Borrows and Christie in Canada are intent on firmly challenging the radical title of the Crown as an appropriate source for Indigenous entitlements to land and resources. They thus also refuse to accept overarching governance powers of the Crown in decisions relating to aboriginal title lands. In line with their thinking are the arguments, eloquently put by Ani Mikaere over a long period, that the starting point for the elucidation of Māori customary rights always should be the values and conceptual regulators of *tikanga Māori* that comprised the first legal system of Aotearoa.[42] *Tikanga* has evolved (whether recognised by the State legal system or not) to be relevant to the contemporary constitutional canon. A living tree approach in New Zealand would find ways and means to give substance to *tikanga* as a primary source of the New Zealand common law. There are dicta, but not yet decisions, that suggest such developments may be emerging.[43]

V. Interpretations of the Treaty of Waitangi

The second major element of this chapter is that, while agreeing with much in Borrows' critique of originalist fictions, there yet remains important work to be done to understand the origins of the Treaty of Waitangi. We may have gained some insights into the perceptions and beliefs of the *rangatira* who signed the Treaty.[44] Yet the original meaning and intent of those British people who drafted and proffered that Treaty to Māori has been much neglected until recently and deserves much more attention than it has been given. This is the position advanced towards the end of this chapter but, to be candid, I have not always thought so. My scholarship has been informed by direct participation in political activism on Treaty issues since 1974, and my writings reflect the changing focus of Treaty activists over the years. In evaluating the significance of the Treaty of Waitangi in the law and the constitutional canon of New Zealand, mine is a very chequered record.

In a doctoral thesis written between 1978 and 1983 I concluded that the Treaty was irrelevant to the imposition of British sovereignty over New Zealand. At that time, the slogans of Nga Tamatoa and the Waitangi Action Committee were that "The Treaty is a Fraud." The thesis concluded that British rule over New Zealand could not be justified by the recognised grounds of European international law at that time: conquest, cession, or discovery followed by occupation of vacant territory. There was no conquest. Indeed, as at 1840, the balance of military might was firmly in favour of the musket-owning *iwi* (tribal federations) rather than the small body of officials and a naval ship that represented the British Empire in these parts. There was no cession by treaty. When doubts about the sovereignty of Britain over all Māori, whether parties to the Treaty or not, were raised in 1842 by William Swainson, the colonial Attorney-General, his objections were emphatically overruled. British sovereignty had been proclaimed and that was that. Paradoxically, I suggested, the most acute comments on the Treaty were the trenchant criticisms of it by New Zealand Company advocates. As for discovery and occupation, New Zealand was not an uninhabited, uncultivated or "desart" land. Blackstone could not be used to justify the imposition of British rule and English law. What occurred was simply an imperialist usurpation wresting control from Māori to establish a colonial state.[45]

As the political tide turned from 1984 onwards towards 'Honour the Treaty', most of us in what later became called the 'Treaty industry' adopted the line taken by Ruth Ross in her 1972 essay cited at the outset of this chapter. The Treaty was hastily and inexpertly drawn up, the English text differed significantly in meaning to that of the Māori text, but the Māori text was the primary text and in the primary language of the day. Weight should be given only to te Tiriti o Waitangi and the meaning of its *te reo Māori* (Māori language) text. The missionary and biblical context of that language was emphasised and the guarantee of *tino rangatiratanga* in article 2 was of more importance and weight than the cession of sovereignty in the English text article 1.[46] Putting stress on the text in te Tiriti o Waitangi was also a vehicle for promoting more discussion on the values of legal pluralism within the legal system by upholding the ongoing relevance of *tikanga Māori* in a bicultural jurisprudence.

In 1989, as the nation prepared for the sesquicentenary of the Treaty, Chief Judge Eddie Taihakurei Durie (now Sir Edward) put forward the notion that the Treaty enabled a relationship based on the fact that "if we are the Tangata Whenua, the original people, then the Pakeha are the Tangata Tiriti, those who belong to the land by the right of that Treaty."[47] That is a position I found appealing at the time, and I still do – although I note that Borrows in his contribution to this book has expressed some concern that the politics of "firstness" may be a "dangerous metaphysics". He suggests that Durie's approach "potentially replaces one *a priori* assumption with another. Crown-*aprioricity* may simply be substituted for Māori firstness under the Treaty as the foundation of legal order in New Zealand."[48] Acknowledging that Borrows is seeking to move us all beyond State-centric assumptions, there is still much to be said, I would urge, for another Durie statement made in 1996. Promoting the notion that the laws of the country are drawn from two streams, not one, Durie said that "a mono-legal regime had not been contemplated during the execution of the Treaty of Waitangi. On the contrary, Māori were specifically concerned that their own laws would be respected."[49]

In addition to te Tiriti o Waitangi as written, and noting the signal importance of oral debate for Māori participating in Treaty debates in 1840, emphasis could also be given to an oral 'fourth article' or 'protocol' that added significance to Crown assurances that *tikanga Māori* would continue to prevail within *hapū* after the proclamation of British sovereignty. This was taken to be more than an oral assurance, at the instance of the Catholic bishop, on religious toleration as between the Christian denominations in the new colony. The reference to "*ritenga Māori*" (customs or rituals) together with the mention of *tikanga* in article 3 of te Tiriti helped to build an argument for legal pluralism. *Hapū* would retain their laws and customs. There need not be the rapid "amalgamation of the races" favoured by some in Britain, and later by Governor Grey, so that Māori would be "civilised" in the manner of Pākehā and should abide by English laws as applied by colonial institutions. Submissions along these lines on this 'fourth article', in a report prepared on behalf of Ngāti Tama ki Te Tau Ihu for the Waitangi Tribunal, were favourably received and commended in the Tribunal's report.[50]

The basic thread of my writings through to about 2007 continued to stress the paramountcy of the Treaty text in *te reo* and to argue for unique Treaty-based relationships between Crown and Māori.[51] It was a diversion from that political imperative to pursue aboriginal title remedies based on the radical title of the Crown and a sui generis fiduciary duty that the Crown might owe to Māori. It was likewise a diversion to allow the centrality of te Tiriti to be downplayed by a focus on the statutory phrase 'the principles of the Treaty of Waitangi'. The focus on principles permitted contemporary judges, in a pragmatic manner, to craft what those principles should be – thus avoiding political and legal pathways seeking to honour te Tiriti itself. What I had not counted on until recently was the possibility that the *English text* of the Treaty might be a platform for a strong argument in favour of legal pluralism. Two sources on interpretations of the Treaty, neither of them of recent provenance, have required a reassessment of previously held views: first, an 1856 judgment of Acting Chief Justice Stephen and, second, two articles published in 1949 and 1941 by one Trevor Williams.

VI. The lost cases project

New Zealand's Lost Cases project was an extraordinarily important contribution to legal history funded by the New Zealand Law Foundation.[52] The project involved the systematic search for, and collation of, early New Zealand cases. Only a selection of cases was formally reported in early colonial New Zealand, but the project found many more in newspapers, manuscript collections, archives, and judges' notebooks. It was my exciting privilege to write up one such case – *McLiver v Mackie* – fully reported in an Auckland newspaper, *The Southern Cross*.[53] My original interest was in ascertaining the background to and reasons for the enactment of the English Laws Act 1858. That Act retrospectively declared that English law had applied to New Zealand since 14 January 1840 – a date, it may be noted, prior to the Treaty of Waitangi.[54] For present purposes, though, the fascination of the case lies in Acting Chief Justice Stephen's reasoning on how New Zealand came to be acquired as a British colony. He started with these propositions derived from *Clark's Colonial Law*,[55] which were reported as the following:[56]

> All writers on colonial law agree in classifying Colonies under three heads: 1st "those acquired by conquest; 2ndly, those acquired by cession under treaty; 3rdly, those acquired by occupancy, viz., where an uninhabited country is discovered by British subjects, and is upon such discovery adopted or recognised by the Crown as part of its possessions" see Clarke p. 4.

The judge then observed:[57]

> It is not easy to determine, under which of the three before mentioned classes of Colonies New Zealand must be considered. It is beyond a doubt, not a conquered colony. Is it a ceded Colony? I cannot consider it as such; certainly not within the meaning of the writers on Colonial law. The only treaty which ever existed between the Crown and the inhabitants of New Zealand (the Māories) was that of Waitangi. But was that a cession of the territory? So far from it, that that treaty recognises the continued right of the Maories over all the lands, and provides that no sales of the lands shall be made by the Māories, except to her Majesty. And, for this last mentioned reason, New Zealand cannot be considered as a plantation, acquired by occupancy.

This provides a rather different approach to the Treaty of Waitangi, relying on the English text, compared to that usually attributed to colonial judges in the nineteenth century. It does not constrain the Treaty within the parameters of the common law on aboriginal title as *Symonds* did. It does not dismiss the Treaty as a simple nullity as *Parata* did. Rather, it is a much fuller recognition of Māori rights "over all the lands" than either of those two cases. Noting also the dictum of Gillies J in an 1884 case[58] that the Treaty "is no such 'simple nullity' as it is termed in" *Parata*, I concluded that[59]

> there are a number of diverging views on the status and significance of the Treaty of Waitangi to be found in pronouncements by members of the colonial judiciary in the nineteenth century. The recovery of the *McLiver v Macky* judgment now adds a further complexity to our understanding of that aspect of our legal history.

VII. Trevor Williams

As noted in the introduction to this chapter, an English scholar named Trevor Williams, in papers published in 1940 and 1941 on the centenary of the Treaty, offered deep insights into Colonial Office thinking and the work of its Under-Secretary, James Stephen, as to an understanding of the aims and purposes of those who drafted the English text of the Treaty. His papers have been generally neglected in New Zealand historical scholarship. So incisive are his remarks, and so little known, that I think a number of his gems should be quoted in full. From his article on the Treaty of Waitangi:[60]

- Waitangi has been the target for the interpretations of politicians, missionaries, officials, landsharks, even historians; of men with axes to grind, pamphlets to sell, or companies to float. Controversy about it has dragged its weary length along for a hundred years. In addition, the Treaty received the sober and more frigid examination of the law-courts of three countries.
- The Treaty was not just a legal document; indeed, there are many who assert that it was never a legal document at all. In the history of the Early-Victorian Empire it marked a new method, or the coherent enlargement of an older more tentative method, of attempting to protect a native race from the inrush of a new and essentially different culture.
- The Company had relied on Cook's rediscovery as an excuse for colonising occupied territory. Instead, it was faced with a Treaty which aimed not at furthering British settlement but controlling it: to protect a native race from its deleterious effects.
- But in the first five years of the colony, the period of the Company's argument against the Treaty, British sovereignty meant the protection of the natives, whereas the Company's purchases, on the other hand entailed native deprivation.
- The Treaty of Waitangi was honoured too often in the breach, and not usually because it was irrelevant. Despite its many disadvantages, the main difficulties in the relationship between European and Māori in the years which followed 1840 were due to the non-observance or evasion of its conditions and, most particularly, of the spirit in which they had been formulated.

From Williams's article on James Stephen and British intervention in New Zealand:[61]

- [Stephen] saw his task as more than compassing British annexation. To him it was a humanitarian opportunity. The treaty of Waitangi was the product of several aims and carried the difficulty of a mixed cargo.
  Hobson was served formally with his instructions on August 14. Through them peep the three clauses of the subsequent treaty. Hobson was to secure a cession of sovereignty. Land titles were to derive only from the crown. The natives were to be left in the practice of their own customs.
- [T]he intention [was] to treat the natives, though now to be British, as subject to different usages and therefore to different treatment from that accorded to the rest of the new community. From the outset, then, the instructions introduced the notion of discrimination.
- Slowly the colonial office had found a policy beyond the makeshift and was eventually putting it into practice. It was almost wholly Stephen's own handiwork. He had ignored Coates's pompous jeremiads as well as Wakefield's hot certainties.
- Hobson's instructions are a signpost in the history of the second British empire, for they advanced the conception of the wardship of native races, a doctrine which formed its major contribution to the theory of native administration, shoddy and bloodsoiled though its practice was often to be.

There are important arguments in these papers that deserve critical scrutiny. They point in a completely different direction from the consensus for the last few decades based on the analysis by Ruth Ross. Far from being hastily crafted by people with no relevant qualifications, the Treaty texts derive from the precise instructions to Hobson in August 1839 written by the legal expert who administered the Colonial Office for the entire empire. The English text closely followed those instructions. The Treaty did not foresee wholesale settlement by British migrants in the short term, but rather a government administration committed primarily to protection of Māori. Even if, over generations to come, the missionaries would be agents of civilisation and amalgamation, the Treaty texts guaranteed Māori the continuation of their own governance, and (with very few exceptions) under their own laws. The proclamation of British sovereignty in New Zealand (as in many British territories acquired in the latter half of the nineteenth century) was entirely compatible with ongoing legal pluralism and parallel dispute settlement jurisdictions within the colony.

VIII. So who was Trevor Williams?

When Ned Fletcher first alighted upon the Trevor Williams papers during the course of his extensive research into archival sources and literature relevant to the drafting of the Treaty of Waitangi for which I was a supervisor, I had no idea who the author was. Further inquiries revealed, however, that Trevor Williams was the same person as ET [Bill] Williams, later knighted and known as Sir Edgar Williams.[62] I knew him well. He was the Warden of Rhodes House when I was a Rhodes Scholar and a fellow of the same college that admitted me to Oxford University. His distinguished war record as senior intelligence officer in the Eighth Army and 21st Army Group, and his long service to the Rhodes Trust were well known. His scholarly contributions as a junior research fellow at Merton College Oxford from 1937, working on a doctorate about the Treaty of Waitangi as it reached its centenary, were entirely unknown to me. Further inquiries revealed a number of links with New Zealand and New Zealanders that then made sense of Williams's decision to research a history thesis on the Treaty that he titled "Prelude to Waitangi".[63] He was close to five New Zealanders studying in Oxford in the 1930s – James Bertram, Geoffrey Cox, Dan Davin, Ian Milner, and John Mulgan – and shared their strong sentiments against appeasement of the Nazi government in Germany.[64] He was a life-long correspondent with Wellington's eminent history professor, JC Beaglehole.[65] His first marriage was to Monica Robertson, whom he had met in Wellington, in 1938. She was the daughter of PW Robertson – New Zealand's second Rhodes Scholar, who went up to Oxford in 1905, and was professor of chemistry in Wellington.[66] Despite these connections in his earlier years, Williams made little of them later on, except for the friendship with Beaglehole.[67] The archives of Rhodes House, Balliol College, and Merton College contain material relating to various aspects of his public life, but not to his work as a historian of the Treaty of Waitangi.

IX. Ned Fletcher's thesis conclusions

The Fletcher thesis, cited at the outset of this chapter, sought to uncover the meaning of the English text of the Treaty of Waitangi for those who had a hand in framing it. The English draft texts (and the text that is now the official English text) are of course the primary evidence of what the British personnel at Waitangi had in mind when commissioning the translation into *te reo Māori* that was proffered to *rangatira* in 1840. Despite the large body of scholarship devoted to the Treaty, the meaning and intent of the English words in the English drafts has been comparatively neglected. Their meaning has variously been treated as self-evident or irredeemably ambiguous, and therefore unrewarding as an object of study in itself. Most recent writing, as noted above, has taken the view that the Māori and English texts differ significantly. That has led to considerable focus on whether the differences were the result of deliberate mistranslation, indeed intentional deception, to make the Treaty acceptable to Māori. This was the line taken by the Waitangi Tribunal in its 2014 Te Paparahi o Te Raki report (Wai 1040) previously cited. The Tribunal report is a comprehensive and compelling report of Ngā Puhi perceptions and perspectives concerning He Whakaputanga and te Tiriti.[68]

Fletcher's thesis, however, offers a significantly different perspective from an alternative starting point. The thesis abstract includes these remarks:[69]

> This thesis is concerned with the anterior question of the meaning of the English text to its framers. It therefore begins by identifying the framers and reconstructing the English text, which has been treated by some historians as lost and unknowable. The meaning of the English text requires consideration of the text itself (itself a neglected topic) but also of the context in which it was drawn up. That context includes the backgrounds and motivations of the framers and the wider experience of Empire and the currents of thought of the time.
>
> The thesis concludes that the English and Māori texts of the Treaty appear to reconcile. It takes the position that the principal framers, William Hobson, James Busby, and James Stephen, understood the Treaty in much the same way and that such understanding was one generally shared by contemporaries. That shared understanding was in part because the Treaty followed British imperial practice elsewhere, and in part because the Instructions given to Hobson in the name of the Secretary of State for the Colonies, but almost entirely the work of Stephen, were clear and were faithfully carried out in the English text. The principal conclusions of the thesis are that British intervention in New Zealand in 1840 was to establish government over British settlers, for the protection of Māori. British settlement was to be promoted only to the extent that Māori protection was not compromised. Māori tribal government and custom were to be maintained. British sovereignty was not seen as inconsistent with plurality in government and law. Māori were recognised as full owners of their lands, whether or not occupied by them, according to custom.

The Fletcher thesis is likely to be published in an abbreviated form in the near future. It is my hope and expectation that this will provoke further inquiry into the history and historiography of the Treaty, and deeper concern as to the meaning and effect of te Tiriti and its relationship to the English language Treaty drafts.[70] I am confident that such inquiries will further undermine the Treaty interpretation positions that I adopted earlier in my career.

X. New instances of legal pluralism possibilities

Perhaps then, the Treaty was indeed a document intended to be protective of Māori rights, rather than a usurpation of those rights. It may well have been that the Treaty in both its English drafts and the text of te Tiriti was supportive of the ongoing application of *tikanga* Māori after the proclamations of British sovereignty in May 1840, rather than imposing the suppression of *tikanga* under the supremacy of English law. That did not prevent what Trevor Williams called the "shoddy and bloodsoiled" practice of colonial law and administration that followed after 1846. Yet, to be reminded of a different original context for the nation's founding document may have important implications for contemporary law and administration. There are a number of recent initiatives in New Zealand law that arguably are Treaty-consistent in ways that few have recognised previously. The examples include the establishment of a separate legal personality for the totality of the Whanganui River that is now Te Awa Tupua and is 'owned' by no-one.[71] Te Urewera is no longer a Crown-owned national park, but a legal person administered by a co-governance entity with a statutory obligation to promote *mana motuhake o Ngāi Tūhoe* (self-determination or government of Ngāi Tūhoe).[72] *Tikanga* rights in respect of the coastal marine area/*te takutai moana* are now being heard in a number of court applications.[73] Title to the volcanic cones of Tāmaki Makarau is vested in an *iwi* collective and administered by a co-governance entity with the Auckland Council.[74] These are all instances of important legal developments that are fully consistent with the living tree approach to interpreting constitutional arrangements and precepts with which this paper commenced. Political constitutionalism has enabled those outcomes to emerge from Crown–Māori negotiations that led to the parliamentary enactments. My hope is that the courts – the third branch of government – will be inspired by such executive and legislative developments to find opportunities to enhance further the status of the Treaty and of *tikanga* in New Zealand common law and in the constitutional canon of Aotearoa New Zealand.

Notes

1 Faculty of Law, University of Auckland.

2 John Borrows "(Ab)Originalism and Canada's Constitution" (2012) 58 *Supreme Court Law Review* 351. See also the chapter with the same title in John Borrows *Freedom & Indigenous Constitutionalism* (University of Toronto Press, Toronto, 2016).

3 *Mabo v Queensland (No 2)* [1992] HCA 23; (1992) 175 CLR 1 (High Court of Australia) [*Mabo (No 2)*].

4 *Edwards v Attorney-General (Canada)* [1930] AC 124 (Judicial Committee of the Privy Council). See Borrows "(Ab)Originalism", above n 2, at 352–358.

5 Ruth Ross "Te Tiriti o Waitangi: Texts and Translations" (1972) 6(2) *New Zealand Journal of History* 129. See also Rachael Bell "Texts and Translations: Ruth Ross and the Treaty of Waitangi" (2009) 43(1) *New Zealand Journal of History* 39.

6 The two texts of the Treaty of Waitangi comprise the Schedule to the Treaty of Waitangi Act 1975 (as amended). See also the Appendix (including translations by I. H. Kawharu) in Michael Belgrave, Merata Kawharu and David Williams (eds) *Waitangi Revisited: Perspectives on the Treaty of Waitangi* (Oxford University Press, Melbourne, 2005) at 388–393.

7 Trevor Williams "Historical Revision No XCV: The Treaty of Waitangi" (1940) 25(99) *History* 237; Trevor Williams "James Stephen and British Intervention in New Zealand, 1838–40" (1941) 13(1) *The Journal of Modern History* 19.

8 Ned Fletcher *A Praiseworthy Device for Amusing and Pacifying Savages? What the Framers Meant by the English Text of the Treaty of Waitangi* (PhD thesis, University of Auckland, 2014).

9 As to the constitutional canon in New Zealand, see Kenneth Keith "On the Constitution of New Zealand: An Introduction to the Foundations of the Current Form of Government" in *Cabinet Manual 2008* (Cabinet Office, Wellington, 2008) at 1–6; Paul Rishworth "The New Zealand Bill of Rights" in Paul Rishworth and others (eds) *The New Zealand Bill of Rights* (Oxford University Press, Auckland, 2003) at 2–3.

10 John Borrows *Canada's Indigenous Constitution* (University of Toronto Press, Toronto, 2010).

11 Steven G. Calabresi (ed) *Originalism: A Quarter-Century of Debate* (Regnery, Washington, DC, 2007) cited in Borrows "(Ab)Originality", above n 2, at 359; Keith Whittington *Constitutional Construction: Divided Powers and Constitutional Meaning* (Harvard University Press, Cambridge, MA, 1999); and critiques of originalism by Paul Brest "The Misconceived Quest for the Original Understanding" (1980) 60 *Boston University Law Review* 204; Mitchell N. Berman "Originalism Is Bunk" (2009) 84(1) *New York University Law Review* 1; David A. Straus *The Living Constitution* (Oxford University Press, New York, NY, 2010); Robert W. Bennett and Lawrence B. Solum *Constitutional Originalism: A Debate* (Cornell University Press, Ithaca, NY, 2011); Thomas Colby "The Sacrifice of the New Originalism" (2011) 99 *Georgetown Law Journal* 713.

12 Borrows "(Ab)Originality", above n 2, at 356–357; *Reference re Secession of Quebec* [1998] 2 SCR 217 (Supreme Court Canada).

13 Borrows "(Ab)Originality", above n 2, at 360–361 (footnote numbers omitted).

14 At 369 quoting from *Guerin v Canada* [1984] 2 SCR 335 (Supreme Court Canada) at 378; *R v Sparrow* [1990] 1 SCR 1075 (Supreme Court Canada) at 1103; *Delgamuukw v British Columbia* [1997] 3 SCR 1010 (Supreme Court Canada) at para 145.

15 *Tsilhqot'in Nation v British Columbia* [2014] SCC 44, [2014] SCR 256 (Supreme Court Canada) [*Tsilhqot'in Nation*]; *Calder v British Columbia* [1973] SCR 313 (Supreme Court Canada).

16 Gordon Christie "Who Makes Decisions Over Aboriginal Title Lands?" (2015) 48(3) *University of British Columbia Law Review* 743. See also Michael Adams "Towards Reconciliation: A Proposal for a New Theory of Crown Sovereignty" (2016) 49(1) *University of British Columbia Law Review* 1.

17 *Tsilhqot'in Nation*, above n 15, at para 69.

18 Christie, above n 16, at 770.

19 At 784.

20 John Borrows "The Durability of *terra nullius*: *Tsilhqot'in Nation v British Columbia*" (2015) 48(3) *University of British Columbia Law Review* 701 at 702–703. See also John Borrows "Aboriginal Title in the Tsilhqot'in Nation" (2014) *Māori Law Review* 4 at 8–10.

21 Stuart Macintyre and Anna Clark *The History Wars* (Melbourne University Press, Melbourne, 2003); Stuart Macintyre and Anna Clark *The History Wars* (2nd ed, Melbourne University Press, Melbourne, 2004) with a foreword by Sir Anthony Mason (former Chief Justice of Australia).

22 *Cooper v Stuart* (1889) 14 App Cas 286 [1889] UKPC 1 (Judicial Committee of the Privy Council).

23 *Milirrpum v Nabalco Pty Ltd* (1971) 17 FLR 141 (Supreme Court Northern Territory).

24 Henry Reynolds *The Law of the Land* (Penguin, Ringwood, 1987) was cited in *Mabo (No 2)* by Justices Deane and Gaudron at para 53 & 54; Justice Dawson at para 41; and Justice Toohey at para 18.

25 *Wik Peoples v Queensland* [1996] HCA 40, (1996) 187 CLR 1: Chief Justice Brennan at fn 170 and Justice Kirby at fn 573, fn 598 and fn 640.

26 Bain Attwood "*The Law of the Land* or the Law of the Land? History, Law and Narrative in a Settler Society" (2004) 2 *Historical Compass* 1 at 18. See also Bain Attwood *Telling the TRUTH About Aboriginal History* (Allen & Unwin, Crows Nest, 2005).

27 Michael Connor *The Invention of Terra Nullius: Historical and Legal Fictions on the Foundation of Australia* (Macleay Press, Paddington, 2005). See David V. Williams "Historians' Context and Lawyers' Presentism: Debating

Historiography or Agreeing to Differ" (2014) 48(2) *New Zealand Journal of History* 136.

28 William Blackstone *Commentaries on the Laws of England, Book I* (Clarendon Press, Oxford, 1765) at 104–105.

29 *Attorney-General v Ngati Apa and Others* [2003] NZCA 117, [2003] 3 NZLR 643 at para 69 [*Ngati Apa*].

30 Jacinta Ruru "Lenses of Comparison Across Continents: Understanding Modern Aboriginal Title in *Tsilhqot'in Nation* and *Ngati Apa*" (2015) 48(3) *University of British Columbia Law Review* 903 at 940–941.

31 *Wi Parata v Bishop of Wellington* (1877) 3 New Zealand Jurist (New Series) 72 (Supreme Court – now High Court) [*Parata*].

32 David V. Williams *A Simple Nullity? The Wi Parata Case in New Zealand Law and History* (Auckland University Press, Auckland, 2011) at 205–229.

33 *R v Symonds* [1847] NZHC 1, (1847) NZPCC 387 (Supreme Court – now High Court) [*Symonds*].

34 *Johnson v M'Intosh* 21 US 543 (1823) (United States Supreme Court).

35 *Parata*, above n 31, at 78.

36 *Paki v Attorney-General (No 2)* [2014] NZSC 118, [2015] 1 NZLR 67 (New Zealand Supreme Court) [*Paki (No 2)*]. See Elias CJ at para 42 (fn 76); para 160. See David V. Williams "The Role of Legal History in Developing New Zealand Common Law Following *Paki (No 2)*" (2016) *New Zealand Law Review* 755.

37 Robert FitzRoy *Remarks on New Zealand, in February 1846* (W. and H. White, London, 1846) at 9–10. (Magna Charta, rather than Magna Carta, was the more usual spelling until recently.) Accessed from the database *Early New Zealand Books* <www.enzb.auckland.ac.nz>.

38 See Mark Hickford "'Decidedly the Most Interesting Savages on the Globe': An Approach to the Intellectual History of Māori Property Rights, 1837–53" (2006) 27(1) *History of Political Thought* 122; Mark Hickford *Lords of the Land: Indigenous Property Rights and the Jurisprudence of Empire* (Oxford University Press, Oxford, 2011) at 202–215.

39 John Salmond "Notes on the History of Native-Land Legislation" in H. A. Palmer and J. Christie (eds) *Public Acts of New Zealand (Reprint) 1908–1931* Vol VI (Government Printer, Wellington, 1932) at 87–94 (emphasis added). See also ss 84–87, Native Land Act 1909 on the non-justiciability on Māori claims that customary title had not been properly extinguished.

40 The Native Land Act 1909 definition of 'customary land' was re-enacted in the Native Land Act 1931 and the Māori Affairs Act 1953. It was not until Te Ture Whenua Māori Act 1993 that the reference to customary land being vested in the Crown was repealed and a tikanga-based definition inserted. In the 1993 Act "Land that is held in accordance with tikanga Māori shall have the status of Māori customary land" [s 129(2)(a)] and (since 2002) "tikanga Māori means Māori customary values and practices" [s 4].

41 David V. Williams "*The Queen v Symonds* Reconsidered" (1989) 19(4) *Victoria University of Wellington Law Review* 385.

42 Ani Mikaere *Colonising Myths – Māori Realities: He Rukuruku Whakaaro* (Huia Publishers, Wellington, 2011).

43 *Takamore v Clarke* [2012] NZSC 116, [2013] 2 NZLR 298; *R v Mason* [2012] NZHC 1361 (High Court). See also *Paki (No 2)*, above n 36.

44 Waitangi Tribunal *He Whakaputanga Me te Tiriti The Declaration and the Treaty: The Report on Stage 1 of the Te Paparahi o Te Raki Inquiry* (Wai 1040) (Waitangi Tribunal, Wellington, 2014); *Ngāpuhi Speaks: He Wakaputanga and Te Tiriti o Waitangi Independent Report on Ngāpuhi Nui Tonu Claim* (Te Kawariki & Network Waitangi Whangarei, Kaitaia/Whangārei, 2012).

45 David V. Williams *The Use of Law in the Process of Colonization: An Historical and Comparative Study With Particular Reference to Tanzania (Mainland) and New Zealand* (PhD Thesis, University of Dar es Salaam, 1985) at 43–95; David V. Williams "The Annexation of New Zealand to New South Wales in 1840: What of the Treaty of Waitangi?" (1985) 2(2) *Australian Journal of Law and Society* 41.
46 David V. Williams "Te Tiriti o Waitangi" in Arapera Blank, Manuka Henare and Haare Williams (eds) *He Kōrero Mo Waitangi, 1984* (Te Runanga o Waitangi, Ngaruawahia, 1985) at 159–170.
47 E. T. Durie "A Special Relationship: Tangata Whenua and Tangata Tiriti" in Hilary Bower (ed) *New Zealand 1990: Official Souvenir Publication* (Dow Publishing, Auckland, 1989) at 18.
48 John Borrows "Origin Stories and the Law: Treaty Metaphysics in Canada and New Zealand", in this book.
49 E. T. Durie "Will the Settlers Settle? Cultural Conciliation and Law" (1996) 8(4) *Otago Law Review* 449 at 460.
50 Waitangi Tribunal *Te Tau Ihu o te Waka a Maui: Report on Northern South Island Claims, Volume I* (Legislation Direct, Wellington, 2008) at 290, citing David V. Williams *The Crown and Ngati Tama ki Te Tau Ihu: An Historical Overview Report* (Crown Forestry Rental Trust, Wellington, 2000) (Wai 785, doc A70) at 16–17.
51 David V. Williams "Te Tiriti o Waitangi – Unique Relationship Between Crown and Tangata Whenua?" in I. H. Kawharu (ed) *Waitangi: Māori and Pakeha Perspectives of the Treaty of Waitangi* (Oxford University Press, Auckland, 1989) at 64–91; David V. Williams "Unique Treaty-based Relationships Remain Elusive" in Belgrave, Kawharu and Williams, above n 6, 366–387. See also David V. Williams "The Constitutional Status of the Treaty of Waitangi: An Historical Perspective" (1990) 14(1) *New Zealand Universities Law Review* 9; David V. Williams "Indigenous Customary Rights and the Constitution of Aotearoa New Zealand" (2006) 14 *Waikato Law Review* 120; David V. Williams "The Treaty of Waitangi – A 'Bridle' on Parliamentary Sovereignty?" (2007) 22(4) *New Zealand Universities Law Review* 596.
52 New Zealand's Lost Cases Project <www.victoria.ac.nz/law/nzlostcases/>.
53 "Supreme Court, Civil Sittings" *The Southern Cross* (26 September 1856) at 3; "Supreme Court" *The Southern Cross* (14 October 1856) at 3; "Supreme Court" *The Southern Cross* (14 November 1856) at 3; "Supreme Court" *The Southern Cross* (18 November 1856) at 3–4. <paperspast.natlib.govt.nz/cgi-bin/paperspast>.
54 David V. Williams "The Pre-history of the English Laws Act 1858: *McLiver v Macky* (1856)" (2010) 41(3) *Victoria University of Wellington Law Review* 361.
55 Charles Clark *A Summary of Colonial Law* (Sweet, Maxwell, and Stevens & Sons, London, 1834).
56 "Supreme Court" *The Southern Cross* (18 November 1856) at 4 ('Clarke' is a misspelling); Williams, "Pre-history", above n 54, at 370.
57 "Supreme Court" *The Southern Cross* (18 November 1856) at 4; Williams "Pre-history", above n 54, at 371.
58 *Mangakahia v The New Zealand Timber Company Ltd* (1884) 2 NZLR 345 (Supreme Court – now High Court) at 350.
59 Williams "Pre-history", above n 54, at 372.
60 Williams "The Treaty of Waitangi", above n 51, at 237–238; 238; 243; 244; 251.
61 Williams "James Stephen and British Intervention", above n 7, at 31–32; 33; 34; 34.
62 C. S. Nicholls "Williams, Sir Edgar Trevor [Bill] (1912–1995), Intelligence Officer and Historian" in *Oxford Dictionary of National Biography* (Oxford University Press, Oxford, 2004; online ed, May 2011).
63 Williams "The Treaty of Waitangi", above n 51, at 237 cites *Prelude to Waitangi* as an essay Williams wrote, "the meat of which will be found in my article . . . in *The Journal of Modern History*", but no original copy has been found thus far.

64 James McNeish *Dance of the Peacocks: New Zealanders in Exile in the Time of Hitler and Mao Tse-Tung* (Random House, Auckland, 2003). In addition to McNeish's narrative, I found evidence of Williams's anti-appeasement attitudes prior to the outbreak of war in Merton College, Oxford, archives: ET Williams Material, Wil 1. Two of the three film reviews by 'ETW' in *The Oxford Magazine* feature comments deeply critical of Germany and its war plans.
65 Tim Beaglehole (ed) *"I Think I Am Becoming a New Zealander": Letters of JC Beaglehole* (Victoria University Press, Wellington, 2013).
66 Brian Halton "Some Unremembered Chemists: Philip Wilfred Robertson (1884–1969)" (2015) *Chemistry in New Zealand* 51.
67 Beaglehole (ed), above n 65, at 424 (Beaglehole to Williams, 4 June 1962, seeking advice on the offer to Beaglehole of the Beit chair in history in Oxford). I found a number of Beaglehole items in the ET Williams file then held in the Rhodes House library: MSS.Brit.Emp.s.554.
68 David V. Williams "He Whakaputanga me Te Tiriti. The Declaration and the Treaty: The Report on Stage 1 of the Te Paparahi o Te Raki Inquiry" (2014) *Māori Law Review* 28.
69 Fletcher, above n 8, at iii–iv.
70 See Anne Salmond *Tears of Rangi: Experiments Across Worlds* (Auckland University Press, Auckland, 2017) at 285.
71 Te Awa Tupua (Whanganui River Claims Settlement) Act 2017.
72 Tūhoe Claims Settlement Act 2014 and Te Urewera Act 2014. See Māmari Stephens "Tūhoe-Crown Settlement – A Transforming Dawn? The Service Management Plan" (2014) *Māori Law Review* 21.
73 Marine and Coastal Area (Takutai Moana) Act 2011.
74 The Tūpuna Maunga o Tāmaki Makaurau Authority is the statutory authority established under the Ngā Mana Whenua o Tāmaki Makaurau Collective Redress Act 2014 to co-govern the Tūpuna Maunga. See also the Orakei Act 1991 with respect to co-governance of *whenua rangatira* Ngāti Whātua title land.

Part II

Giving meaning to the Treaty through time

4 The Treaty of Waitangi in historical context

Saliha Belmessous

One of the main concerns of this volume regards the value and limits of history in examining the Treaty of Waitangi. The assumption behind that concern is that historical investigation could question or even undermine the value of the Treaty – that it could strengthen it is not considered. Any history of the Treaty is necessarily presentist, insofar as it would have political and legal repercussions and therefore be relevant to present-day discussions of the Treaty. The problem, though, is not history itself, but the role one wishes history to play in present-day debates. Historical methodologies are dependent upon the agenda pursued by historians: whereas juridical history intends to use the past to further contemporary claims at the cost, sometimes, of distorting it, contextual history aims at understanding past peoples on their own terms and showing the complexities of their experiences rather than simplifying them.

The aim of this chapter is to contextualise the Treaty of Waitangi. To do so, I will first consider the long historical tradition of treaty-making between European and non-European polities to negotiate European expansion. I will then examine the ways in which the Treaty of Waitangi was or was not coherent with conventional practices of expansion in the nineteenth-century British Empire. After that, I will consider the possible impact of the Treaty, particularly in the neighbouring Australian colonies; finally, I will discuss historiographical assessments of colonial treaties.

I. The Treaty of Waitangi in the history of colonial treaties

European and non-European societies used warfare, trade, diplomacy, and treaty-making to deal with each other. Although concluding treaties with non-Christians was contentious in the early-modern period, Dutch colonial promoters, soon followed by other European states, adopted treaty-making as the basis of their overseas expansion from the early 1600s. Compelling reasons explain the use of treaty-making to support European expansion, reasons with roots implanted in European debates about what constituted political legitimacy. In the Middle Ages, it was commonly believed that Christianity was central to political legitimacy and that only Christian princes held sovereign rights over the lands they ruled. Consequently, non-Christian rulers did not hold sovereignty over the territories they occupied and European states could legitimately conquer those lands. Although that opinion was rejected by eminent theologians (including Thomas Aquinas, Pope Innocent IV, and Francisco de Vitoria) and jurists (including Hugo Grotius), European states based their claim to overseas lands on that principle from the late fifteenth century onward. They assumed and stated that Christian princes could acquire any land that was not ruled by a Christian sovereign. The discovery of those lands gave the Europeans 'rights of acquisition' against other European competitors, which they had to turn into 'rights of possession' through conquest, cession, or occupation whenever those lands were not vacant.[1] In America, Asia, Africa, and later Oceania, European states used these three methods to build and extend their empires. In their direct dealings with native societies, European powers rarely based their title on the claim of occupation. Rather, they negotiated their entitlements through conquest and cession – the United States Supreme Court Chief Justice Marshall acknowledged that pattern in both the *Johnson v McIntosh* case (1823) and the *Worcester v Georgia* case (1832). Both arguments required treaty-making to formalise the kind of rights (including territorial rights) and duties European and non-European peoples obtained from those agreements.

European powers concluded, throughout their expansion, treaties with non-European polities that were contractual agreements, binding agreements, aimed for different ends. The first treaties signed were concerned with establishing commercial relationships and providing military assistance against competitors, whether they were native or European. Trade and military aid often worked hand in hand. There were also treaties aimed at providing resources such as land and labour to European groups; these agreements anticipated European settlements and the transfer of property. Finally, there were treaties establishing the transfer of sovereignty (treaties of cession and treaties following conquest) such as the Treaty of Waitangi and the 1874 Fijian Deed of Cession.

In the early-modern era, at a time when European state formation was not completed, the ability to conclude treaties was not exclusive to the sovereign, even though states were making that claim. Treaties could be negotiated and signed by home governments, colonial administrators, chartered corporations, or even individuals acting on behalf of their ruler or on their own. Europeans signed treaties that were public, formal, and written agreements between sovereigns; they also concluded treaties that were private agreements between individuals that would and sometimes would not be endorsed by their rulers. On both European and non-European sides, the issue of who was empowered to treat was critical. It encompassed the question of authority within one's group and one's representativeness of the group's interests.[2] In the nineteenth-century British Empire, the Crown claimed her exclusive right to make treaties with native peoples and used that right to create and consolidate her imperial sovereignty.[3] That claim was not as inflexible as it sounds, and the Crown supported at times private initiatives to conclude treaties in newly settled territories. On the non-European side, the issue was also critical. In societies where power was strictly organised, delegates were generally endorsed by their ruler. In societies where power was shared more horizontally, things could get very tricky. Individuals could negotiate a treaty on their behalf or that of their group but without being entrusted by their whole community. In North America, for example, conflicts arose within native groups for this reason. Yet, Europeans refused generally to take into account that fact and considered the whole community bound to comply with the treaty negotiated.[4]

Since treaties were used to further European expansion, they were very heterogeneous both in form and content. Treaties concluded in areas where contact, especially commercial contact, with local peoples had long been established tended to be concerned with conquest and transfer of sovereignty. On the other hand, treaties signed in areas where the European presence was weak and dependent upon local assistance were generally more concerned with trade, military assistance, and transfer of property.[5]

The fact that treaty-making was critical to European expansion does not mean that it was exclusively promoted by Europeans or always detrimental to native peoples. Historians have uncovered ample evidence that local rulers initiated contract agreements with Europeans to further their own interests, whether it was to support their rivalries with other local or European groups, strengthen their authority, extend their territory, obtain commercial rights, and so on.[6] I have previously mentioned that the Dutch were the first Europeans to engage in treaty-making overseas to further their expansionist agenda in Southeast Asia. But it also needs to be said that they did so at the invitation of local rulers who were looking for ways to constrain Portuguese control in the region.[7] In the nineteenth-century Gold Coast (West Africa), the Fante people concluded treaties with the British that were more beneficial to them than to their allies. Those treaties allowed them first to free themselves from their Asante neighbours and gain their political independence; in later years, the Fante obtained, through treaty, multiple commercial and material benefits that proved costly to the British.[8]

There is also evidence showing that native groups could be the prominent party in treaty negotiations. In colonial America, English and French agents adjusted to native diplomatic ways and although they recorded treaty negotiations in writing, they also adopted native treaty protocol, using native rhetoric based on metaphors to make their speeches, and offer and receive strings and belts of wampum (shell beads) to convey messages and record agreements.[9]

Figure 4.1 Iroquois belt traditionally used to record a peace treaty. The two squares symbolise the two nations involved in the agreement, while the long line connecting them represents a peace treaty.[10]

In the seventeenth-century north–east North America, the Iroquois (Haudenosaunee) Confederacy extended its alliance system to the English colonies and set up a Covenant Chain, that is, an alliance comprising native tribes under the leadership of the Iroquois, and the English colonies under the supervision of the governor of New York. Since the Mohawks had declared that Albany, in the Mohawk Valley, was the geographical centre of the alliance, English governors, including the governors of Pennsylvania and Virginia, had to travel there almost every year until 1777 to renew the terms of the alliance with the Iroquois and their native allies.

From the mid-eighteenth century onwards, Europeans greatly increased their use of treaty-making to negotiate their overseas expansion. They favoured cession through treaty above all other possible titles such as conquest, discovery, and occupation because cession was the least challengeable title in imperial politics. Cession could also be used in ways that were complementary with the other bases for title, for example conquest followed by a treaty, and occupation of sovereignty followed by treaties for property.[11] Cession was perceived to be the strongest title because it was based on the doctrine of consent to which they were historically attached.

The idea of consent had developed through medieval conciliarism and French Protestant resistance to Catholic rule. English political contract theorists such as Thomas Hobbes and John Locke argued, in the seventeenth century, that only consent could legitimate authority.[12] Although European philosophers disagreed on whether colonial expansion required indigenous consent – for example Locke and Hume thought it superfluous, whereas it was central for Adam Ferguson and Immanuel Kant – many nineteenth-century international jurists claimed that it did and they promoted treaties as the most legitimate way of expanding European empires and constructing political legitimacy.[13] Europeans pursued treaty-making because it was consistent with dominant political ideas on the significance of consent to legitimise political sovereignty and whenever the reality of colonial power relations dictated the necessity of treaties, that is, when the peoples with whom they treated also pursued agreements.

While they were attached to the principle of consent, European polities waived that principle whenever they were unable to gain native consent. In the eighteenth-century New Holland (Australia), for example, Lieutenant James Cook claimed to take possession of the eastern coast of Australia without gaining the consent of the Aboriginal population, which his instructions required him to obtain.[14] For various reasons, which I have examined elsewhere, he considered that he could not conclude an agreement with the Aboriginal people whereby they would have consented to his taking of possession. Cook's move was accepted at home despite being in contradiction with British policies.[15] To conciliate the principle of consent, critical to the establishment of political legitimacy, to colonial realities, European states, including the British in Australia, employed Locke's theory of tacit consent to claim they did after all obtain native consent. According to Locke,[16]

> **every man, that hath any possessions, or enjoyment, of any part of the dominions of any government, doth thereby give his tacit consent, and is as far forth obliged to obedience to the laws of that government, during such enjoyment, as any one under it; whether this his possession be of land,

> to him and his heirs for ever, or a lodging only for a week; or whether it be barely travelling freely on the highway; and in effect, it reaches as far as the very being of any one within the territories of that government.

Tacit consent implied that by entering into contact with European settlers, walking along colonial settlements, living within the limits of those settlements or the regions claimed by the Europeans, trading with them, or accepting military assistance or protection, native peoples had implicitly given their consent to European governments and agreed to obey them. The use of tacit consent testifies to the continuing significance of consent in European thought and imperial practice. Tacit consent also shows that, in the absence of formal consent, imperial agents constructed consent as a process of legitimation.[17]

In the late nineteenth century, the Berlin Conference participants would push things further and re-affirm the importance of consent in European expansion. They reaffirmed treaty-making as the normative process legitimating European expansion in international law. They would do so while acknowledging that European powers also manipulated the idea of consent to suit their purposes.[18] In many contexts, the Europeans concluded fraudulent treaties, treaties whose terms were not explained to the indigenous signatories, treaties with added clauses, and treaties signed under pressure. Fraudulent treaties show that behind many expressions of consent, one could find imposed authority. In any case, even twisted, the appearance of consent still mattered for only consent, in the absence of conquest, could provide a legitimate title over an uninhabited territory.

Colonial treaties were binding agreements, and each side, sometimes non-European, but in most contexts European, used intimidation and violence to force compliance. Historians have questioned what appears to be a paradox – the promotion of a non-violent form of expansion founded on consent as an alternative to violence, while, at the same time, using violence to enforce that non-violent practice.[19] To overcome that stumbling block, we need to reconsider the relationship between force and treaty-making. According to the Prussian general Carl von Clausewitz, who famously theorised the principles of war in the aftermaths of the Napoleonic wars, "war is not merely an act of policy but a true political instrument, a continuation of political intercourse, carried with other means." Therefore, "war should never be thought of as *something autonomous* but always as an instrument of policy."[20] Similarly, violence and treaty-making should not be opposed because they are part of the same process and serve the same political objective. The possibility and the usage of violence are instrumental to treaty-making, which, in turn, is itself instrumental to the exercise of politics.

Seeking the consent of local peoples and then using violence to make them comply with the terms of the agreement is therefore not inconsistent. It is even at the heart of what constitutes a political community in European political thought. In the eighteenth century, the Scottish philosopher David Hume rejected the social contract argument, that is, the idea that consent was the only source of political legitimacy, and he asserted that consent was "so much intermixed with fraud or violence, that it cannot have any great authority".[21]

II. Treaty-making in the nineteenth-century British Empire

After they lost their North American colonies in 1783, the British established colonies in Western Africa, Madagascar, Malaysia, North-Western America, and New Holland (or Botany Bay). In all of these places, with the exception of Botany Bay, they negotiated their settlements through agreements of purchase or rent. Their property rights resulted from their purchase, real or fictive, of native lands, while they based their claim to sovereignty by right of discovery, conquest, occupation, or cession. While American policy-makers used extensively Swiss philosopher Emer de Vattel's justification of the expropriation of native peoples for the reason that they were claiming more land than they were exploiting, even adding that purchasing those lands was "laudable" but not necessary, the British continued to promote treaty-making as their preferred way to obtain overseas lands – that preference could, however, give way to the dismissal of indigenous rights in certain contexts. Permanent Under-Secretary for the Colonies James Stephen (1836–1847) allegedly said that transferring Māori sovereignty through treaty was "much wiser" than relying on past discoveries or "the language of Vattel".[22]

In the mid-1830s, British philanthropic concerns about the worrying situation of native peoples, particularly in South Africa and Australia, contributed to a greater public awareness of the denial of native rights. Observers started questioning the kinds of titles the Crown claimed on overseas lands and made conflicting recommendations on the issue of treaty-making. The Select Committee on Aborigines, a parliamentary committee set up in 1835 and chaired by Thomas Fowell Buxton, recommended, in its report, British removal from Xhosa territory on the Cape frontier and stated that all acquisitions of Aboriginal land by settlers within the entire British Empire were illegal, even those obtained by purchase or grant. The Report endorsed the position that the Crown had affirmed in its 1763 Royal Proclamation about North American territories. The Proclamation established that all land located in the West of the Appalachian Mountains belonged to native peoples who could either cede it by treaty or sell it to the Crown, and that settlers could only acquire land through the Crown. The Report also advised the government to prohibit colonial governors from acquiring new territories without its approval. The Committee acknowledged British sovereignty over colonised territories, even though it admitted that the British had acted illegally and unjustly in places such as Australia.[23]

The discussion on the opportunity to conclude treaties with native peoples showed that there was not one unambiguous position on the subject. Since those engaged in moralising British imperial politics were not anti-colonialists, they had to conciliate indigenous rights with British interests. The discussion concerned the transfer of native property rights only and ignored the issue of sovereignty. It was assumed that the British had established their title by right of discovery or conquest and that it was absolute.

The parliamentary Committee's recommendation on treaty-making was radical and at odds with British conventional practices: it rejected treaties with native peoples, characterising them as "inexpedient", because they were detrimental to native interests as witnesses before the Committee, such as Saxe Bannister, New South Wales first Attorney-General, had shown:[24]

> As a general rule, however, it is inexpedient that treaties should be frequently entered into between the local Governments and the tribes in their vicinity. Compacts between parties negotiating on terms of such entire disparity are rather the preparatives and the apology for disputes than securities for peace: as often as the resentment or the cupidity of the more powerful body may be excited, a ready pretext for complaint will be found in the ambiguity of the language in which their agreements must be drawn up, and in the superior sagacity which the European will exercise in framing, in interpreting, and in evading them. The safety and welfare of an uncivilized race require that their relations with their more cultivated neighbours should be diminished rather than multiplied.

That position was, however, contested by the Aborigines Protection Society, the philanthropic organisation founded in 1836 by Thomas Hodgkin, Reverend JJ Freeman (foreign secretary to the London Missionary Society), and Saxe Bannister. The Society's position was consistent with Saxe Bannister's recommendation to the Select Committee to promote treaty-making as the most legitimate and just way to establish relations with native peoples. Within British dominion, Bannister promoted the compensation of those who had been dispossessed illegally and the purchase, approved by the Crown and formalised by treaties, of new land at a fair price for the Aboriginal sellers. The question of the fair price was critical, since, although a great proportion of British settlements had been obtained by treaty and purchase instead of conquest, native peoples received very little for the lands they ceded.[25]

According to Bannister, regulating British expansion also required that the Home government concluded "treaties of amity and commerce" with native peoples before they came into contact with settlers so that relations between both groups would be based on the rule of law. He ultimately promoted before the Select Committee the set-up of a "pacific coalition . . . under British influence and mediation" in the South Seas, a suggestion which the Aborigines Protection Society would endorse. The Society rejected the Select Committee's opposition to treaty-making because it left native peoples with no possibility to claim their rights. Yet, they ought to be enabled to "put themselves in a position of defending themselves and their rights", and they "may be encouraged to form treaties of friendship not only with the British Government, but with one another, for their own mutual defence and protection".[26]

Since, it was believed, dispossession could not be undone in places such as Australia, it was critical that British expansion in the Pacific would take place on the right footing. The government was concerned both with the preservation of British economic activities in the South Seas and the need to protect Māori people against the growing number of British settlers (there were about 2,000 settlers in

New Zealand, principally in the North Island) who were multiplying encroachments over Māori lands and abuses against Māori people.[27] The government then authorised the colonisation of New Zealand and soon followed the Society's advice to conclude a treaty with the Māori.[28] Recent scholarship has shown that the British project to treat with Māori chiefs the transfer of sovereignty (and not just property rights) over New Zealand was not a novelty, but rather consistent with British practices in Western Africa: to create the colony of Sierra Leone, for example, the British concluded treaties of cession with local rulers whereby they acquired the cession of sovereignty.[29] The acknowledgement of native sovereignty was actually consistent with British practices in North America following the Proclamation of 1763 and the progressive closing of frontier military forts. Before 1763, the British had denied that native peoples could hold sovereign rights over their lands: they had claimed territorial sovereignty on north-eastern North America, while acknowledging that they did not hold sovereignty over native peoples themselves. Native nations were independent and self-governed. To claim sovereignty over native peoples, the British went to great lengths to give the impression that native peoples had accepted their submission to British rule – colonial agents even forged treaties of submission to formalise the full extent of British sovereignty over claimed possessions.[30]

By the Treaty of Waitangi, the British Crown acquired sovereign rights over the Northern Island of New Zealand, claimed her exclusive pre-eminence over the transfer of Māori property rights, and finally granted "to the Natives of New Zealand Her royal protection and imparts to them all the Rights and Privileges of British Subjects".[31] About 45 Māori leaders signed the Treaty in February 1840, soon followed with more than 500 chiefs. Whereas the English text of the Treaty gave full sovereignty to the British Crown, the Māori text was more limiting and granted the Crown rights of governorship only. Although the Crown claimed to hold sovereign rights over the Māori people themselves, it would not try to impose its rule over Māori society, which remained governed by Māori law and authorities.

To account for the signature of the Treaty of Waitangi, especially in the context of a British refusal to enter into treaty-making in Australia, historians have emphasised British reliance on anthropology and the progressive theory of history.[32] It has been argued that Europeans assessed indigenous entitlements on the basis of cultural stereotypes, and they consequently accepted or dismissed treaty protocol accordingly. For the Treaty of Waitangi to be concluded, the Māori were to be included into the family of nations, which was made possible because the Colonial Office believed the Māori to be cultivators capable of rudimentary government. This explanation, which has become increasingly conventional, needs to be reconsidered. If we look at the British Empire in its globality, we find that the British signed treaties in Upper Canada with nomadic societies, which they considered as having basic political structures, while they did not enter into such agreements with the Iroquois of the Saint Lawrence River Valley or the Wendats (Hurons), even though they were sedentary and agricultural societies that had more complex political organisations.[33] To explain that contrast, we also need to take into consideration each context. As I wrote above, even though the British, like their European counterparts, favoured expanding their empire by treaty, they did not feel constrained by this principle. The balance of power mattered too. The British acknowledged indigenous entitlements and signed treaties when they were in a position of weakness and ignored those entitlements when they were in a stronger position and whenever they believed that they could not enter into treaty-making with the local populations. They used anthropology subsequently to validate their respect or disregard of native entitlements, as we can see in the Pacific area. The British did not conclude a treaty in Eastern Australia because they believed, at the time of Cook's expedition, that they were unable to negotiate indigenous consent to their possession. They justified their decision to disregard Aboriginal claims subsequently with reasons such as the extent of so-called wastelands and anthropological descriptions stressing the brutishness and harmlessness of the supposedly scarce Aboriginals. Those descriptions served then to rationalise the exclusion of Aboriginal peoples from the family of nations. In New Zealand, on the other hand, the balance of power was favourable to the populous and formidable Māori. The British used descriptions emphasising Māori agricultural and political activities to rank them on a higher point of the human ladder imagined by theorists of progressive history. They would consequently qualify Māori people as partners capable of entering into a treaty protocol. Elsewhere in the Pacific, the British concluded several treaties of cession from the 1840s onwards. Waitangi was therefore consistent with both European and British imperial practices.

III. The reception of the Treaty of Waitangi in Australia

During the weeks preceding the signature of the Treaty on 5 and 6 February 1840, the governor of New South Wales Sir George Gipps issued three proclamations pre-dated 14 January 1840, in which he extended his jurisdiction over New Zealand if a treaty of cession was to be concluded, appointed Captain William Hobson Lieutenant-Governor of the territory to be ceded, forbade the purchase of Māori lands unless authorised by the Crown, and announced the appointment of land commissioners in charge of investigating past land transactions.

Sydney newspapers echoed popular discussions about the validity of a treaty and the regulations governing land transactions. Proponents of the legal status quo existing in the Australian colonies argued that they saw

> no reason why Her Britannic Majesty should not take possession of these islands by right of prior discovery, and sustain her absolute sovereignty over the entire territory, as she has done in colonizing Australia, by the conscious power she possesses to defend her empire against hostile interference.[34]

Since New Zealand was annexed to New South Wales – and it would remained so until 1841 – settlers found the existence of different rules governing relations with native peoples troubling. Possessors of New Zealand lands were concerned about the validity of their deeds and wanted reassurance that they would be confirmed. Those who had acquired tracts of land in New Zealand with little regard for Māori property rights argued that Māori people used the land without owning it. Proprietors of huge tracts of land for which they had paid very little contested the Crown's decision to review all transactions – most famously, barrister William Charles Wentworth and whaler station owner John Jones contested the Crown's cancellation of their purchase, dated 15 February 1840, of almost the whole of South Island (around ten million acres), Stewart Island and other adjacent islands, and 200,000 acres in the Northern Island for about £220 and the promise to pay a life annuity of £110 to the vendors.[35]

The prevalent opinion was that the Crown could not cancel the titles Sydney proprietors held because the Crown had, at the time those purchases were made, no right over New Zealand. The Crown could not, therefore, claim retrospective rights on New Zealand. One settler contrasted the situation in New Zealand with what had happened in Port Phillip (Australia) five years earlier.[36] There, settlers of Van Diemen's Land had concluded a treaty of purchase with the Kulin people without consulting the Crown, claiming that Port Phillip fell beyond the pale of the Crown's possessions, an argument which the Crown rejected for the reason that Port Phillip was part of New South Wales and therefore Crown land.[37] When Wentworth and his acolytes bought land in the Southern Island, the British Crown had not claimed sovereignty yet on that part of New Zealand. To contest Wentworth's purchase and include the Southern Island of New Zealand within British new dominion, Governor Gipps used the so-called discovery of Captain James Cook of 1769 to claim sovereignty on the island on 21 May. A week later, he presented the New Zealand Land Claims bill to the New South Wales Legislative Council. That bill, which would be adopted a few weeks later, established that all land purchases from Māori sellers before 1840 would be investigated to check the conditions with which those purchases were made: only acquisitions that were equitable and not detrimental to the Crown's interests would be confirmed.

The conclusion of the Treaty of Waitangi had also an impact, although limited in time, on the discussion over the legal status of Australian Aboriginal peoples. Indeed, proponents of a treaty between Aboriginals and colonial governments tried to exploit the apparent inconsistency of the Colonial Office to defend indigenous entitlements. In 1841, the resident judge of Port Phillip, Justice John Willis, used the Treaty of Waitangi to question British title. He contested British jurisdiction over Aboriginal peoples on the grounds that no transfer of sovereignty had taken place in contrast with New Zealand where the Treaty of Waitangi had allegedly achieved that process. In Western Australia, the great majority of the settlers rejected the idea of concluding a treaty despite earlier considerations of doing so.[38] Entering into a treaty would have resulted in the reassessment of their property titles, and they would have had to purchase the lands they had settled. To rule out any threat to their titles, the settlers argued that the Crown was responsible for buying the land she had distributed, a move which the home government did not support anyhow.[39]

IV. Historiographical assessments of colonial treaties

Historians have generally given little attention to colonial treaties for the reason that many treaties were fraudulent or signed under coercion. Importantly, they have disagreed on the question of the legal inclusiveness of the European *ius gentium* (the law of nations), that is, the inclusion of non-European sovereigns on the same footing as their European counterparts in that legal system. Rather than focusing on the law of nations as a system, I suggest we consider the reality of international relations in the early-modern period. Even though most political theorists opposed treating with non-Christians before the eighteenth century, European states engaged in treaty-making with non-Christian powers whenever it suited their interests. They were able to do so because they considered that "the law of nations", to quote Hugo Grotius, "regulates those which look to the common association of the human race".[40] Because Christian and foreign powers belonged to a common political world, they were able to negotiate common affairs such as war and peace, cession of territories, borders, trading and navigation rights. In 1507, for example, King Louis XII of France concluded a treaty of alliance and friendship with Egypt. Less than 30 years later, King François I – infamously for his contemporaries – concluded a treaty with the Ottoman Sultan Suleiman the Magnificent to oppose the Habsburgs. The outcry that alliance provoked in Europe – Giovanni Botero described the treaty as "a vile, infamous, diabolical treaty" – did not prevent French sovereigns from regularly renewing their alliance with the Sublime Porte and, between 1536 and the end of the eighteenth century, France would sign eleven other treaties with the Ottomans.[41] In the seventeenth and eighteenth centuries, the French kingdom also concluded seven treaties with Morocco, fourteen with the Regency of Tunis, seven with the Regency of Tripoli, and three treaties with Persia.[42] Over the same period of time, Great Britain concluded *at least* ten treaties with Morocco, fourteen treaties with the Regency of Algiers, five treaties with the Regency of Tunis, nine treaties with the Regency of Tripoli, two treaties with the Sublime Porte, and thirty-seven with South Asian kingdoms (fourteen with Bengal and Awadh, three with the nizam [ruler] of the princely state of Hyderabad, four with the *nawab* of Arcot, six with the rajah of Tanjour, five with the rulers of the kingdom of Mysore, and five with the Maratha confederacy) – comparatively and at the same period, Great Britain concluded twenty-four treaties with Spain, nine with Portugal, another nine with Sardinia, and two with Genoa and Venice.[43]

According to legal historian CH Alexandrowicz, the law of nations relied, prior to the rise of positive law in the nineteenth century, on natural law which embraced all political communities, whether they were European or non-European.[44] Since native societies, whether in America or in Asia, were organised in a way consistent with natural law, hence showing that they understood natural law principles, as Francisco de Vitoria and Grotius had both argued, these societies were part of the law of nations.[45] Treaties between European and non-European rulers were inclusive, that is, they were reciprocal and binding compacts between sovereigns of equivalent legal status, an argument Grotius had already made in the early 1600s when justifying the treaties concluded between the Dutch East India Company (VOC) and the sultan of Johore.[46] Yet, other historians have recently argued that treaties concluded with non-Europeans "belonged to a distinct legal universe".[47] The publication of these treaties in French and English collections in the eighteenth and nineteenth centuries, mixed among treaties with other European powers and not separated as later nineteenth-century jurists were inclined to argue, indicates that they were not. The content of these treaties in general seems also not to be different from inter-se European treaties: parties exchange maritime rights, trading privileges, military assistance, and promises of peace. Yet, it has been recently argued that peace treaties between European and non-European societies could include an important variation from inter-se treaties: whereas peace treaties among Europeans were political compromises with no commentary on the justice of the war, peace treaties with non-Europeans differed when the European power was in a position of strength. Then, non-European peoples were blamed for waging war, and peace was granted as a unilateral act of European clemency which the indigenous parties would acknowledge through political subjection and/or the payment of a tribute.[48] Although significant this variation is, the fact is that this kind of treaty was not systematic, contingent rather than normative.

Those who claim that the European law of nations did not incorporate non-European societies also argue that Europeans did not value treaties signed with non-Europeans because of cultural prejudice. Cultural stereotypes attached to non-European societies – the barbarism and treachery of Muslim rulers, the savagery of American, Australian, and Māori peoples – were allegedly powerful enough to influence political relations and qualify them. Yet, the history of treaty-making within Europe shows that European powers could not be relied upon and broke as many agreements as they signed, while also resorting to claims based on national stereotypes. Already in the early sixteenth century, Dutch theologian Erasmus denounced the opportunism and hypocrisy of European sovereigns who used treaties to pursue aggressive aims instead of furthering peace. Treaty-making, as Macchiavelli, Justus Lipsius, and Grotius argued, was a political device useful to promote one's interests. European powers used it accordingly and it is unsurprising that they expected non-European societies to use it in the same way. The French diplomatic archives contained endless denunciations, for example, of British violations of treaties. Such was French distrust of the British whose alleged perfidy was infamous that already in the seventeenth century, they called Britain the Perfidious Albion. In true reciprocal fervour, British politicians called the French "treacherous".[49] Early-modern Europeans, especially in the sixteenth century during the Wars of Religion, located barbarity among themselves rather than outside Europe.[50] No European states suggested, however, that their counterparts belonged to a parallel legal universe, and they continued concluding treaties with each other.

Historians have also pointed to the inequality of colonial treaties and suggested that European powers considered their non-European partners as inferior or minor sovereigns. Yet, the same can be said once again of inter-European relationships. The formal equality contained in the law of nations did not result in a de facto equality, and powerful sovereigns looked condescendingly at their European counterparts, some of whom could be their dependents. Equality was not a question of dignity according to Vattel: it lied primarily in the benefits each party obtained from the treaty. Equal treaties provided equal or proportionate benefits to the contracting parties, whereas unequal treaties did not. The confusion, Vattel continued, was due to the fact that unequal treaties were mostly contracted by sovereigns of unequal status. Fraud, intimidation, and inequality: those were real aspects or components of a great number of treaties, but they were not exclusive to colonial treaties. Europeans also concluded with each other treaties that were marred by dishonesty, fraud, and intimidation. They also signed treaties that were so unequal that, according to Vattel, they prejudiced the sovereignty of the inferior power.[51] European diplomatic history abounds with such treaties, including the series of treaties Napoléon imposed on the European powers – from the Treaty of Campoformio in 1797 to the Treaty of Tilsit in 1807 – and the Treaty of Vienna of 1864, whereby the Danish Crown was forced to renounce its sovereignty over the duchies of Schleswig and Hostein in favour of Austria and Prussia.

Recent assessments of international law have also emphasised the deep connections between colonial expansion and the construction of international law, although the extent to which colonialism influenced international law is still debated.[52] A recent and important account argues that seventeenth- and eighteenth-century jurists were marginally concerned with colonial expansion and the distinction between Europeans and non-Europeans when theorising law, and that the entanglement of colonial law and international law was a mid-nineteenth-century phenomenon.[53] Whereas Third World Approaches to International Law (TWAIL) scholars have denounced "the uses of international law as a medium for the creation and perpetuation of a racialised hierarchy of international norms and institutions that subordinate non-Europeans to Europeans" and suggested that Western legal conventions could be tainted because they were used to support the dispossession of non-European peoples, recent studies have shown how wrong it would be to assume that non-European peoples were not involved in legal debates over European expansion at the time it was taking place.[54] It would also be wrong to ignore the many European voices who opposed colonialism and dispossession in those debates.[55] Contextual studies provide ample evidence that those discussions were not conducted in exclusively Western terms, that non-European peoples also drew upon their own legal traditions when they negotiated with European countries, and finally that both European and non-European groups created legal forms borrowing from their legal systems in order to work together.[56]

The suggestion that the law of nations, or international law, was committed to European interests from the sixteenth century onwards, has led to the exclusion of non-European peoples from the history of international law both as objects and subjects of study. That thinking results from an epistemological inability to overcome what we know of dispossession as a historical process. Because scholars know that colonial treaties would be used to dispossess indigenous peoples, they become blind to the processes that shaped these developments and to the moments when the outcome was still in question – not to mention cases where it remains in question. They also become blind to the actors who negotiated these treaties and tend to simplify the dynamics of relations between non-European and European peoples. Yet, it is important to break with this continuous vision of empire-building and focus on contingencies, to look at these treaties contextually rather than dismissing them on the grounds that they were mere legal fictions if only because some of these treaties, including the Treaty of Waitangi, still shape the lives of many indigenous peoples around the world. It is, at the same time, also important not to shy away from the complex and historical natures of colonial treaties in pursuit of a past more conveniently adjusted to present-day concerns. An important and recurrent question raised by legal scholars, including the editors of this volume, concerns the value of history in working with colonial treaties: as historian Richard White has perceptively reasoned, "For history to do effective work in the world over the long term, it has to be true to the complexity of the past."[57] If we seek to examine the continuing value of colonial treaties that still have a bearing on their post-colonial societies, we need to understand their past, that is, the various contexts in which they were concluded. History is not an obstacle preventing the re-evaluation of the Treaty of Waitangi: it is rather the platform from which we gain a broader vision of the meanings and possibilities of the Treaty.

Notes

1 M. F. Lindley *The Acquisition and Government of Backward Territory in International Law, Being a Treatise on the Law and Practice Relating to Colonial Expansion* (Longmans, Green and Co, London, 1926) at 12–15, 17–18, 26–27.
2 G. F. de Martens *Précis du droit des gens moderne de l'Europe fondé sur les traités et l'usage* Vol 1 (3rd ed, JP Aillaud Libraire, Paris, 1831) (ed M. S. Pinheiro-Ferreira) at 133–138.
3 Robert Travers "A British Empire by Treaty in Eighteenth-Century India" in Saliha Belmessous (ed) *Empire by Treaty: Negotiating European Expansion, 1600–1900* (Oxford University Press, New York, NY, 2015) at 132–160.
4 Saliha Belmessous "Wabanaki Versus French and English Claims in North-Eastern North America c 1715" in S. Belmessous (ed) *Native Claims: Indigenous Law Against Empire, 1500–1920* (Oxford University Press, New York, NY, 2012) at 107–128.
5 Isabelle Surun "Une souveraineté à l'encre sympathique?: Souveraineté autochtone et appropriations territoriales dans les traités franco-africains au XIXe siècle" (2014) 2 *Annales. Histoire. Sciences Sociales* 313.
6 Belmessous (ed), above n 3, at chapters 2, 5–8; Daniel K. Richter and Troy L. Thompson "Severed Connections: American Indigenous Peoples and the Atlantic World in an Era of Imperial Transformation" in Nicholas Canny and Philip Morgan (eds) *The Oxford Handbook of the Atlantic World, 1450–1850* (Oxford University Press, Oxford, 2011) at 500.
7 Arthur Weststeijn "'Love Alone Is Not Enough': Treaties in Seventeenth-Century Dutch Colonial Expansion" in Belmessous (ed), above n 3, at 30.
8 Rebecca Shumway "Palavers and Treaty-Making in the British Acquisition of the Gold Coast Colony (West Africa)" in Belmessous (ed), above n 3, at 161–185.

9 On the Covenant Chain, see Francis Jennings (ed) *The History and Culture of Iroquois Diplomacy: An Interdisciplinary Guide to the Treaties of the Six Nations and Their League* (Syracuse University Press, Syracuse, NY, 1985) at 38–43; and, more generally, *The Ambiguous Iroquois Empire: The Covenant Chain Confederation of Indian Tribes with English Colonies, From Its Beginnings to the Lancaster Treaty of 1744* (Norton, New York, NY, 1984).

10 Onondaga Nation "Alliance Belt" <www.onondaganation.org/culture/wampum/alliance-belt/>.

11 See Andrew Fitzmaurice *Sovereignty, Property and Empire, 1500–2000* (Cambridge University Press, Cambridge, 2014).

12 Thomas Hobbes *Leviathan, or the Matter, Forme and Power of a Commonwealth, Ecclesiastical and Civil* (1651); and John Locke *Second Treatise of Government* (1690). On Locke, see John Dunn "Consent in the Political Theory of John Locke" (1967) 10(2) *The Historical Journal* 153.

13 On Locke, see David Armitage "John Locke: Theorist of Empire?" in Sankar Muthu (ed) *Empire and Modern Political Thought* (Cambridge University Press, Cambridge, 2012) at 105; on Ferguson's critique of colonisation, see Fitzmaurice, above n 11, at chapter 5. Kant's argument for indigenous consent can be found in M. Gregor (ed) *Practical Philosophy* (Cambridge University Press, Cambridge, 1996) at 490, VI: 353 MM §62. On consent more generally, see James Tully "Consent, Hegemony, and Dissent in Treaty Negotiations" in Jeremy Webber and Colin M. Macleod (eds) *Between Consenting Peoples: Political Community and the Meaning of Consent* (University of British Columbia Press, Vancouver, 2010) at 235–237.

14 National Library of Australia "Secret Instructions for Lieutenant James Cook Appointed to Command His Majesty's Bark the Endeavour 30 July 1768" <http://foundingdocs.gov.au/resources/transcripts/nsw1_doc_1768.pdf>.

15 Saliha Belmessous "The Tradition of Treaty-Making in Australian History" in Belmessous (ed), above n 3, at 188–191.

16 John Locke *The Two Treatises of Civil Government* (London, 1689) at book 2, ch 8, 119.

17 On this question, see also Jeremy Webber "The Meaning of Consent" in Webber and Macleod (eds), above n 13, at 17–20.

18 Martti Koskenniemi *The Gentle Civilizer of Nations: The Rise and Fall of International Law, 1870–1960* (Cambridge University Press, Cambridge, 2004) at 138–139.

19 See, for example, Belmessous (ed), above n 3, at 1–15, 40–41.

20 Carl von Clausewitz *On War* (1832, Princeton University Press, Princeton, NJ, nd) (edited and translated by Michael Howard and Peter Paret) at book 1, ch 1, § 24, p 87; and §27, p 88.

21 David Hume "Of the Original Contract" in *Essays and Treatises on Several Subjects* (London: printed for A. Millar; and A. Kincaid and A. Donaldson, at Edinburgh, 1758) at 254.

22 Emer de Vattel *Le Droit des Gens ou Principes de la Loi Naturelle Appliqués à la Conduite et aux Affaires des Nations et des Souverains* (1758, Carnegie Institution of Washington, Washington, DC, 1916) at book 1, ch 7, § 81; ch 18, § 208. For Stephen's reaction to the Treaty of Waitangi, see Ned Fletcher *A Praiseworthy Device for Amusing and Pacifying Savages?: What the Framers Meant by the English Text of the Treaty of Waitangi* (PhD Thesis, University of Auckland, 2014) at 791.

23 Great Britain, Parliament, House of Commons *Report from the Select Committee on Aborigines (British Settlements); With the Minutes of Evidence, Appendix and Index*. Ordered by the House of Commons to be printed, 26 June 1837 (London, 1837) at 78–79, 82–83.

24 At 80.

25 On the importance of treaty and purchase in British expansion, see Lindley, above n 1, and Belmessous (ed), above n 3; compare with Stuart Banner "Conquest by Contract: Wealth Transfer and Land Market Structure in Colonial New Zealand" (2000) 34(1) *Law & Society Review* 47.

26 Aborigines Protection Society (Great Britain) *The First Annual Report of the Aborigines Protection Society Presented at the Meeting in Exeter Hall, May 16th, 1838* (London, 1838) at 19.

27 Saxe Bannister "An Account of the Changes and Present Condition of the Population of New Zealand" (1838) 1(6) *Journal of the Statistical Society of London* 362 (the figure can be found at page 363).

28 *Select Committee 1837* "Minutes of Evidence of Bannister" at 11, 13–14, 18, 20.

29 Fletcher, above n 22, at 1–2, 263–269.

30 See for example, Belmessous, above n 4, at 121, 123–125.

31 "Te Tiriti o Waitangi" <www.tiritiowaitangi.govt.nz/treaty/translation.pdf>.

32 Mark Hickford "'Decidedly the Most Interesting Savages on the Globe': An Approach to the Intellectual History of Māori Property Rights, 1837–53" (2006) 27(1) *History of Political Thought* 122; Stuart Banner *Possessing the Pacific: Land, Settlers, and Indigenous People from Australia to Alaska* (Harvard University Press, Cambridge, MA, 2007). On the Māori legal system, see Bannister, above n 27, at 366.

33 Alain Beaulieu "The Acquisition of Aboriginal Land in Canada: The Genealogy of an Ambivalent System (1600–1867)" in Belmessous (ed), above n 3, at 103–104.

34 Quoted in Fletcher, above n 22, at 815.

35 Harry Evison "The Wentworth-Jones Deeds of 15 February 1840" (1995) 28 *The Turnbull Library Record* 43.

36 Fletcher, above n 22, at 815–820.

37 Lord Glenelg to Governor Bourke, 13 April 1836, in Michael Cannon (ed) *Historical Records of Victoria, vol 1: Beginnings of Permanent Government* (Victorian Government Printing Office, Melbourne, 1981) at 25.

38 Belmessous, above n 15, at 186–213.

39 At 206–207.

40 Hugo Grotius "Defense of Chapter V of the Mare Liberum" in David Armitage (ed) *The Free Sea* (Liberty Fund, Indianapolis, IN, 2004) at 107.

41 Giovanni Botero *The Reason of State* (Routledge, London, 1956) (translated by P. J. Waley and D. P. Waley) at 223–224.

42 Ferdinand de Cornot baron de Cussy and Pierre-Louis-Auguste-Bruno Blanc de Lanautte comte d'Hauterive *Recueil des traités de commerce et de navigation de la France avec les puissances étrangères depuis la paix de Westphalie en 1648*, part 1, vol 2 (Rey et Gravier, Paris, 1835), and part 9 (Rey, Paris, 1844).

43 George Chalmers *A Collection of Treaties Between Great Britain and Other Powers* (London, Printed for J. Stockdale, 1790).

44 C. H. Alexandrowicz "Mogul Sovereignty and the Law of Nations" (1955) 4 *Indian Yearbook of International Affairs* 318, and *An Introduction to the History of the Law of Nations in the East Indies (16th, 17th and 18th Centuries)* (Clarendon Press, Oxford, 1967). See also Frederika Hackshaw "Nineteenth-Century Notions of Aboriginal Title and Their Influence on the Interpretation of the Treaty of Waitangi" in I. H. Kawharu (ed) *Waitangi: Māori & Pakeha Perspectives of the Treaty of Waitangi* (Oxford University Press, Auckland, 1989) at 101; and Lauren Benton *Law and Colonial Cultures: Legal Regimes in World History, 1400–1900* (Cambridge University Press, New York, NY, 2002) at 247–252.

45 Francisco de Vitoria "On the American Indians" in Anthony Pagden and Jeremy Lawrance (eds) *Political Writings* (Cambridge University Press, Cambridge, 1991) at 250; Grotius, above n 40, at 13.

46 Grotius, above n 40, at 99–100; see also Peter Borschberg "Hugo Grotius, East India Trade and the King of Johor" (1999) 30(2) *Journal of Southeast Asian Studies* 225. On Vitoria and Grotius's discussions of natural law arguments in relation to non-European peoples, see Fitzmaurice, above n 11, at 40–58, 87–101.

47 Jennifer Pitts "Empire and Legal Universalisms in the Eighteenth Century" (2012) 117(1) *American Historical Review* 103; Travers, above n 3, at 134–135.

48 Randall Lesaffer "Alberico Gentili's ius Post Bellum and Early Modern Peace Treaties" in Benedict Kingsbury and Benjamin Straumann (eds) *The Roman Foundations of the Law of Nations: Alberico Gentili and the Justice of Empire* (Oxford University Press, Oxford, 2010) at 225–226, and "Peace Treaties and the Formation of International Law" in Bardo Fassbender and Anne Peters (eds) *The Oxford Handbook of the History of International Law* (Oxford University Press, Oxford, 2012) at 90.

49 See, for example, Great Britain *The Parliamentary History of England from the Earliest Period to the Year 1803* Vol 20 (T. C. Hansard, London, 1814).

50 Saliha Belmessous "Greatness and Decadence in French America" (2012) 26(4) *Renaissance Studies* 559.

51 Vattel, above n 22, at book 2, ch 12, para 172, 175.

52 See Anthony Anghie *Imperialism, Sovereignty and the Making of International Law* (Cambridge University Press, Cambridge, 2005) and Fitzmaurice, above n 11, for contrasting discussions of the colonial origins of international law. Emmanuelle Tourme-Jouannet has questioned the importance of colonialism in the making of international law in "Des origines coloniales du droit international: à propos du droit des gens moderne au 18ème siècle" in Pierre-Marie Dupuy and Vincent Chetail (eds) *The Roots of International Law/Les fondements du droit international* (M. Nijhoff, Leiden and Boston, 2014) at 649–672.

53 Tourme-Jouannet, above n 52, at 655–656, 668.

54 On TWAIL, see Makau Mutua and Antony Anghie "What Is TWAIL?" (2000) 94 *Proceedings of the Annual Meeting (American Society of International Law)* 31 at 31.

55 See Sankar Muthu *Enlightenment Against Empire* (Princeton University Press, Princeton, NJ, 2003); and Fitzmaurice, above n 11.

56 See, for example, the scholarship in Native American history and more particularly Francis Jennings *The Ambiguous Iroquois Empire: The Covenant Chain Confederation of Indian Tribes with English Colonies* (Norton, New York, NY, 1984); and Richard White *The Middle Ground: Indians, Empires, and Republics in the Great Lakes Region, 1650–1815* (Cambridge University Press, Cambridge, 1991). See also Belmessous, above n 4; and Adam Clulow "The Art of Claiming: Possession and Resistance in Early Modern Asia" (2016) 121(1) *The American Historical Review* 17.

57 Quoted in Bain Attwood "*The Law of the Land* or the Law of the Land?: History, Law and Narrative in a Settler Society" (2004) 2 *History Compass* 19.

5 Towards a post-foundational history of the Treaty

Bain Attwood

In 1989, the historian JMR Owens observed that very little of the historical writing about the Treaty of Waitangi had been executed in the tradition of history championed by the English historian Herbert Butterfield who had famously argued that historians should seek to understand the past in its own right and on its own terms. Instead, Owens pointed out, nearly all of the historical work done on the Treaty was profoundly influenced by the present and driven by a concern to produce politically useful pasts. In the last 25 years, there has been an enormous upsurge in historical writing about the Treaty and yet very little of it would satisfy Butterfield's dictum. In this chapter, I proceed on the assumption that this is a problem with which historians would do well to grapple.[1]

In doing so, I take for granted something that historians have long acknowledged, namely that moral or political commitment on the one hand and scholarly detachment on the other are in equal measure part of the historical craft, or, to put this another way, the pursuit of objectivity is inescapably conditioned by the perspectives historians bring to their work. At the same time, however, I argue that there is a razor-thin line that separates historical scholarship from political advocacy, and that in striving for historical knowledge historians must struggle to sustain a fruitful tension or a delicate balance between the conflicting demands of commitment and detachment, lest by the slightest misstep to either side the integrity not only of the historian, but of the historian's society or culture, is imperilled. In so doing, the historian is better able to encompass the complex, heterogeneous, and even chaotic flow of events in the past.[2]

I. Foundational history

The principal reason why so much of the historical work done on the Treaty fails to maintain that razor-thin line between political advocacy and scholarly objectivity can be said to lie in the fact that it amounts to *foundational history*. By this I mean that historians try to discern in a particular historical event, in this case the Treaty of Waitangi, some norm or another that they believe created, or should have created, or could still create, the foundations of the nation. It could be argued that foundational history also amounts to a mode of thinking that tends to both configure the past in terms of some self-same essence that is deemed to be invulnerable to historical change and even prior to its representation in historical knowledge, and resist the chaos of heterogeneity.[3]

Foundational history can also be said to resemble myth. As everyone knows, the word *myth* in everyday parlance implies something that has been fabricated or is false. My use of the term does not exclude this connotation but is more ambiguous. In terms of intention, the story historians tell is fundamentally different from the story myth-makers tell. As the historian Paul A Cohen has explained, the primary objective of scholarly historians is to construct as accurate and truthful an understanding of the past as is possible. Mythologisers do the reverse because, while they start out with an understanding of the past, their purpose is not to enlarge upon or deepen that understanding, but to draw upon it to serve the needs of the present. In actual practice, Cohen points out, the distinction between history and myth is nowhere near so clear-cut because, however much the seeking of historical truth may be the goal of the scholarly historian, their work is profoundly shaped, as noted earlier, by perspectives shaped by moral and political values. Nevertheless, differences remain. While myth-makers may present accounts that they sincerely believe to be true, usually their narratives distort and oversimplify the past and omit material contrary to their purpose, and so tend to be one-dimensional, in Cohen's terms, "wrenching from the past characteristics or traits or patterns that are then portrayed as the essence of past reality". By contrast, scholarly historians tend to deal in complexity, ambiguity and nuance, or at least we should do.[4]

For some time, the norms that historians espied in the Treaty were moral. Perhaps the most famous example of this is to be found in the work of Keith Sinclair, commonly regarded as the doyen of the post-war generation of New Zealand historians. In the late 1950s, he argued that the British approach to the Treaty had been honest and honourable since it sought to lay the basis for a just society in which Māori and Pākehā could live together in peace and harmony. More recently, historians, following lawyers and legal scholars, have sought to discover in the Treaty norms that are legal and constitutional in nature. Probably the best example of this is Claudia Orange's *The Treaty of Waitangi*, first published in 1987.[5]

However, prior to this, in the 1960s and 1970s, several historians had become highly critical of any attempt to regard the Treaty as foundational (at the same time that they probably still accepted that foundational history could serve a valuable role in national life).[6] In 1968, Ian Wards argued that the Treaty could not be regarded as the foundation of New Zealand's race relations, since the historical record demonstrated that the British government had never intended it to be anything more than a short-term step to counter a French threat; that the government's aim in making the Treaty was simply to acquire sovereignty in the country; and that there was no evidence that the government had given any attention to the actual terms of the Treaty since no draft had been prepared and no legal opinion sought.[7]

Ruth Ross was even more critical of the notion that the Treaty had created the foundations of the nation. In two polemical essays published in 1972, she argued that if one examined the circumstances in which the Treaty was made, considered the people involved, and studied its various texts, it simply could not support the interpretations that had been placed upon it. Indeed, it can be said that Ross sought to cut the Treaty down to size, for she famously concluded: "However good [the] intentions [of the British government and its officials] may have been, a close study of events shows that the Treaty of Waitangi was hastily and inexpertly drawn up, ambiguous and contradictory in content, chaotic in execution." More specifically, Ross contended that the English and Māori texts of the Treaty differed radically from one another, most importantly in the meaning of key concepts, especially but not only that of sovereignty; and she alleged that a leading missionary, Henry Williams, who was chiefly responsible for translating the Treaty into Māori, had deliberately mistranslated it and thereby misled the Māori *rangatira* (chiefs or people of high rank) whom he and his fellow missionaries encouraged to sign.[8] Not surprisingly perhaps, Ross dismissed the possibility that the Treaty could be ratified and thus serve a foundational purpose: ratification was a legal and constitutional process that would have to be done in the terms in which the Treaty was signed, yet the signatories were divided in their understanding of what it meant.[9]

In 1973, Alan Ward similarly drew into question the claim that the Treaty could be said to have provided the nation with a good start. He accepted Ross's argument that the Māori *rangatira* would not have seen the Treaty in the way the British had because they had little understanding of the British concept of sovereignty; and he endorsed her contention that those responsible for drafting and translating the Treaty had deliberately avoided using the term *mana* (prestige or status) in translating the concept of sovereign power and authority and so had failed to give the *rangatira* a clear indication of what they were ceding. Ward's critical take on the Treaty is most apparent in these damning remarks: "At Waitangi [the British Consul William Hobson] accepted the signatures of the chiefs, well aware that they were signing in trust of missionary assurances as to their future position and without clear understanding of the Treaty's implications," and "His instructions to officers who subsequently hawked the Treaty about the country also suggest that he saw the task as an exercise in public relations rather than a weighty mission."[10]

In 1977, Peter Adams was less damning of those responsible for drawing up the Treaty, but he nevertheless argued that its provisions did not follow wholly or even predominantly from a humanitarian desire to benefit Māori, and he suggested that the second clause of its second article had not been inserted to protect Māori from land speculators, but to finance systematic colonisation. Echoing Ross, Adams concluded that the British government had intended to protect Māori "only in so far as their rights were compatible with British dominance", and that consequently the belief that "the treaty enshrined a true equality between the races, powerfully demonstrate[d] the degree to which a historical myth can serve as a cloak against the cold wind of reality."[11]

In the light of this historical scholarship, one might have anticipated that the Treaty's days as a foundational history were numbered. However, testifying to the fact that myths are more powerful than any scholarly history because of their highly rhetorical and emotional content, the standing of the Treaty was about to enjoy a spectacular revival in New Zealand public life. This was largely the result of two developments that began in the early to mid-1970s. First, Māori advocates abandoned their claim that the Treaty was merely a fraud devised by the British colonisers and adopted instead the position that the Treaty was a binding historical agreement on the grounds that it had been entered into genuinely by both the Crown and *rangatira*. They now called on the New Zealand state to uphold what they represented as a sacred covenant designed to protect the special rights of Māori as the *tangata whenua* or Indigenous people of the land. Second, the New Zealand state accepted that it had to address Māori claims in regard to what came to be called the Crown's breaches of the Treaty in order to be able to renew the nation's moral, legal, and constitutional foundations and thus provide it with the legitimacy that any nation requires. Consequently, the Treaty became a touchstone of debate about relations between Māori and Pākehā as well as the subject of a new foundational history of New Zealand.[12]

This new foundational history, which was formulated between the early and mid-1980s, can be characterised as the tale of two treaties. This story, which took up Ross's contention that the English and Māori texts of the Treaty differed on fundamental matters at the same time as it ignored her swingeing attack on the Treaty's status as a sacred compact, went like this. In the English text the Māori *rangatira* ceded to the British Crown "all the rights and powers of sovereignty" they possessed; the British confirmed and guaranteed to the *rangatira* the "exclusive and undisturbed possession of their lands and estates, forests, fisheries and other properties", while the *rangatira* agreed to cede to the Crown "the exclusive right of pre-emption over such lands" they might be prepared to sell; and the British gave an assurance that Māori would have the Crown's "protection" and "all the rights and privileges of British subjects". But in the Māori text, the *rangatira* merely granted the British Crown *te Kawanatanga katoa* or the right of governance or government over the land, which is to say that they ceded an authority considerably less than that of sovereignty; and the Crown confirmed *te tino rangatiratanga* or the full exercise of Māori chieftainship over their lands and the like, which is to say that it guaranteed Māori ownership of all natural resources.

The work of legal scholars and legal bodies played an important role in formulating the Treaty as the nation's foundational text. Legal scholars such as Paul McHugh and David Williams, drawing on changing interpretations of international law and important legal decisions in other settler state jurisdictions such as Canada, challenged the long-standing legal orthodoxy that the Treaty had no standing in the law; contended that the British government had a long tradition of making treaties in which it recognised that status of Indigenous peoples and their rights; argued that these were deemed cognisable in colonial law; and drew attention to recent legal judgments that assenting parties to treaties were required to pay attention to the Indigenous language texts and to the promises that the British Crown made in those languages.[13] Legal bodies, most importantly the Treaty of Waitangi Tribunal under the chairmanship of Edward Durie, used the exclusive authority it had been granted by the New Zealand parliament to determine the meaning and effect of the Treaty as embodied in its two texts and decide issues raised by the differences between them to articulate what it called the *principles* of the Treaty. The status of the Treaty as the nation's foundational history was deepened after the Tribunal was given the authority to hear claims about breaches of the Treaty dating back to its signing and began to commission historical reports by professional historians in regard to these historical claims.[14]

Academic historians were not far behind in this new line of storytelling about the Treaty. The most important account was Orange's best-seller, *The Treaty of Waitangi*. In much the same manner as Whig history, her account suggested that a new foundation for New Zealand could be found in a history she told, which placed the beginnings of the New Zealand nation-state in a contract, namely the Treaty of Waitangi, called the New Zealand state to account for its breaches of the Treaty, and urged it to redeem itself by honouring this agreement. The tale of the two treaties was articulated further in the 1990s by other academic historians such as Judith Binney and James Belich, even though their accounts of the treaty-making at Waitangi diverged in some respects from Ross's influential account, as indeed had Orange's.[15]

II. Challenges to the new foundational history

In the 1990s and 2000s, this new foundational history of the Treaty might be said to have been challenged on various grounds. First, a number of historians, most notably Andrew Sharp and WH Oliver, described the nature of the historical work undertaken by the Waitangi Tribunal as juridical history, by which they meant a form of history that seeks to represent the past in such a way that legal and quasi-legal judgments can be made about it in the present. They argued that juridical history requires historians to discover in the past timeless norms and principles that constituted just and proper relationships but which might well have been broken, in order to enable the law to resolve contemporary problems. As a result, Sharp and Oliver alleged, juridical history was fundamentally ahistorical: it was presentist since it was designed from a contemporary perspective that sought to address present-day problems; it was anachronistic because it made findings about the British Crown's breaches of the Treaty without considering sufficiently the actual historical context in which it acted; and it was counterfactual since much of its inquiry required a construction of what *might* have happened had the Crown acted in accordance with the so-called principles of the Treaty. Indeed, Sharp and Oliver went so far as to question whether juridical history should be considered history at all.[16]

Second, there were scholars such as the historian Keith Sorrenson who drew into question the proposition that the Treaty was peculiar to New Zealand by arguing that it was an expression of an old colonial policy that had been applied in various parts of the British Empire. "Indeed", he remarked, "I would go further and say that there was little in the Treaty, at least in its English text, that had not already been expressed in earlier treaties." In support of this contention, Sorrenson pointed to the similarities in language between the Treaty and treaties that the British had made elsewhere. Yet, even as historians like Sorrenson drew attention to these treaties to note that agreements such as the Treaty of Waitangi were common fare, the arguments they made tended to have a normative ring to them. In Sorrenson's case, he acknowledged that treaties were "cobbled together as a typically pragmatic response by the Colonial Office to yet another crisis on a far-flung imperial frontier", only to insist that there was something he called "British colonial policy".[17]

Third, Michael Belgrave convincingly demonstrated that the Treaty had been understood very differently at different points over time. More particularly, he argued that at the moment of its signing the Treaty was not understood by those principally responsible for making it as a treaty of rights, as the Treaty had been represented since the 1970s, but rather as a treaty of relationships. Most importantly, by paying more thorough attention to the context in which the Treaty was made, Belgrave challenged the tale of the two treaties by querying whether the Māori and English texts were in fact all that different and by suggesting that the way in which Māori signatories understood the Treaty was actually very similar to the way it was perceived by the British figures who had variously drafted the document in English, translated it into Māori, and urged *rangatira* to sign. However, Belgrave's account might be said to accept the premises of foundational history given his insistence on the importance of scholarly historians recovering what he called "the original treaty" by peeling back the layers of interpretation that have resulted from the many attempts to use the Treaty for political ends.[18]

A more thoroughgoing challenge to the new foundational history of the Treaty awaited, paradoxically some might say, the work of several legal historians who sought to play down the role that the law, at least in any normative sense, played in its making. The most important work along these lines has been that by Stuart Banner and Mark Hickford. Banner brought into question the role of any normative factors in the making of treaties that involved the acquisition of land by demonstrating that the methods by which land was acquired in Anglophone settler colonies were remarkably diverse and were dictated by conditions on the colonial peripheries rather than by so-called humanitarian impulses or governmental policy-making at any imperial centre. Hickford drew into question the contention that there was a settled legal view about the nature of aboriginal people's property rights, let alone that there was any common law legal doctrine or understanding of native title which informed or underpinned imperial practices. He suggested that, while ideas about native property rights were important, they are best regarded as intellectual resources that were drawn upon and deployed by a range of imperial and colonial stakeholders who were seeking to advance their political and economic agendas in what amounted to intra-British contests or debates. The Colonial Office, and more especially the colonisation companies and their assorted critics, used philosophical and legal arguments about property rights to obtain leverage in their political negotiations and settlements, without seeking to resolve more abstract questions about the nature of native title.[19]

III. Towards a post-foundational history of the Treaty

Building on the work of Belgrave, Hickford, and Banner, I will now consider what an attempt to produce post-foundational histories of the Treaty requires and then give an example of what may result if one adopts this approach. This is an approach, as I implied earlier in this chapter, that historicises the past in such a way that it unsettles any notion of the past being comprised of self-same essences over time and instead reveals that forms of knowledge are contingent and therefore unstable as they are constructed by historical processes and relationships, especially relationships of power.[20]

I begin with the matter of *historical perspective*. By this I mean viewing things in the past in terms of their relative historical importance or what we might call their true relation to the past. In this sense, historical perspective requires the historian to stand back from an intensely national discussion about the Treaty. This allows us to recognise that the importance or significance that has been attributed to the making of the Treaty in 1840 is excessive, even absurd. It was but one event among many that occurred in the islands of New Zealand in the course of the early to middle decades of the nineteenth century,[21] and its import quickly receded among all parties, rose once more in the mid to late 1840s, only to recede again.[22]

We are more able to grasp the Treaty's historical significance if we adopt the methods of comparative history. As Marc Bloch famously observed, unless we do comparative history, "the historian risks attributing an exaggerated explanatory value to certain facts which are in reality of mediocre importance." One example must suffice to demonstrate this point. The Treaty of Waitangi was one of hundreds of such treaties that were made in the eighteenth and nineteenth centuries, and its content is remarkably similar to some that the British made elsewhere (as we noted above). Yet few, if any, of those other treaties have assumed the kind of place in the history of colonial or post-colonial nations that the Treaty has done in New Zealand's case. This very fact suggests that the significance that the Treaty has come to have in New Zealand's history is not so much a function of its text or texts, or even the contexts in which it was made, but is instead the result of the interpretations that have been spun around it at some later point in time, beginning as early as the mid-1840s. The example of the American Declaration of Independence, which occupies a similar kind of place in that country's politics and culture to that of the Treaty in New Zealand's, is instructive. As several scholars, such as David Armitage, have pointed out, the Declaration had a highly particular purpose at the moment that it was proclaimed, and only later did it come to acquire the very different meanings and significance that we now associate with it.[23]

Arguably, a comparative perspective can also help draw into question an assumption that has informed most of the historical accounts of the treaty-making, namely that common or mutual understanding is the prerequisite for good relations between settlers and natives. The American historian Richard White, in his study of the relationships between Indians, the British, and the French in the area of the Great Lakes over a period of more than 150 years between the mid-seventeenth century and the early nineteenth century, has argued that the process by which these culturally diverse peoples met one another and tried to accommodate their differences was largely characterised by *creative misunderstanding* on the part of all the parties. In his words, "[people] often misinterpret and distort both the values and practices of those they deal with, but from these misunderstandings arise new meanings and through them new practices."[24]

Historical perspective can also enable historians to grasp the fact that the Colonial Office was not the creature that has been figured in foundational histories, including, most recently, a remarkable doctoral thesis by Ned Fletcher. In other words, this government department was not staffed by men whose decisions were determined by principle, policy, precept, or precedent. The Colonial Office, as several historians across several generations have pointed out, was very small and struggled to manage a vast empire. As a result, it was highly reactive to contemporary political pressures, producing what John W Cell once called "an unsettled and changing set of responses". This means that historians make a profound mistake when they seek to generalise about so-called colonial policy or principles on the basis of remarks made by its officials in highly particular circumstances. In the case of the islands of New Zealand, a careful reading of the most relevant historical sources reveals that the Colonial Office acted in reference to a long chain of correspondence from figures and bodies such as the British Resident in New Zealand, governors of New South Wales, churchmen, and, most of all, missionary societies such as the Church Missionary Society and colonisation companies such as the New Zealand Company. Indeed, the pronouncements of its officials often amount to a kind of bricolage from that correspondence. Paying attention to what we might call the highly contextual (in the sense of intertextual) nature of the positions that were adopted by the Colonial Office can help bring to the surface some striking facts. For example, the Colonial Office only began to represent the islands of New Zealand as falling under the sovereignty of Māori *rangatira* after the Church Missionary Society and the New Zealand Company had done so.[25]

Once a historian abandons the mindset that accompanies foundational history and sets about trying to see the Treaty as it was perceived at the time it was made, he or she is able to recognise that the significance that has been attributed to its making is unwarranted. One example must suffice. Many historians have sought to discern in the treaty-making the seeds of a policy of amalgamation or assimilation, but this policy only began to be formulated later. If one focuses specifically on what the agents of the imperial government were saying at the time, it is evident that they primarily had one purpose in mind in making a treaty, that of persuading the natives to cede sovereignty to the British Crown so it could assert some control over unruly colonists and meet a chorus of calls demanding that greater protection be provided to both aboriginal and British subjects in the islands of New Zealand. Before the interpretation of treaties like the Treaty of Waitangi fell into the grip of lawyers and legal scholars in the 1980s and 1990s, it was taken for granted by historians that imperial powers regarded treaties first and foremost in this kind of way, that is, primarily as diplomatic or political rather than legal or constitutional instruments.[26]

To be able to produce a post-foundational history, which is say a more properly historical account, of the Treaty, it is necessary to adopt a methodological approach that has been recommended by a couple of English historians, Timothy Ashplant and Adrian Wilson. After reminding us that there are major difficulties inherent in the very project of history because the historian approaches the past from the substantive perceptual and conceptual categories of the present, they argue that this epistemological problem has not been addressed by many standard practices in the discipline of history. Instead, many historians fail to attend to the invariable disjunction between the category systems of the past and the present, tending instead to use sources or more commonly just fragments of sources to answer the questions that *they* are seeking to answer. Consequently, they fail to pay attention to the inevitable discrepancy between their use of any given historical source and the use or uses that it originally served. To address these problems, Ashplant and Wilson urge historians to conduct a detailed investigation of the very nature of the historical processes that generated any particular body of historical sources. By seeking to elucidate the genesis of our historical sources the historian is better able to comprehend the category systems that underlie those sources as well as the original use(s) of them. The historian can turn from asking what a given source might mean today to asking what that source meant in the past. To put this simply, the historian must ask how and why any particular source came into being at all, which is to investigate how it came into being at a particular time at a particular place, at the hands of a particular author rather than another, and with a particular content and no other.[27]

Here is an example of this methodology at work. Numerous historians have used a memorandum penned by the permanent Under-Secretary of the Colonial Office, James Stephen, in November 1839 on the matter of sovereignty in New Zealand to argue that it had long been and still was the policy of the British government to recognise the islands of New Zealand as a territory that fell under the sovereignty of the native peoples and so lay beyond British dominion, and that this was the result of the Colonial Office upholding a particular legal principle or a doctrine regarding the sovereignty held by native peoples such as Māori.[28] In making this argument, historians have paid little, if any attention to the nature of the author who wrote this memorandum, the context in which he did so, and the uses that the Colonial Office meant it to serve.[29]

A close examination of the text and context of the memorandum suggests the following. The directors of the New Zealand Company had been calling upon the Colonial Office to assert British sovereignty over New Zealand, and thus allow it to colonise the country, by arguing that the British Crown had the right to do so on the grounds that Cook had claimed possession of the country in 1769–1770 on the basis of the doctrine of discovery. However, the Colonial Office refused to accede to the Company's demand. The Company's chairman, Joseph Somes, had then sought to use the Company's powerful political connections to bypass the Colonial Office and present its case to the Foreign Secretary, Lord Palmerston. In turn, Palmerston called upon the newly appointed Secretary of State for the Colonies, Lord John Russell, to explain the position that the Colonial Office had adopted on the matter of sovereignty in the islands of New Zealand. This was a situation that demanded that the Colonial Office defend itself by providing the best possible gloss on its decision in 1839 to negotiate with Māori *rangatira* for the cession of sovereignty rather than simply assert British sovereignty on the basis of Cook's unilateral claim of possession for the British Crown. It required that it explain its decision in a manner that would persuade the Foreign Secretary that it had acted in accordance with a coherent set of principles. Stephen chose to do this by constructing a historical account in which he claimed that it was simply a matter of fact that the British Crown had repeatedly acted in ways that recognised New Zealand as both a foreign and independent state. However, his interpretation of many of those acts was tendentious, so much so that it really amounts to a fiction. Furthermore, the tone of Stephen's letter was scathing at times, revealing both the antipathy and anger he felt towards the directors of the New Zealand Company, and suggesting that he struggled to treat matters objectively. (Stephen recognised this later and it led him to withdraw from any major involvement in New Zealand's affairs.) In short, a careful reading of both the text and the context of this memorandum indicates that historians have erred in treating it as a reliable source of information about the stance that the Colonial Office took on the matter of sovereignty and that we must look elsewhere if we are discover the nature of the position it had adopted in the past and the reasons why it had done so.[30]

I have two further suggestions as to how we might historicise the Treaty and its making. First, historians must grasp a crucial point about the nature of language, namely that words are often used in a performative fashion in order to change the world rather than to represent it truly. In other words, historians of the Treaty ought to recognise the importance of rhetoric and realise when, why, and how it is being used. Take for example the instructions that the Colonial Office drew up for the British Consul to New Zealand, William Hobson, in 1839, which included an instruction to make a treaty with the natives. It is abundantly clear that the Colonial Office had several audiences in mind when it drew up those instructions and that its most famous passages were crafted by Stephen for putative critics that included, at the very least, the missionary societies and the advocates of systematic colonisation of New Zealand. One might add that scrutiny of these instructions reveals that in the part that dealt with the making of a treaty the Colonial Office made no reference whatsoever to any requirement to guarantee to the natives "the full, exclusive and undisturbed possession of their lands".[31]

Second, we will better grasp the relative importance of the Treaty if we pay careful attention to the moments in which it became significant and seek to explain why that occurred. To illustrate this point, I will present an interpretation of what seems to have happened in the two and more years after the signing of the Treaty.[32] In July 1840 the Colonial Office received a brief dispatch from Sir George Gipps, the Governor of New South Wales, relaying a report by Hobson that he had been successful in making a treaty with the natives. Stephen, who, as we have seen, had been under attack by the New Zealand Company for the Colonial Office's treatment of the matter of sovereignty in regard to the islands of New Zealand, seized upon this news as an endorsement of the position the Colonial Office, and he in particular, had claimed it had adopted on this matter (as discussed above), scribbling:

> It seems to me to prove, if proof were wanting, how much wiser was the course taken of negotiating for a cession of the sovereignty than would have been the course of relying on the proceedings of Captain Cook [in claiming possession on the grounds of the doctrine of discovery] or the language of Vattel [legitimating such a move]

(which is what the New Zealand Company had urged). Note that this remark of Stephen pertains to the matter of sovereignty and to that alone, rather than to matters such as native title. More importantly, there is no evidence to suggest that the Colonial Office's senior members examined closely the English text of the Treaty that accompanied Gipps's despatch, let alone pondered the possible implications of the first clause of its second article. They made no further reference to the Treaty for some time. Moreover, in November 1840, the Colonial Office made an agreement with the New Zealand Company by which it granted it a very large amount of land subject to its meeting some merely technical requirements, disregarding the fact that it had previously ruled that all purchases of land made prior to the cession of British sovereignty by those such as the Company were to be subject to investigation by a Land Claims Commission based in New Zealand. In making this agreement, there is no evidence to suggest that the so-called guarantee of native possessions in the first clause of the second article of the Treaty figured in the Colonial Office's considerations. But, as I have just argued, the absence of any reference to the Treaty in the Colonial Office's negotiations of this agreement should not surprise us, since the Colonial Office at this time had not given the Treaty any further thought. To their mind, it had served the purpose for which it had been conceived.[33]

Now, let us move across to the islands of New Zealand and some 18 months later. In April 1842, after William Spain arrived in Port Nicholson (which came to be called Wellington) to begin his work as one of the Land Claims Commissioners, Hobson called on him to investigate more than a hundred claims to land by British claimants on the basis of their purchase from Māori, the most important of which were the claims of the New Zealand Company. Why were the Company's claims included? Hobson recognised that the provisions of the November 1840 agreement between the Colonial Office and the Company overrode the terms of the Land Claims Commission inasmuch as the Colonial Office had more or less guaranteed the Company title to land in many of the areas it had claimed to purchase it. However, he held that that guarantee was conditional upon the Company proving that it had in fact extinguished native title.[34]

It appears that Spain was of the same mind. In June 1842, he reasoned as follows:

> if it had been intended by Her Majesty's Government at once to admit the Company's title to be good and the native one extinct, then surely

> instructions would have been sent to [the Governor] to [exempt] that body from the operation of the [Land Claims] Commission, and to make them a grant of land . . . without further inquiry.

Spain confessed that he was unable to believe that the Colonial Office could have possibly intended the Company's claims to be exempt from such an investigation. It would, he wrote, be "so totally inconsistent and irreconcilable with the profession made to [the natives] that Her Majesty would afford equal protection to all her subjects". (This was, of course, to take the Colonial Office's high-flown rhetoric at face value rather than in the more nuanced way the Colonial Office meant its officials to receive its instructions.) Having formed this opinion, Spain, being the methodical man that he was, scoured official papers and correspondence to find support for it. Heading the numerous pieces of evidence that he adduced was the first clause of the second article of the Treaty: he argued in effect that Secretary of State for the Colonies Lord John Russell had approved a treaty "guaranteeing to the natives all their lands &c". (This, as I indicated earlier, is an unconvincing argument.) Sometime later, Spain, in presenting a report about his work to Hobson's successor as governor, returned to the matter. Once more, he speculated about what the imperial government *must* have had in mind as it made the agreement with the Company, but this time he made no specific reference to any particular clause in the Treaty, referring instead to what he called the spirit of the agreement, which was a new way of construing the agreement:

> It appears to me that a consent on the part of the [imperial] government to grant to the [New Zealand] company the land . . . without obliging [it] to prove the extinction of the native title would have been a direct contravention of and in utter opposition to the *spirit* of the treaty of Waitangi, and in violation of all the assurances of Her Majesty's government to the aborigines of affording them justice and protection.[35]

Let us shift now to London. There, by November 1842, the Colonial Office was becoming embroiled in a bitter conflict with the New Zealand Company. At this time, Russell's successor as the Secretary of State for the Colonies, Lord Edward Stanley, raised the stakes in this conflict by choosing to play what we might call the trump card of rights (in the sense of doing something in a morally right way rather than in the sense of rights as we understand these today).[36] In doing so, he invoked the first clause of the second article of the Treaty, asserting emphatically:

> even if such an interpretation [of the November 1840 agreement between the government and the New Zealand Company] could be shown to be the true one, [I consider] it impossible to maintain that the right of the natives of New Zealand to the soil, which has been recognised as indisputable by Her Majesty's government in [its instructions to Hobson], could be thereby affected; or that the Crown either intended thereby to deprive them, or did

> in fact deprive them, of the 'full, exclusive, and undisturbed possession of their lands and estates', which had been 'confirmed and guaranteed' to them by the treaty of Waitangi.[37]

This was the first time that the Colonial Office had ever chosen to make reference to this clause of the Treaty or even betrayed any knowledge that this agreement had a clause that might contain such a meaning. Why did Stanley do so now, especially given that the more obvious source of authority for the position that he, Hobson, and Spain were adopting in respect of the Company's claims was not the terms of the Treaty, but those of the Land Claims Commission? In the light of the fact, noted earlier, that the Colonial Office tended to be highly reactive in the way it went about its work, the answer to this question probably lies in the following sequence of events.

In May 1842, the New Zealand Company's principal agent in New Zealand, William Wakefield, who clearly misunderstood the Treaty, erroneously claimed that its terms, rather than those of the Land Claims Commission, were responsible for the fact that the government had failed to award the Company the lands to which it held it was entitled under the November 1840 agreement. The Company's directors followed suit in a letter to Stanley, and its attack on the Treaty seems to have sent Stanley or his staff at the Colonial Office off to read it carefully for the first time. They then decided to embrace the first clause of its second article, which the Colonial Office had never sought to insert in the Treaty and whose presence it had not previously even registered, as a means to embarrass and thereby bring into line the Company and its directors, whom Stanley, his deputy George Hope, and Stephen hated with a vengeance. This is to argue more generally that the Colonial Office only came to regard the Treaty as being of continuing importance some time after the event of its signing and that it did so in highly particular, which is to say contingent, circumstances, and for reasons that are both complex and mundane.[38]

Concluding remarks

A post-foundational history of the Treaty, I have suggested here (and in another recent essay),[39] reveals that both its making in 1840 and the significance (in both senses of that word) it came to acquire in the years that followed was highly contingent upon particular historical circumstances. By uncovering the deeply historical processes and relationships that made and remade the Treaty, post-foundational history demonstrates that there is nothing essential, let alone stable, in the significance of the Treaty, just as it helps explain why it has continued to be the subject of so much debate. Consequently, unlike foundational history, post-foundational history does not readily lend itself to being politically useful. Yet, by disclosing that the past or the pasts of the Treaty are heterogeneous and thus richer than that presented by foundational history, it can furnish us with new historical horizons that could enable New Zealanders to imagine alternative futures.

Notes

I wish to thank Claudia Haake and Miranda Johnson for reading a draft of this chapter and for their stringent criticisms and fruitful suggestions.

1 Herbert Butterfield *The Whig Interpretation of History* (G. Bell and Sons, London, 1931) at 16; JMR Owens "Historians and the Treaty of Waitangi" (1990) 1 Archifacts 18. Owens, it might be noted, was not especially troubled by this. Indeed, he applied to the Treaty an argument that an English medieval historian, JC Holt, had made in 1969 in regard to the Magna Carta, namely that there was little point trying to establish the precise historical meaning of the phrases or clauses of a historical text of this kind since there was little hope that the historian would succeed and any attempt to do so could only lead to distortion (at 4). I doubt the pertinence of Holt's argument since it seems to me that there *is* some prospect of being able to establish something like the historical meaning or meanings of a text made in the nineteenth century (as compared to being able to do this for one forged in the thirteenth century, for which the historical sources are much sparser) as well as some value in undertaking this task.

2 Here I have drawn heavily on Wolfgang Mommsen "Moral Commitment and Scholarly Detachment: The Social Function of the Historian" in Joep Leersen and Ann Rigney (eds) *Historians and Social Values* (Amsterdam University Press, Amsterdam, 2000) and Thomas L Haskell's discussion of this book, "Objectivity: Perspective as Problem and Solution" (2004) 43(3) *History and Theory* especially 350.

3 Gyan Prakash "Writing Post-Orientalist Histories of the Third World: Perspectives From Indian Historiography" (1990) 32(2) *Comparative Studies in Society and History* 384 at 397.

4 Paul A Cohen *History in Three Keys: The Boxers as Event, Experience, and Myth* (Columbia University Press, New York, NY, 1997) at 211–214.

5 Keith Sinclair *A History of New Zealand* (Penguin, Harmondsworth, 1959) at 73, *The Origins of the Māori Wars* (1957, 2nd ed, New Zealand University Press, Wellington, 1961) at 28; Claudia Orange *The Treaty of Waitangi* (Allen & Unwin New Zealand/Port Nicholson Press, Wellington, 1987).

6 Perhaps it is unsurprising that two of these historians, Ian Wards and Ruth Ross, took this position, since they were both closely associated with a leading New Zealand historian, JC Beaglehole, who had previously looked askance at the deployment of the Treaty in the nationalist myth-making. In 1936, he had remarked that it was puzzling to see the veneration in which it was being held, given what he described as "the troubled career of the Treaty, its uncertain observance, [and] the ambiguities of its interpretation" (John Beaglehole *New Zealand: A Short History* (George Allen & Unwin, London, 1936) at 38–39).

7 Ian Wards *The Shadow of the Land: A Study of British Policy and Racial Conflict in New Zealand 1832–1852* (Historical Publications Branch, Department of Internal Affairs, Wellington, 1968) at ix–x.

8 Some of Ross's argument is prefigured by Trevor Williams "The Treaty of Waitangi" (1940) 25(99) *History* 246.

9 Ruth Ross "The Treaty on the Ground" in *The Treaty of Waitangi: Its Origins and Significance*, foreword by Guy Powles (University Extension Publications, Wellington, 1972) at 16–34, and "Te Tiriti o Waitangi: Texts and Translations" (1972) 6(2) *New Zealand Journal of History* 129. For a useful discussion of Ross's work on the Treaty, see Rachael Bell "'Texts and Translations': Ruth Ross and the Treaty of Waitangi" (2009) 43(1) *New Zealand Journal of History* 39.

10 Alan Ward *A Show of Justice: Racial 'Amalgamation' in Nineteenth Century New Zealand* (Auckland University Press/Oxford University Press, Auckland, 1973) at 42–45.

11 Peter Adams *Fatal Necessity: British Intervention in New Zealand 1830–1847* (Oxford University Press/Auckland University Press, Auckland, 1977) at 11–15.

12 Andrew Sharp "The Problem of Māori Affairs, 1984–1989" in Martin Holland and Jonathan Boston (eds) *The Fourth Labour Government: Politics and Policy in New Zealand* (2nd ed, Oxford University Press, Auckland, 1990) at 251–269.

13 Both McHugh and Williams have since become advocates of an approach that seeks to historicise these matters. For McHugh, see, for example, "Time Whereof: Memory, History and Law in the Jurisprudence of Aboriginal Rights" (2014) 77(2) *Saskatchewan Law Review* 207; for Williams, see, for example, his chapter in this volume.

14 MPK Sorrenson "Towards a Radical Interpretation of New Zealand History: The Role of the Waitangi Tribunal" (1987) 21(2) *New Zealand Journal of History* 173.

15 Judith Binney "The Māori and the Signing of the Treaty of Waitangi" in David Green (ed) *Towards 1990: Seven Leading Historians Examine Significant Aspects of New Zealand History* (GP Books, Wellington, 1989) at 20–31; Judith Binney, Judith Bassett and Erik Olssen *The People and the Land: Te Tangata Me Te Whenua: An Illustrated History of New Zealand* (Bridget Williams Books, Wellington, 1990); James Belich *Making Peoples: A History of the New Zealanders From Polynesian Settlement to the End of the Nineteenth Century* (Allen Lane/Penguin, Auckland, 1996); Paul McHugh "Law, History and the Treaty of Waitangi" (1997) 31(1) *New Zealand Journal of History* 46 at 54. See also DF McKenzie *Oral Culture, Literacy and Print in Early New Zealand: The Treaty of Waitangi* (Victoria University Press with the Alexander Turnbull Library Endowment Trust, Wellington, 1985).

16 Andrew Sharp "History and Sovereignty: A Case of Juridical History in New Zealand/Aotearoa" in Michael Peters (ed) *Cultural Politics and the University in Aotearoa/New Zealand* (Dunmore Press, Palmerston North, 1997) at 159–181; WH Oliver "The Future Behind Us: The Waitangi Tribunal's Retrospective Utopia" in Andrew Sharp and Paul McHugh (eds) *Histories, Power and Loss: Uses of the Past – A New Zealand Commentary* (Bridget Williams Books, Wellington, 2001) at 9–29. See also Kerry Howe "Two Worlds?" (2003) 37(1) *New Zealand Journal of History* 56; Michael Belgrave "The Tribunal and the Past: Taking a Roundabout Path to a New History" in Michael Belgrave and others (eds) *Waitangi Revisited: Perspectives on the Treaty of Waitangi* (Oxford University Press, Auckland, 2005) at 35–55.

17 MPK Sorrenson "Treaties in British Colonial Policy: Precedents for Waitangi" in William Renwick (ed) *Sovereignty & Indigenous Rights: The Treaty of Waitangi in International Contexts* (Victoria University Press, Wellington, 1991) at 15–17, 28–29. See also Tom Bennion "Treaty-Making in the Pacific in the Nineteenth Century and the Treaty of Waitangi" (2004) 35(1) *Victoria University of Wellington Law Review* 165.

18 Michael Belgrave *Historical Frictions: Māori Claims and Reinvented Histories* (Auckland University Press, Auckland, 2005), especially Chapters 1 and 2. See also Lyndsay Head "The Pursuit of Modernity in Māori Society: The Conceptual Bases of Citizenship in the Early Modern Period" in Sharp and McHugh, above n 16, at 97–121, and *Land, Authority and the Forgetting of Being in Early Colonial Māori History* (PhD Thesis, University of Canterbury, 2006).

19 Stuart Banner *Possessing the Pacific: Land, Settlers and Indigenous People From Australia to Alaska* (Harvard University Press, Cambridge, MA, 2007) at 2, 4–5, 316–318; Mark Hickford *Making 'Territorial Rights of the Natives': Britain and New Zealand, 1830–1847* (DPhil Thesis, University of Oxford, 1999), "'Vague Native Rights to Land': British Imperial Policy on Native Title and Custom in New Zealand, 1837–53" (2010) 38(2) *Journal of Imperial and Commonwealth*

History 175, and *Lords of the Land: Indigenous Property Rights and the Jurisprudence of Empire* (Oxford University Press, Oxford, 2011), Chapters 2–4.

20 Here, once more, I am following Prakash, above n 3, at 399–400.

21 In this chapter, I use the term 'the islands of New Zealand' as part of my attempt to draw attention to fact that in a post-foundational history this area would not be treated as a prehistorical and unified given that the term 'New Zealand' tends to imply. In the historical sources for the period I examine in this chapter, the term 'islands of New Zealand' is how British players tended to refer to this place, and they distinguished between the islands, especially the northern and what they called the middle island (now the South Island). It is also the case, as John Gillis has argued, that islands at this time continued to be an important organising principle for understanding imperial space and that this was only in the process of being supplanted in the transition to land-based empires (*Islands of the Mind: How the Human Imagination Created the Atlantic World* (Palgrave MacMillan, New York, NY, 2004)). For more on this point, see Lauren Benton *A Search for Sovereignty: Law and Geography in European Empires, 1400–1900* (Cambridge University Press, New York, NY, 2010) especially Chapter 4.

22 I chart some of these changes in a book I am currently writing, tentatively titled *Claiming Possession: A Colonial Tale.*

23 Marc Bloch "Comparaison" (1930) in his *Histoire et historiens* (Armand Colin, Paris, 1995) (ed Ètienne Bloch) at 93; David Armitage *The Declaration of Independence: A Global History* (Harvard University Press, Cambridge, MA, 2007) at 3, 6, 15–18, 26–30, 33, 63–64, 66.

24 Richard White *The Middle Ground: Indians, Empires, and Republics in the Great Lakes Region, 1650–1815* (Cambridge University Press, New York, NY, 1991) at x.

25 John W Cell *British Colonial Administration in the Mid-Nineteenth Century: The Policy-Making Process* (Yale University Press, New Haven, CT, 1970), especially at xi; Ned Fletcher *A Praiseworthy Device for Amusing and Pacifying Savages? What the Framers Meant by the English Text of the Treaty of Waitangi* (PhD Thesis, University of Auckland, 2014).

26 Ward, above n 10, at 34–37; Orange, above n 5, at 2; Dorothy V Jones *License for Empire: Colonialism by Treaty in Early America* (University of Chicago Press, Chicago, IL, 1982) at xi–xii.

27 TG Ashplant and Adrian Wilson "Whig History and Present-Centred History" (1988) 31(1) *Historical Journal* 11 at 13, 15, "Present-Centred History and the Problem of Historical Knowledge" (1988) 31(2) *Historical Journal* 255 at 265–270.

28 See, for example, John Manning Ward *British Policy in the South Pacific* (Australasian Publishing Company, Sydney, 1948) at 75. For this argument more generally, see Paul McHugh "'A Pretty Gov[ernment]': The 'Confederation of United Tribes' and Britain's Quest for Imperial Order in the New Zealand Islands during the 1830s" in Lauren Benton and Richard J Ross (eds) *Legal Pluralism and Empires, 1500–1850* (New York University Press, New York, NY, 2013) at 239. Compare Bain Attwood "Protection Claims: The British, Māori and the Islands of New Zealand, 1800–40" in Lauren Benton and others (eds) *Protection and Empire: A Global History* (Cambridge University Press, Cambridge, 2018) at 153–174.

29 My argument here is informed by the distinction the historian Alan Megill makes between 'historical *traces*' and 'historical *sources*'. He has argued: "A trace is anything remaining from the past that was not made with the intention of revealing the past to us, but simply emerged as part of normal life. A source, on the other hand, is anything that was intended by its creator to stand as an account of events. . . . [T]here is a sense in which inadvertent evidence is a far more solid foundation for historical knowledge than is the evidence that people in the past

have intended to stand as evidence" (*Historical Knowledge, Historical Error: A Contemporary Guide to Practice* (University of Chicago Press, Chicago, IL, 2007) at 25–26).

30 *Colonial Gazette* 2 October 1839; Joseph Somes to Lord Palmerston 7 November 1839, *British Parliamentary Papers* (henceforth *BPP*), 1840, Paper no 238, Correspondence with the Secretary of State Relative to New Zealand, 66–68; James Stephen to Lord John Russell 21 November 1839, National Archives of the United Kingdom (henceforth NA), CO 209/5; Stephen to GW Hope 28 December 1842, NA, CO 209/18; Paul Knaplund *James Stephen and the British Colonial System* (University of Wisconsin Press, Madison, WI, 1953) at 82, 91.

31 Stephen, Drafts of Instructions to William Hobson undated, 24 January 1839, and 9 July 1839, NA, CO 209/4; Lord Normanby to Hobson 14 August 1839, *BPP*, Paper no 238, 37–42.

32 Strikingly, Orange's classic account fails to register the fact that there was very little discussion of the Treaty during this period.

33 Stephen, Minute on Sir George Gipps to Russell 19 February 1840, 9 July 1840, NA, CO 209/6; Agreement between the British Government and the New Zealand Company, 18 November 1840, *BPP*, 1841, Paper no 311, Copies or Extracts of Correspondence Relative to New Zealand, 85–87.

34 Colonial Secretary to Spain 19 March 1842, National Archives of New Zealand, Series IA 4/253; Hobson, Instructions to Spain and Colonial Secretary to Spain 26 March 1842, National Archives of New Zealand, Series IA 4/253.

35 Spain to Hobson 22 June 1842, in Spain to Colonial Secretary, 12 September 1843, *BPP*, 1844, Paper No 556, Appendices of the Report of the 1844 Select Committee (henceforth Appendices of the Report of the 1844 Select Committee), 292–295, my emphasis; Spain to Governor Robert FitzRoy 19 November 1843, Appendices of the Report of the 1844 Select Committee, 280.

36 For a discussion of this point, see Richard Dagger "Rights" in Terence Ball and others (eds) *Political Innovation and Conceptual Change* (Cambridge University Press, New York, NY, 1989) at 294.

37 Hope to Somes 7 November 1842, Appendices of the Report of the 1844 Select Committee, 14.

38 William Wakefield to EJ Ward 30 May 1842, Appendices of the Report of the 1844 Select Committee, 558–559; Lord Edward Stanley to Sir Robert Peel 17 December 1844, 14th Earl of Derby Papers, Liverpool Record Office, 920 Der 14, 129/4/29.

39 See "Protection Claims", above n 28.

6 The failing modern jurisprudence of the Treaty of Waitangi

Jacinta Ruru

This chapter explores the scope of the modern jurisprudence of Te Tiriti o Waitangi/the Treaty of Waitangi to be a legal anchor in the courts to recognise Māori interests, rights, and responsibilities to care for and nourish treasured lands and waters. In December 1986, just shy of 150 years since Māori chiefs signed the Treaty, Aotearoa New Zealand's Parliament enacted legislation – the State-Owned Enterprises Act 1986 – with a statement in section 9 that reads: "Nothing in this Act shall permit the Crown to act in a manner that is inconsistent with the principles of the Treaty of Waitangi." Six months later, on 29 June 1987, the Court of Appeal handed down a landmark decision interpreting the Treaty as no longer a "dead letter"[1] or a "simple nullity",[2] but rather as "the foundation for the future relationship between the Crown and the Māori race",[3] and that the principles require Crown and Māori to work together as partners in good faith. This case, *New Zealand Māori Council v Attorney-General*, has been described as "perhaps as important for the future of our country as any that has come before a New Zealand Court",[4] "arguably . . . New Zealand's most important 20th-century constitutional decision",[5] and "a circuit-breaker which founded New Zealand's modern Treaty jurisprudence".[6] Thirty years on, the Treaty principles have been integrated into many key statutes, are guiding the Treaty claim settlement process, and are the subject of many court cases.

New Zealand's modern Treaty jurisprudence is in many respects expansive and certainly sits aligned with other legal systems seeking to reconcile with their Indigenous peoples.[7] But is this comparatively more respectful contemporary government stance transpiring into more enhanced opportunities than in the colonial past for Māori to make and inform decisions for lands and waters? Are all three branches of government – the executive, legislature, and the judiciary – similarly re-calibrating colonial foundations to recognise the Treaty intent for partnership? This chapter considers these questions by focusing specifically on one arm of government: the courts. It examines judicial cases concerning water under the Resource Management Act 1991 (RMA) and concludes that New Zealand's High Court Justice Joe Williams's warning in 2012 about one specific case as "probably represent[ing] a missed opportunity to adapt and mould RMA processes in a new and innovative way"[8] is a far more apt observation for a whole suite of contemporary RMA cases and in fact is suitable as a broad statement for the entire body of Treaty jurisprudence to date.

I. Why water?

It is worthwhile to focus on water as a test resource for reconciliation and restitution because water is fundamentally important to all peoples and all legal systems, has an increasing economic value, and often moves in a flowing nature through different geographical and political boundaries. Also, in New Zealand, the government has entered into significant groundbreaking Treaty of Waitangi claim settlement statutes regarding water that have attracted world attention, importantly recognising that the legislature is at least recasting a new direction for some waterways.

Throughout the world, including in New Zealand, water is essential for the welfare of people, plants, livestock, farming activities, industry, and power generation.[9] In New Zealand, water, which is abundant but in some regions is becoming scarce due to over allocation of use rights,[10] is described as an essential resource for the country's economic, environmental, cultural, and social well-being.[11] State law takes this seriously. The statute that regulates water use, the RMA, requires that water be safeguarded for its life-supporting capacity and is discussed more fully later in this chapter. Māori law also takes seriously water and is discussed in brief here.

All of the approximately 40 distinct tribal federations and hundreds of tribes that constitute the Māori people derive their identity from the mountains, rivers, and lakes.[12] For instance, in greeting someone new, we might ask, "*Ko wai koe?*" which queries "Who are you?", but more literally translates as "Who are your waters?" The answer will depend on which tribal federation and tribe that person belongs to. All tribes have these geographical identity markers linked to water. The link between land and water and humans is a common feature of the Māori language. For instance, *iwi* means both 'tribal federation' and 'bone'; *hapū* means both 'tribe' and 'to be pregnant'; *whānau* means both 'extended family' and 'to give birth'; *whenua* means 'land' and 'afterbirth'; and *wai* means 'water', but also 'memory' and 'who'.

The Māori legal system has developed strong rules for protecting the *mauri* (life force) of water. For instance, according to Māori law, it is often abhorrent to artificially force the mixing of waters from different catchments and to mix waters with human sewage (the preference being for sewage to be treated on land).[13] For example, as presented to the Environment Court in evidence in 2016:[14]

> To Iwi Māori, discharge of human bodily waste into natural waterways, no matter how minute or miniscule, is culturally and environmentally offensive, has always been opposed by Māori, because of the offence caused to the mauri or life-force of water.

Moreover, the importance of water for Māori in a modern context has been captured in this 12-point 'indicia of ownership' framework encapsulated by the Waitangi Tribunal as[15]

1 The water resource has been relied upon as a source of food.
2 The water resource has been relied upon as a source of textiles or other materials.
3 The water resource has been relied upon for travel or trade.
4 The water resource has been used in the rituals central to the spiritual life of the *hapū*.
5 The water resource has a *mauri*.
6 The water resource is celebrated or referred to in *waiata* (song).
7 The water resource is celebrated or referred to in *whakatauki* (proverb).
8 The people have identified *taniwha* (water spirit/monster) as residing in the water resource.
9 The people have exercised *kaitiakitanga* (guardianship) over the water resource.
10 The people have exercised *mana* (authority) or *rangatiratanga* (sovereignty/self-determination) over the water resource.
11 *Whakapapa* (genealogy) identifies a cosmological connection with the water resource.
12 There is a continuing recognised claim to land or territory in which the resource is situated, and title has been maintained to 'some, if not all, of the land on (or below) which the water resource sits'.

While New Zealand has yet to recognise Māori ownership of freshwater (politically or legally), preferring instead to assert that either no one owns water or we all own water,[16] many of these Māori laws remain alive and relevant for tribes throughout the country. New Zealand's legal system does not guarantee Māori any general all-encompassing rights to water.[17] However, many tribes have successfully negotiated specific new governance regimes for some waterways through the Treaty claim settlement process.[18] Many of these settlements recognise the importance of freshwater to Māori identity, health, and well-being. Three examples are discussed here.

In 2006, Parliament enacted the first Treaty claim settlement statute focused entirely on water: Te Arawa Lakes Settlement Act 2006.[19] This Act recognises the significant relationship between the North Island tribe Te Arawa and 14 lakes that lie within the Te Arawa traditional geographical boundaries.[20] These lakes are situated in and around Rotorua and have, for more than a century, been a major international and national tourist destination. The Act settles Te Arawa historical claims to these lakes; in doing so, it records a Crown apology to Te Arawa for past wrongdoings, vests the ownership of the lakebeds in Te Arawa, and establishes new relationships between Te Arawa and other government official bodies that have responsibility for the lakes. While the mechanisms used in this Act were not nationally novel – in other regions, other statutes had already recognised Māori tribal ownership of some lakebeds[21] and had begun processes for joint management opportunities[22] – this Act was the first comprehensive statute to separate redress for water from other resources.[23]

In 2010, heralded as revolutionary are the settlements enacted to co-manage the Waikato River – New Zealand's longest river (425 kilometres): the Waikato-Tainui

Raupatu Claims (Waikato River) Settlement Act 2010 and the Ngāti Tūwharetoa, Raukawa, and Te Arawa River Iwi Waikato River Act 2010. In early 2012, another similar and linked statute was enacted for the Waipa River, which is a significant contributor to the Waikato River: Ngā Wai o Maniapoto (Waipa River) Act 2012. These three statutes present an entirely different water redress package than that offered in the Te Arawa Lakes Settlement Act 2006. These statutes are premised on a vision that seeks to restore the health and well-being of the Waikato and Waipa Rivers through providing for cooperative management of the rivers with those tribes that genealogically link to this water. These were the first statutes in New Zealand to elevate Māori to co-management roles with the Crown in regard to fresh water. A key component of the vision is to restore and protect the relevant tribal relationships with the two rivers in accordance with their tribal laws, "including their economic, social, cultural, and spiritual relationships".[24] These statutes rely on co-management tools rather than the mechanisms used in the Te Arawa Lakes settlement.

Then, in 2017, Parliament enacted legislation that recognises Te Awa Tupua as an indivisible and living whole, comprising the country's third longest river, the Whanganui River, and all its tributaries, streams, lakes, and wetlands: Te Awa Tupua (Whanganui River Claims Settlement) Act 2017. Te Awa Tupua became a legal entity with "all the rights, powers, duties and liabilities of a legal person".[25] A formal Te Pou Tupua (guardian) has been created to "provide the human face of Te Awa Tupua".[26] Two people fulfil this guardian role – one appointed by the Crown, the other by the Whanganui iwi.[27] The primary functions of the Te Pou Tupua are to promote and protect the health and well-being of Te Awa Tupua and speak on behalf of Te Awa Tupua.[28] The guardians perform the landowner functions for and on behalf of Te Awa Tupua.[29]

Thus government – particularly the executive and legislature – does not doubt the importance of water to Māori. There are ample official sources and policies that accept that Māori regard water as a *taonga* (treasure) and that water is fundamental to Māori cultural identity and well-being.[30] The political controversies arise in attempting to define and resolve the exact nature of Māori rights to water.[31] Of interest in this chapter is how the courts have dealt with Māori interests in water, specifically in resource consent cases heard under the RMA. This is important because it goes to the heart of understanding how the Treaty jurisprudence is developing in everyday decisions being made in New Zealand and the Māori experience of being heard (or not) in the courts.

II. The legislature and the Resource Management Act 1991

New Zealand has a unicameral legislature. Under its constitutional system, Parliament is supreme and has no formal limits to its law-making power.[32] The Treaty of Waitangi is not part of the domestic law. Since the 1980s, the Treaty is commonly said to form part of the country's informal constitution along with the New Zealand Bill of Rights Act 1990, the Electoral Act 1993, and the Constitution

Act 1986.[33] But for the judiciary or those acting under the law, the Treaty itself usually only becomes relevant if it has been expressly incorporated into statute.[34] Even so, statutory incorporation of the Treaty has been a relatively recent phenomenon. It was once endorsed in the courts "as a simple nullity".[35] It was not until the 1970s that the long Māori struggle calling for action to remedy Treaty breaches began to gain mainstream recognition and, in turn, the attention of those in Parliament and the judiciary.[36]

The Treaty of Waitangi Act 1975 was the first statute to use the term 'the principles of the Treaty of Waitangi' and the first statute to permit interpretation of the Treaty of Waitangi. Hence, the Treaty jurisprudence was initially developed in the Waitangi Tribunal.[37] The courts entered this terrain post 1986 via the opening provided in section 9 of the State-Owned Enterprises Act 1986:[38] "Nothing in this Act shall permit the Crown to act in a manner that is inconsistent with the principles of the Treaty of Waitangi." This wording was unique – no other statute had ever confined those with statutory power to have some level of regard to the Treaty of Waitangi.

Today, there are more than 100 statutes referencing the Treaty of Waitangi, but there are various reasons and methods for the incorporations. For example, the Treaty of Waitangi settlement statutes reference the historical signing of the Treaty and record Crown apologies for breaching the principles of the Treaty of Waitangi. Those statutes that actually direct decision-makers acting under a statute to have some level of regard to the Treaty principles do not use uniform orders. Section 9 of the State-Owned Enterprise Act is obviously one example of a directive. However, it is more common for the Treaty principles directive to be positioned as a positive, rather than a negative, duty. The directives usually take one of the following forms:[39]

- *Give effect to* the Treaty principles[40]
- *Give particular recognition to* the Treaty principles[41]
- *Take into account* the Treaty principles[42]
- Ensure *full and balanced account* of the Treaty principles[43]
- *Have regard to* the Treaty principles[44]
- *Acknowledge* the Treaty principles[45]
- *Recognise and respect* the Treaty principles[46]

The latest trend for statutory incorporation of the Treaty principles is to be more prescriptive. For example, section 5 of the Environmental Reporting Act 2015 reads:

> In order to recognise and respect the Crown's responsibility to take appropriate account of the Treaty of Waitangi/Te Tiriti o Waitangi, –
>
> (a) sections 8(1)(c) and 11(1)(c) provide for te ao Māori to be an impact category in preparing synthesis and domain reports, to ensure that those reports, and the topics, are informed by a Māori perspective; and

(b) section 19(3) requires consultation with iwi authorities before regulations may be made, to ensure that the Ministers are informed of the views of those organisations before regulations are made.

The central statute that manages the use of water in New Zealand is the RMA and it is inclusive of the Treaty principles.[47] The RMA is the pre-eminent natural resources statute.[48] It puts forward an all-encompassing regime for the sustainable management of land, air, and water.[49] Central government retains some responsibility to influence this regime, primarily through setting national environmental standards, national policy standards, and the New Zealand coastal policy statement.[50] However, day-to-day control is vested in regional government and territorial authorities.[51] These bodies prepare plans that contain rules concerning the use of land, air, and water where appropriate, and stipulate when and where proposed activities may require resource consents permitting use. The RMA requires that these decision-makers and the courts have some level of regard for Māori, including their relationship with water as is now briefly explained.

The common starting point is that no person may do anything with land (including their privately owned land), air, or water that contravenes a rule in a district plan, unless the activity is expressly allowed by a resource consent or coastal permit, granted by the territorial authority responsible for the plan, or contravenes a rule in a regional, or regional coastal, plan.[52] The RMA gives regional and local councils the power to assert rules and guidelines for taking, using, damming, and diverting freshwater.[53] Regional councils have specific duties in regard to water. These include controlling the use of land for the purpose of the maintenance and enhancement of the quality and quantity of water in water bodies.[54] The councils' functions also include control over taking, using, damming, and diverting of water for the purposes of setting maximum and minimum, and controlling the range of change, of water levels and flows.[55] Regional councils need to control discharges of contaminants into water, and discharges of water into water. Regional councils can also, if appropriate, establish rules in a regional plan to allocate the taking or use of water, as long as the allocation does not affect the activities authorised in the Act.[56] Resource consents relating to water can be issued for a maximum of 35-year terms.[57]

In formulating district and regional plan rules and issuing resource consents, the RMA directs local authorities to recognise the Māori relationship with water. Section 6(e) mandates that all persons exercising functions and powers in relation to managing the use, development, and protection of natural and physical resources must recognise and provide for matters of national importance, including the relationship of Māori and their culture and traditions with water. However, this is one of several factors that local authorities must weigh in reaching decisions. Section 6 in full reads (with emphasis added):

6 Matters of national importance

In achieving the purpose of this Act, all persons exercising functions and powers under it, in relation to managing the use, development, and protection of natural and physical resources, shall recognise and provide for the following matters of national importance:

(a) the preservation of the natural character of the coastal environment (including the coastal marine area), wetlands, and lakes and rivers and their margins, and the protection of them from inappropriate subdivision, use, and development:
(b) the protection of outstanding natural features and landscapes from inappropriate subdivision, use, and development:
(c) the protection of areas of significant indigenous vegetation and significant habitats of indigenous fauna:
(d) the maintenance and enhancement of public access to and along the coastal marine area, lakes, and rivers:
(e) *the relationship of Māori and their culture and traditions with their* ancestral lands, *water*, sites, waahi tapu, and other taonga:
(f) the protection of historic heritage from inappropriate subdivision, use, and development:
(g) the protection of protected customary rights:
(h) the management of significant risks from natural hazards.

Additionally, section 7(a) of the RMA directs that all persons exercising functions and powers in relation to managing the use, development, and protection of natural and physical resources, shall have particular regard to ***kaitiakitanga*** (the exercise of guardianship by Māori).[58] Again, it is one of several factors that must be considered. Section 7 in full reads:

7 Other matters

In achieving the purpose of this Act, all persons exercising functions and powers under it, in relation to managing the use, development, and protection of natural and physical resources, shall have particular regard to –

(a) Kaitiakitanga:
(aa) The ethic of stewardship:
(b) The efficient use and development of natural and physical resources:
(ba) The efficiency of the end use of energy:
(c) The maintenance and enhancement of amenity values:
(d) Intrinsic values of ecosystems:
(e) [Repealed]
(f) Maintenance and enhancement of the quality of the environment:
(g) Any finite characteristics of natural and physical resources:
(h) The protection of the habitat of trout and salmon:
(i) The effects of climate change:
(j) The benefits to be derived from the use and development of renewable energy.

Moreover, section 8 states:

> **8 Treaty of Waitangi**
>
> In achieving the purpose of this Act, all persons exercising functions and powers under it, in relation to managing the use, development, and protection of natural and physical resources, shall take into account the principles of the Treaty of Waitangi (Te Tiriti o Waitangi).

Sections 6(e), 7(a), and 8 provide a strong base for Māori to voice their concerns relating to the use of fresh water. In addition, several other sections in the RMA create mandatory requirements for local authorities to listen to Māori and even negotiate the transfer of power to tribal authorities (not that any local authority has actually actioned such a transfer to any tribal authority despite it being an option now for more than 25 years).[59] Importantly, the legislature through section 8 of the RMA has provided the plank for the courts to take into account the Treaty principles in resource management decision-making. Is such recognition influencing the outcome of at least some judicial cases?

III. The judiciary and the resource management Act 1991

In New Zealand, persons can appeal local government decisions relating to issuing or not issuing resource consents to the Environment Court.[60] Thereafter, appeals are restricted to points of law, and go, in order, to the High Court, Court of Appeal, and lastly to the Supreme Court.[61] There are several instances where Māori, as objectors, have appealed council decisions that approved resource consents to take water, discharge wastewater into water, or dam water. In all of these cases, Māori speak of the importance of the water to them culturally, including the belief that water has its own *mauri* and the importance of these places for food gathering, namely fishing.

In a survey of RMA cases concerning Māori and water, few resulted in clear wins for Māori and often do not concern the typical water take facts of most of the other cases.[62] While the RMA was enacted in 1991, the first clear win did not occur until 2002. This case concerned an argument posed by the Federated Farmers of New Zealand in the North Canterbury Province that a human-made drain channel was not subject to minimum flow requirements.[63] The Environment Court accepted Te Rūnanga o Ngāi Tahu's argument that it was subject to the requirements because the drain was linked to the Cust River and had capacity to support traditional use and values. The other case involved Ngāti Tamaoho Trust's concern that the decision to grant resource consent to the Papakura District Council to construct and operate tidal gates on a specific tidal estuary inlet for the purposes of creating recreational opportunities would interfere with the natural flow of the tide.[64] The Court agreed that to Ngāti Tamaoho, if the water was interfered with, the *wairoa* (spirit) of the water would decay. The resource consent was revoked.

Several of the identified cases did result in, at best, partial wins for Māori. The most recent one concerned the Bay of Plenty Regional Council reissuing to the Rotorua District Council a resource consent to take up to 3,500 cubic metres of water per day over the summer months from the Taniwha Springs.[65] Ngāti Rangiwewehi appealed the decision, relying on section 6(e), stating that their relationship with this water was a matter of national importance. The Court partially agreed by reducing the term of the resource consent from 25 to 10 years. The maximum daily volume and rate were not reduced. Another case, decided back in 1996, involved the Mangakahia Māori Komiti challenging the resource consents issued to 17 diary farmers to take water from the Opouteke River for irrigation.[66] The Komiti contended that the water permits would adversely affect their right to catch fish in the river. The Court found a middle ground where the consents in most cases were slightly increased by one year, but the total level of water take permitted was reduced. Ngāi Tahu were partially successful in a case where they argued that the issuing of resource consent to a particular jetboat company to operate ten additional trips on the Dart River for tourism purposes would adversely impact on their relationship with the river. The Court reduced the number of jetboat trips to four.[67] In another handful of cases, Māori were successful in protecting part of a lake from an aerial spray of weedkiller,[68] and a fish passage where consent had been granted for flashboards to be replaced by hydraulically controlled gates to manage a dam's water levels.[69]

However, in some cases, Māori lost their appeals outright. For example, Tautari lost their challenge of a resource consent that had been granted for the construction of a farm irrigation dam on the Waiopitotoi Stream. The consent also allowed the applicant to take up to 2,700 cubic metres of water per day. Tautari appealed on behalf of the interests of the Māori people living only six kilometres downstream of the proposed dam. Tautari argued that they had not been adequately consulted and that the terms of the consent would disrupt the migration of traditional fish species and have a general effect on fish life as traditional sources of food. The Court disagreed.

In a case where Contact Energy appealed the Waikato Regional Council's refusal to grant resource consents for a proposed geothermal power station, Tauhara Middle Trust argued that the power station should not proceed because consultation had been inadequate and the geothermal resource is a *taonga*. The Environment Court found in favour of Contact Energy permitting the power station to be built. In another case, Tainui argued that the resource consents issued to build a 86-hectare engineered landfill would have potential adverse effects on the tributaries of the Waikato River, particularly the Clune Stream. The Court concluded that the existing conditions that the design is subject to "will adequately protect the Māori interests".[70]

In another set of cases, Calter Holt Harvey was issued a 21-year-term resource consent for discharge-to-water permits for its pulp and paper plant. Ngāti Tūwharetoa did not agree with that term. The Environment Court had some sympathy for the tribe and held that they must be given more of a participatory role by reporting to them issues arising.[71] However, the High Court disagreed and held that Tūwharetoa have no consultation interests in the resource consent.[72]

In another case concerning water where a Māori tribe opposed the issuing of consents to Genesis Power to enable the Tongariro hydroelectric power development scheme to continue operating, the Māori tribe lost. Ngāti Rangi Trust opposed the consents primarily because it involved diversion of water from the Whangaehu, Whanganui, and Moawhango riveres in Lake Taupō and then into the Waikato River, and that their cultural traditions have been inhibited by a reduced flow of water, reduced water levels, degraded water quality, and a change to the ecological system that affects the food chain in the water. While the Environment Court restricted the consents from 35 years to 10 years,[73] the High Court overruled that decision,[74] and the Court of Appeal has since endorsed the High Court's judgment.[75] Importantly, it is this series of cases that led Justice Joe Williams to make the observation that the judiciary had perhaps missed an opportunity to adapt and mould the RMA.[76] He observed extra-judicially in 2012:[77]

> The result is disappointing in terms of the Act's overall effectiveness in mediating Māori concerns that impact on the wider community and economy. If the reforms contained in the RMA were about anything, they were about providing a platform upon which the two systems could engage in civilised conversation about their differences and mutual interests. Given Whanganui's hundred year history of claims in respect of the river and their opposition to the power development since its inception, their anger at and distrust of Genesis was, with respect, understandable. Make no mistake, the decisions in the High Court and Court of Appeal were orthodox on the law, but in practical terms the Genesis Energy case probably represents a missed opportunity to adapt and mould RMA processes in a new and innovative way. As Ellen France J noted in dissent, an adjournment for further discussion between the parties over acceptable mitigation measures would probably have been unobjectionable and would have achieved the same result. I am told that despite the result on appeal, the parties did meet and discuss appropriate accommodations and common ground was eventually found as the Environment Court had hoped.

Another Environment Court decision concerning Māori and water illustrates the frustration that Māori often experience in these cases. In *Wakatu Inc v Tasman District Council*,[78] the Wakatu Incorporation and other Māori tribal groups appealed a resource consent issued by the Tasman District Council to permit the local authority to take a large amount of groundwater per day from an aquifer hydraulically connected to the Motueka River to provide for a community water scheme. The scheme would supply piped water to unreticulated homes in the wider region. Māori opposed the proposal because they believed the taking of water from one catchment and using it in another "would have significant impacts upon the mauri of the river".[79] The Council agreed that

Māori valued the Motueka River as a treasure and ancestor, and they have "kaitiaki [guardian] responsibilities to protect the mauri and mana of the river".[80] The dispute was whether the use of the water would affect the life force of the river. The Council argued no; Māori of this region said yes; or as the Environment Court framed it:[81]

> What is essentially at issue is whether in the absence of any physical effect on the river that is more than negligible, there can be a spiritual effect on the mauri of the river, or on the relationship of the tangata whenua [people of the land/Indigenous people] with it.

The case addressed the Māori law about transferring water between catchments and "whether any broad principle in *tikanga* [protocol/Māori law] could be applied to a new situation enabled by more advanced technology",[82] namely pipes. The Court concluded in favour of the resource consent (thus against Māori) by resolving that any spiritual or metaphysical effects could be addressed by requiring the Council to establish a Māori "consultation group convened regularly by the Council to consider matters relating to the exercise and monitoring of the consent".[83]

Thus, while the RMA does provide a platform for Māori to air their concerns, these concerns constitute just one of several factors that the decision-makers and the courts have to consider. The fact that Māori often lose in the courts is perhaps not because the courts lack the awareness of the importance of the RMA protections to Māori. For example, Aotearoa New Zealand's then top appeal court, the Privy Council in the United Kingdom, stated in 2002, that sections 6(e), 7(a) and 8 provide "strong directions to be borne in mind at every stage of the planning process"[84] and that if alternative proposals exist that do not significantly affect Māori, then preference should be given to those alternatives even if they are not ideal. However, in that case, which concerned the laying of roads and not the take of water, Māori still lost. Moreover, the courts have been clear in stipulating that section 6(e) "does not create a right of veto"[85] for Māori and that it does not trump other matters.[86] The Environment Court accepts, though, that section 6(e) "should not be given lip service to".[87] Nonetheless, overall the case law illustrates that while it is definitely a strong starting point to have legislative rights, those rights remain fundamentally vulnerable to a judicial decision-making balancing act. This then begs the question: is there tangible worth for Treaty inclusive legislation? Certainly there is, especially in the extra judicial realm where Treaty provisions encourage and facilitate new relationship building between, for example, local government and Māori. But as Aotearoa New Zealand marks more than 175 years of the Treaty, significantly more ought to be expected of the judiciary, our nation-state and our citizens. The balancing of interests to consistently not favour Māori interests, indicates systemic regional and national issues of bias and the deep prevalence of assumed Crown supremacy.

Conclusion

This chapter has provided a glimpse into the judicial machinery of Aotearoa New Zealand, highlighting central themes and outcomes replicated the world over. This survey of domestic RMA cases clearly demonstrates that to date Treaty jurisprudence is falling well short of where this nation ought to be aiming in order to live out the intentions and possibilities inherent within the Treaty itself. Fundamentally new interpretative knowledge and practice is required to change this still colonial reality that includes theoretical constitutional change, displacement of Crown assumptions of superiority, and welcoming of Māori influence *within* the law, including on the highest reaches of judicial decision-making. As Borrows knowingly asserts in his chapter, "Right relationships among peoples and the earth deserve greater attention in our quest to honour the treaties."[88] This must resonate as nations climb their 'highest mountains' of law with grace and dignity.

Notes

1 *New Zealand Māori Council v Attorney-General* [1987] 1 NZLR 641 (CA) at 661 referring to the Treaty of Waitangi Act 1975. For more discussion about this case, see P.G. McHugh "'Treaty Principles': Constitutional Relations Inside a Conservative Jurisprudence" (2008) 39 *VUWLR* 39; and Jacinta Ruru (ed) *'In Good Faith' Symposium Proceedings Marking the 20th Anniversary of the Lands Case* (New Zealand Law Foundation and the University of Otago, Wellington, 2008).

2 *New Zealand Māori Council v Attorney-General*, above n 1, at 715, referring to *Wi Parata v Bishop of Wellington* (1877) 3 NZ Jur (NS) SC 72.

3 At 714 per Bisson J.

4 At 651 per Sir Robin Cooke, the then President of the Court of Appeal; see also Robin Cooke "Introduction" (1990) 14 *NZULR* 1 (Special Waitangi Issue).

5 Nilay Patel "Lord Cooke of Thorndon (1929–2006): 51 Years in the Law" (2006) 32 *Commonwealth Law Bulletin* 443 at 445.

6 Philip A. Joseph *Constitutional & Administrative Law in New Zealand* (4th ed, Brookers Ltd, Wellington, 2014) at 51.

7 See for example *Tsilhqot'in Nation v British Columbia* [2014] 2 SCR 257; *Mabo v Queensland (No 2)* (1992) 175 CLR 1; P. G. McHugh *Aboriginal Title: The Modern Jurisprudence of Tribal Land Rights* (Oxford University Press, Oxford, 2011); Robert J. Miller and others *Discovering Indigenous Lands: The Doctrine of Discovery in the English Colonies* (Oxford University Press, Oxford, 2010); Nigel Bankes and Timo Koivurova (eds) *The Proposed Nordic Saami Convention: National and International Dimensions of Indigenous Property Rights* (Hart Publishing, Oxford, 2013); Ulla Secher *Aboriginal Customary Law: A Source of Common Law Title to Land* (Hart Publishing, Oxford, 2014); Patrick Macklem and Douglas Sanderson (eds) *From Recognition to Reconciliation: Essays on the Constitutional Entrenchment of Aboriginal and Treaty Rights* (University of Toronto Press, Toronto, 2016); John Borrows and Michael Coyle (eds) *The Right Relationship: Reimagining the Implementation of Historical Treaties* (University of Toronto Press, Toronto, 2017).

8 Justice Joe Williams "Lex Aotearoa: An Heroic Attempt to Map the Māori Dimension in Modern New Zealand Law" (2013) 21 *Waikato Law Review* 1 at 20.

9 *Carter Holt Harvey Ltd v Waikato Regional Council* [2011] NZEnvC 380 at [2].

10 See New Zealand Institute of Economic Research *Water management in New Zealand: A Road Map for Understanding Water Value*. NZIER public discussion paper. Working paper 2014/01 (Wellington, 2014).
11 *National Policy Statement for Freshwater Management 2014 (amended 2017)* (ME 1324, Wellington, August 2017).
12 For an introduction to the Māori worldview, see Hirini Moko Mead *Tikanga Māori: Living by Māori Values* (2nd ed, Huia Publishers, Wellington, 2016); Atholl Anderson, Judith Binney and Aroha Harris *Tangata Whenua: An Illustrated History* (Bridget Williams Books, Wellington, 2014).
13 Waitangi Tribunal *The Interim Report on the National Freshwater and Geothermal Resources Claim* (Wai 2358, 2012).
14 *Manawatu District Council v Manawatu District Council* [2016] NZEnvC 53, at [122].
15 Tribunal, above n 13, at 38.
16 See Cabinet Economic and Infrastructure Committee *Fresh Water: Allocation Work Programme* (June 2016) <www.mfe.govt.nz/sites/default/files/media/Fresh%20water/Freshwater%20Allocation%20Work%20Programme%20%20Terms%20of%20Reference%20and%20Appointmen. . . .pdf>.
17 For information about how other countries are recognising (or not) their Indigenous peoples' rights in water, see for example Barbara Cosens and Judith V. Royster (eds) *The Future of Indian and Federal Reserved Water Rights: The Winters Centennial* (University of New Mexico, Albuquerque, NM, 2012); Melanie Durette "A Comparative Approach to Indigenous Legal Rights to Freshwater: Key Lessons for Australia From the United States, Canada and New Zealand" (2010) 27 *Environmental and Planning Law Journal* 296; Kenichi Matsui *Native Peoples and Water Rights: Irrigation, Dams, and the Law in Western Canada* (McGill-Queen's University Press, Montreal/Kingston, 2009); Virginia Marshall *Overturning Aqua Nullius: Securing Aboriginal Water Rights* (Aboriginal Studies Press, Canberra, 2017); Melissa Nursey-Bray "Lore, Law and Water Governance: Insights Into Managing Water for Country, Australia" (2016) 8 *Indigenous Law Bulletin* 12.
18 See Nicola Wheen and Janine Hayward *Treaty of Waitangi Settlements* (Bridget Williams Books, Wellington, 2012); Carwyn Jones *New Treaty, New Tradition: Reconciling New Zealand and Māori Law* (Victoria University Press, Wellington, 2016).
19 Te Arawa Lakes Settlement Act 2006.
20 See Section 12 of the Te Arawa Lakes Settlement Act 2006 for a definition of "Te Arawa".
21 The bed of Lake Taupo was vested in Ngāti Tūwharetoa through a deed dated 28 August 1992. This was superseded by a deed executed on 10 September 2007. See Hon Parekura Horomia, Minister of Māori Affairs, Hon Chris Carter, Minister of Conservation, and Hon Mark Burton, Minister of Local Government "New Deed of Settlement for Lake Taupō" (press release, 10 September 2007). The bed of Te Waihora (Lake Ellesmere), a large lake in the South Island, was vested in Te Rūnanga o Ngāi Tahu ownership. See Ngāi Tahu Claims Settlement Act 1998, s 168. More recently, the bed of Lake Ngākeketo in Northland was vested in Te Rūnanga Nui o Te Aupōuri Trust. See Ngāti Kuri Claims Settlement Act 2015, s 40.
22 See the provisions for joint management of Te Waihora (Lake Ellesmere) between Te Rūnanga o Ngāi Tahu and the Department of Conservation in Sections 177–181 of the Ngāi Tahu Claims Settlement Act 1998. More recently, see the creation of the Rangitaiki River Forum, which is a joint committee of members from different tribes, the Bay of Islands Regional Council and the Whakatāne District Council.

See Ngāti Manawa Claims Settlement Act 2012; Ngāti Whare Claims Settlement Act 2012; Hineuru Claims Settlement Act 2016.

23 The later Affiliate Te Arawa Iwi and Hapū Claims Settlement Act 2008 records the settlement of historical claims to resources including lands and forestry.

24 Nga Wai o Maniapoto (Waipa River) Act 2012, First Schedule, cl (3)(c).

25 Te Awa Tupua (Whanganui River Claims Settlement) Act 2017, s 14(1). See Linda Te Aho "Ngā Whakatunga Waimāori: Freshwater Settlements" in Nicola R. Wheen and Janie Hayward (eds) *Treaty of Waitangi Settlements* (Bridget Williams Books, Wellington, 2012); Linda Te Aho "Indigenous Challenges to Enhance Freshwater Governance and Management in New Zealand – The Waikato River Settlement" (2010) 20 *Journal of Water Law* 285.

26 Te Awa Tupua (Whanganui River Claims Settlement) Act 2017, s 18(2). See Linda Te Aho "Legislation – Te Awa Tupua (Whanganui River Claims Settlement) Bill – The Endless Quest for Justice" (August 2016) *Māori Law Review* <http://Māorilawreview.co.nz/2016/08/legislation-te-awa-tupua-whanganui-river-claims-settlement-bill-the-endless-quest-for-justice/>.

27 In September 2017, the first two guardians were appointed: Dame Tariana Turia and Turama Hawira; see Zaryd Wilson "Whanganui River Representatives Appointed" *New Zealand Herald* (online edition, Auckland, 5 September 2017).

28 Te Awa Tupua (Whanganui River Claims Settlement) Act 2017, s 19.

29 S 19(1)(d).

30 See, RMA, s 6. See also Land and Water Forum reports including *Fourth Report of the Land and Water Forum* (2015); *National Policy Statement for Freshwater Management 2014 (amended 2017)* (ME 1324, Wellington, August 2017).

31 The government executive has accepted Māori rights and interests in water are "unresolved", see Minister for the Environment and Minister of Agriculture *Implementing the New Start for Fresh Water: Proposed Officials' Work Programme* (2009) <www.mfe.govt.nz/more/cabinet-papers-and-related-material-search/cabinet-papers/freshwater/implementing-new-start>.

32 To better understand New Zealand's constitutional system, see Joseph, above n 6; Jacinta Ruru, Paul Scott and Duncan Webb *The New Zealand Legal System: Structures and Processes* (6th ed, LexisNexis, Wellington, 2016).

33 The Constitution Act 1986 sets out New Zealand's system of government, in particular the executive, legislature, and judiciary, and it holds that the Sovereign in right of New Zealand is the Head of State, and the Governor-General is the Sovereign's representative. See generally Geoffrey Palmer and Matthew Palmer *Bridled Power: New Zealand's Constitution and Government* (4th ed, Oxford University Press, Auckland, 2004).

34 *Te Heuheu Tukino v Aotea District Māori Land Board* [1941] NZLR 590, [1941] AC 308 (PC).

35 *Wi Parata v Bishop of Wellington*, above n 2, at 78.

36 See Ranginui Walker *Ka Whawhai Tonu Matou Struggle Without End* (Penguin, Wellington, 1990); Aroha Harris *Hikoi: Forty Years of Māori Protest* (Huia Publishers, Wellington, 2004).

37 For commentary on Treaty principles, see Te Puni Kokiri, Ministry of Māori Development *He Tirohanga o Kawa ki te Tiriti o Waitangi. A Guide to the Principles of the Treaty of Waitangi as Expressed by the Courts and the Waitangi Tribunal* (Te Puni Kokiri, Wellington, 2001).

38 The courts have defined the relationship by stating that the Tribunal's opinions "are of great value to the Court" (*New Zealand Māori Council v Attorney-General*, above n 1, at 662), and "are entitled to considerable weight" *Moana Te Aira Te Uri Karaka Te Waero v The Minister of Conservation and Auckland City Council* HC Auckland M360–SW01, 19 February 2002 at 59, but can be freely dismissed.

39 Note that this table is taken from the Constitutional Advisory Panel *New Zealand's Constitution: The Conversation So Far* (September 2012) at 56. The various provisions are discussed by Matthew Palmer *The Treaty of Waitangi in New Zealand's Law and Constitution* (Victoria University Press, Wellington, 2008) at 182–183 and Ross Carter *Burrows and Carter Statute Law in New Zealand* (5th ed, LexisNexis, Wellington, 2015) at 523–525. See too one of the more recent cases to discuss legislative recognition of the Treaty principles, *Ngaronoa v Attorney-General* [2017] NZCA 351.

40 For example, Conservation Act 1987, s 4, states "This Act shall so be interpreted and administered as to give effect to the principles of the Treaty of Waitangi."

41 For example, Royal Foundation for the Blind Act 2002, s 10, states that one object of the Foundation is to "give particular recognition to the principles of the Treaty of Waitangi and their application to the governance and services of the Foundation".

42 For example, RMA, s 8, requiring that the exercise of functions and powers under the Act "take into account the principles of the Treaty of Waitangi".

43 The Preamble of the Environment Act 1986, states that one purpose of the Act is to "Ensure that, in the management of natural and physical resources, full and balanced account is taken of . . . (iii) The principles of the Treaty of Waitangi".

44 For example, Crown Minerals Act 1991, s 4, requires that the exercise of functions and powers under the Act "shall have regard to the principles of the Treaty of Waitangi".

45 Education Act 1989, s 181, states that one duty of a council of an institution in exercising its functions and powers under the Act will be to acknowledge the Treaty principles.

46 Exclusive Economic Zone and Continental Shelf (Environmental Effects) Act 2012, s 12, outlines what is required "in order to recognise and respect the Crown's responsibility to give effect to the principles of the Treaty of Waitangi for the purposes of this Act".

47 Other statutes are also relevant. See Environment Act 1986; Conservation Act 1987; Fisheries Act 1996; Māori Fisheries Act 2004.

48 David Grinlinton "Contemporary Environmental Law in New Zealand" in Klaus Bosselmann and David Grinlinton (eds) *Environmental Law for a Sustainable Society* (New Zealand Centre for Environmental Law, Auckland, 2002) at 19. See also Derek Nolan (ed) *Environmental and Resource Management Law* (4th ed, LexisNexis, Wellington, 2011); Peter Salmon and David Grinlinton (eds) *Environmental Law in New Zealand* (Thomson Reuters, Wellington, 2015).

49 See RMA, s 5.

50 Ss 24–29A, 43–58A.

51 Ss 30–31.

52 Ss 9–23; see also Karen N. Scott "From the Lakes to the Oceans: Reforming Water Resource Management Regimes in New Zealand" (2006) 17 *Journal of Water Law* 231.

53 RMA, s 14.

54 S 30(1)(c) (ii) and (iii).

55 S 30(1)(e).

56 S 14(3)(b)-(e).

57 S 123.

58 Section 2 of the RMA defines *kaitiakitanga* to mean "the exercise of guardianship by the *tangata whenua* of an area in accordance with *tikanga* Māori in relation to natural and physical resources; and includes the ethic of stewardship".

59 For requirements to listen to Māori, see for example, RMA, ss 61(2A)(a), 74(2A)(a). For powers to make joint management agreements, see RMA, ss 36B–36E. For powers to make *iwi* participation arrangements, see RMA, ss 58L–58U.

60 Kenneth Palmer "Reflections on the History and Role of the Environment Court in New Zealand" (2010) 27 *Environmental Planning Law Journal* 69.
61 Although note that prior to 2004, the Privy Council in London was New Zealand's last judicial bastion. See Supreme Court Act 2003.
62 See Jacinta Ruru *The Legal Voice of Māori in Freshwater Governance: A Literature Review* (Landcare Research, 2009) and Jacinta Ruru "Undefined and Unresolved: Exploring Indigenous Rights in New Zealand's Freshwater Legal Regime" (2010) 20 *Journal of Water Law* 236 at 238–240.
63 *Federated Farmers of New Zealand (North Canterbury Province Inc) v Canterbury Regional Council* (2002) 8 ELRNZ 223 (EnvC).
64 *Ngataki, Ted and Ngati Tamaoho Trust v Auckland Regional Council* [2004] 9 NZED 725 (EnvC).
65 *Te Maru o Ngati Rangiwewehi v Bay of Plenty Regional Council* (2008) 14 ELRNZ 331 (EnvC).
66 *Mangakahia Māori Komiti v Northland Regional Council* [1996] NZRMA 193.
67 See *Kemp & Billoud v Queenstown Lakes District Council* [2000] NZRMA 289 (EnvC) and *Dart River Safaris Ltd v Kemp* [2000] NZRMA 440 (HC).
68 *Walker v Hawke's Bay Regional Council* [2003] NZRMA 97 (EnvC).
69 *Mokau ki Runga Regional Management Committee v Waikato Regional Council* EnvC Auckland A046/06, 10 April 2006 per Whiting J.
70 *Land Air Water Association v Waikato Regional Council* [2001] 7 NZED 26 (EnvC) at [494].
71 *Te Runanga o Tuwharetoa ki Kawerau v Bay of Plenty Regional Council* [2002] 7 NZED 363 (EnvC).
72 *Calter Holt Harvey Ltd v Te Runanga o Tuwharetoa ki Kawerau* [2003] 2 NZLR 349.
73 *Ngati Rangi Trust v Manawatu-Wanganui Regional Council* EnvC Auckland A67/2004, 18 May 2004 per Whiting J.
74 *Genesis Power Ltd v Manawatu-Wanganui Regional Council* [2006] NZRMA 536 (HC). See also *Genesis Power Limited v Manawatu-Wanganui Regional Council* HC Wellington CIV-2004-485-1139, 22 May 2007 per Wild J; *Ngati Rangi Trust v Genesis Power Limited* [2007] NZCA 378.
75 *Ngati Rangi Trust v Genesis Power Ltd* [2009] NZCA 222.
76 Williams, above n 8.
77 Williams, above n 8.
78 *Wakatu Inc v Tasman District Council* [2012] NZEnvC 75.
79 At [4].
80 At [58].
81 At [58].
82 At [65].
83 At [74].
84 *McGuire v Hasting District Council* [2002] 2 NZLR 577 at 594.
85 *Chief Executive of the Ministry of Agriculture and Forestry v Waikato Regional Council* EnvC Auckland A133/06, 17 October 2006 at [49], approach reaffirmed in *Maungaharuru-Tangitu Trust v Hawke's Bay Regional Council* [2016] NZEnvC 232 at [126].
86 *Freda Pene Reweti Whanau Trust v Auckland Regional Council* 11 ELRNZ 235 (EnvC) at [50].
87 *Te Maru o Ngati Rangiwewehi v Bay of Plenty Regional Council* 14 ELRNZ 331 (EnvC) at [132]. For more discussion of this case, see Warren Bangma "The Decision in *Te Maru o Ngati Rangiwewehi* and the Consideration of Alternatives Under the RMA" (April 2009) *Resource Management Journal* 7.
88 John Borrows "Origin Stories and the Law: Treaty Metaphysics in Canada and New Zealand", in this book.

Part III

Diverse sites of the Treaty relationship

7 'Ko te mana tuatoru, ko te mana motuhake'

Rawinia Higgins

Tūhoe did not sign the Treaty of Waitangi. Whether this was a conscious decision or whether they were approached at all to sign the Treaty, what is understood is that Tūhoe were conscious of the Treaty of Waitangi and what it represented. In the 175 years since the signing of the Treaty of Waitangi, Tūhoe's interactions with the Crown have not been overtly premised on a desire for Te Tiriti o Waitangi to be honoured, but as a vehicle to ensure that *te mana motuhake o Tūhoe* is recognised and acknowledged. This chapter will explore the relationship between the Treaty of Waitangi and Tūhoe expressions of *mana motuhake*. Illustrating this relationship are examples of where the negotiated space has supported the realisation of *mana motuhake* and where it has been challenged. In doing so, this chapter will provide a personal Tūhoe perspective about *mana motuhake*.

As a child, I do not recall my elders talking about the Treaty of Waitangi. In fact, the only time I recall the Treaty being mentioned was when they would sing the following song composed by Te Kooti:

> Kāore te pō nei mōrikarika noa!
> Te ohonga ki te ao, rapu kau noa ahau.
> *Ko te mana tuatahi ko te Tiriti o Waitangi,*
> *Ko te mana tuarua ko te Kooti Whenua,*
> *Ko te mana tuatoru ko te Mana Motuhake!*
> Ka kīa i reira ko te Rohe Pōtae o Tūhoe
> He rongo ka houhia ki a Ngāti Awa.
> He kino anō rā ka āta kitea iho
> Ngā mana Māori ka mahue kei muri!
> Ka uru nei au ki te ture Kaunihera,
> E rua aku mahi e noho nei au:
> Ko te hanga i ngā rōri, ko te hanga i ngā tiriti!
> Pūkohu tāiri ki Pōneke rā,
> Ki te Kāinga rā i noho ai te Minita.
> Ki taku whakaaro ka tae mai te Poari
> Hai noho i te whenua e Kootitia nei.
> Pā rawa te mamae ki te tau o taku ate.
> E te iwi nui e, tū ake ki runga rā.

Tirohia mai rā te hē o aku mahi!
Māku e kī atu, 'Nōhia! Nōhia!'
Nō mua iho rā, nō ngā kaumātua.
Nā taku ngākau i kimi ai ki te ture.
Nō konei hoki au i kino ai ki te hoko.
Hī! Hai aha te hoko![1]

In this song, Te Kooti describes three *mana* (aspects of prestige or status): the Treaty, the Land Court, and Mana Motuhake, and when this song is sung, the emphasis is always placed on the last *mana*, *mana motuhake*. This *waiata tohutohu* or song of instruction outlines some of Te Kooti's prophecies and teachings to Tūhoe. Subsequent historical events have been linked to this song as a realisation of these teachings. Judith Binney[2] outlines a number of historical accounts that specifically relate to this song and Tūhoe expressions of *mana motuhake*. The article describes the negotiation of Tūhoe's *mana motuhake* through the Urewera District Native Reserves Act 1896. Although premised on good faith, this was quickly reneged on by Premiere Richard Seddon. The article also describes other historical accounts that are considered realisations of the *waiata*, and as a child I recall my elders continually referring back to this song when instances between Tūhoe and the Crown occurred.

Although *mana motuhake* is classically defined as autonomy or independence, Mason Durie notes that it "embodies a link with customary Māori systems of authority, especially in the face of colonising forces".[3] For Tūhoe, this customary system from which *mana motuhake* is determined features in the sixth line of the *waiata*, "ka kīia i reira ko te Rohe Pōtae o Tūhoe" (It is stated that it is the encircled lands of Tūhoe) or Te Urewera. Richard Boast described *Te Urewera* as the last "major bastion of Māori de-facto autonomy",[4] and historical accounts recall Tūhoe's efforts to ensure that their *mana motuhake* was maintained within Te Urewera:[5]

> Distinctions between mana motuhake and tino rangatiratanga [sovereignty or self-determination] are contextual rather than categorical, but while they have much in common, mana motuhake more strongly emphasises independence from state and crown and implies a measure of defiance.

In this case, the context is always Te Urewera and the rich historical narratives describing the unique relationships that have been fought, loved, and lost between Tūhoe and everyone else, including the Crown, results in a particular perception of Tūhoe as being defiant.

Resistance to hegemony is a key objective in the numerous Tūhoe negotiations for *mana motuhake* and continue to be realised even in a post-Treaty of Waitangi settlement phase. *Mana motuhake* is as fundamental to Tūhoe as Te Urewera. They are inextricably linked and form the basis of Tūhoe identity. In a post-Treaty of Waitangi Settlement phase however, what is the impact of the first *mana* described in Te Kooti's song in achieving the third? Has it altered the way in which Tūhoe understands the Treaty of Waitangi? Or was it just a means to attain the ultimate – *mana motuhake*?

The discourse on Treaty of Waitangi settlements delves deep in to the historical narratives of grievance and achieving some sense of balance as a result of loss through compensation, quantum, assets, apologies, and redress. Negotiation is premised on a deep understanding of the relationships between *iwi* (tribal federation) and the Crown historically and works to form new relationships between the two groups on how future engagements will be handled based on the Principles of the Treaty of Waitangi. For example, Article 2 matters recognise a group's *tino rangatiratanga* over natural resources and this can be negotiated in a number of ways, whether it be inclusion in the governance of such resource or in vested titles. However, since the contemporary settlements process began, there have been shifts in how these negotiations have been settled.

The process of developing policy for settlements and then of negotiating them is still evolving and, while both the government and Māori appear to be looking for some final solution to the problem, the issues have been transformed so quickly that any settlement can be viewed only with the specific context in which it was negotiated.[6]

In this case, the 'specific context' of Treaty of Waitangi negotiations is not determined from a 'partnership' model from which both parties set the parameters. It is premised on the Crown's constructs and only highlight the struggles surrounding coming to agreements in settlement negotiations. David Ritter describes this contested negotiation space:[7]

> 'Practical experience' may well demonstrate the benefits of negotiation, but these relationships are developed on a stage that is constructed atop a legal, economic and political landscape determined at a more fundamental level. The same interests and parties that bitterly clashed in the political sphere and the courts, in attempting to refashion the system to their advantage, have come to embrace negotiating over their differences, but only because of the form in which the strategic terrain has settled and in some cases the absence of realistic alternatives for seeking further change. The deal-making that is now so prevalent reflects underlying power relationships; it does not alter them.

It is a widely accepted fact that all Treaty of Waitangi settlements never fully compensate the historical loss incurred by Māori. Full and final settlements are to be viewed within the context of its negotiation and although the objective is to also build a future relationship with the Crown, the power relationships between them fundamentally do not change. The 'strategic terrain' requires the creation of a Post Settlement Governance Entity (PSGE) that will manage and govern the details of their settlement. These legal structures do not provide Māori with the agency to create structures that are premised on *tikanga Māori* (Māori custom) that sit outside the bounds of law. They are determined by the Crown, and consequently, the constructs force Māori in to a dichotomy whereby they are negotiating "customary Māori systems of authority"[8] and the parameters of a Crown-determined PGSE.

To balance the negotiation process within 'customary systems of authority' has resulted in a number of claimants wrestling among themselves over the Crown-determined mandating processes. The Tūhoe settlement negotiations process was also subjected to this. Judith Binney refers to this in her final chapter of her last book *Stories Without End*,[9] where she discusses the factions between Te Kotahi a Tūhoe (TkaT) and Te Umutaoroa. Although Binney explains that Te Umutaoroa came about as a result of some personalities objecting to others, she failed to highlight the process that is placed upon iwi to create 'mandated large natural groupings' by the Office of Treaty Settlements. Although Te Umutaoroa took Te Kotahi a Tūhoe to the High Court to oppose TkaT's mandate, the settlement systems are not determined by Māori and often contravene *tikanga Māori*, or any 'customary system of authority' which in this case is predicated on what is referred to as the 'Tribal executive'.[10] The governance of Tūhoe has always been determined by the *hapū* (tribes), and *hapū* continue to manage their regions for the wider collective interests. Binney fails to highlight the shortcomings of the construct in which they find themselves negotiating, but rather focuses on the '*vituperative ire*' of some individuals.

The tension described above that is caused by this negotiation process is that the PSGE are viewed as legal, economic, and political structures that reflect a Marxist 'superstructure',[11] created to support a dominant social class and not necessarily addressing the desires, hopes, and aspirations of the people they represent. More often than not, as part of the settlement process the PSGE has divided *iwi* rather than unite them, creating a tension between economic development and 'customary systems of authority'. Yet they continue to be developed in order for the settlement to proceed.

I was first introduced to working on the Tūhoe claims from a relatively young age. I did a summer internship scouring through Māori Land Court Minute Books and archival materials looking for any and all references to Tūhoe as part of the WAI 36 claim. But this was relatively minor compared to being more actively involved as a trustee for Te Kotahi a Tūhoe – the settlement negotiation trust. Whether it was because I was older and got to be more involved beyond photocopying minute books and archival materials, my time and experience on Te Kotahi a Tūhoe provided me with the opportunity to view the terrain related to Treaty of Waitangi settlement processes.

As a consequence of being involved in the Tūhoe Treaty of Waitangi settlement process, I was constantly reminded of the work I had done as an intern and my subsequent research as an academic. Reviewing and identifying examples of historical negotiations between Tūhoe and the Crown provided sign posts for Te Kotahi a Tūhoe. Earlier I referred to the Urewera District Native Reserve Act 1896 that has been comprehensively researched by numerous scholars, where Tūhoe attempt to negotiate their *mana motuhake* with the Crown. The challenge of negotiation often necessitates some form of compromise on the part of one group and challenges whether *mana motuhake* can be realised. Historical responses to these challenges came in the form of Tūhoe protests along the borders retrenchment and resistance to any further encroachment in to Te Urewera. However, failed attempts at negotiation have not always been subject to protestation.

Interestingly, this particular letter to the Government[12] by Te Whitu Tekau in 1872 signalled to the Crown their *mana motuhake* over Te Urewera. It also

No. 33.

TE WHENUANUI and others to the GOVERNMENT.

TO THE GOVERNMENT,— Kohimarama Ruatahuna, 9th June, 1872.

Salutations to you—this is our word to you. The meeting of Tuhoe (Urewera) has taken place at Ruatahuna on the 9th June. The first thing decided were the boundaries of the land. My district commences at Pukenui, to Pupirake, to Ahirau, to Huorangi, Tokitoki, Motuotu, Toretore, Haumiaroa, Taurukotare, Taumatapatiti, Tipare, Kawakawa, Te Karaka, Ohine te Rarakau, Kiwinui, Te Tirina, Omata-roa, Te Mapara, thence following the Rangi Taiki River to Otipa, Whaka-ngututoroa, Tuku-toromiro, Te Hokowhitu, Te Whakamatau, O'kahu, Oniwarima, Te Houhi, Te Taupaki, Te Rautahuri, Ngahuinga, Te Arawata, Pohotea, Makihoi, Te Ahianatane, Ngatapa, Te Haraungamoa, Kahotea, Tukurangi, Te Koarere, Te Ahu-o-te-Atua, Arewa, Ruakituri, Puketoromiro, Mokomirarangi, Maungatapere, Otorangi-pu, and on to Puke-nui-o-raho, where this ends.

2nd. Was the uniting of the tribe—that their words should be one and that they should have one canoe, Matatua.

3rd. Was the apportionment of chiefs among Tuhoe. There are this day seventy chiefs. Their work is to carry on the work of this bird of peace and quietness.

4th. The things that were rejected from these boundaries are roads, leasing and selling land.

Te Whenuanui
Paerau
Haunui
Erueti Tamaikowha Tu
Hetaraka
Te Pukenui
Te Makarini
Ahikaiata
And all the tribe.

Figure 7.1 Letter from Te Whenuanui and others to the Government

contains the phrase that became the underpinning *kōrero* (speech) that would guide our negotiations – 'to carry on the work of this bird of peace and quietness', and this is referred to in the speeches during the signing of the settlement process.

As previously mentioned, I did a summer internship when I was a first-year student for WAI36 the primary Tūhoe claim relating to the confiscation of lands. However, over time, it was recognised that this claim was relatively limited, and consequently approximately 30 other Tūhoe claims were lodged. These claims became the basis of the Waitangi Tribunal hearings that took place in Te Urewera. After these hearings, Te Kotahi a Tūhoe received the mandate to undertake the Treaty negotiations for these claims in 2005, and we completed our work by 2013 when the Deed of Settlement was signed.

Being part of Te Kotahi a Tūhoe, I learnt that there were three non-negotiable issues that the *iwi* wanted – Te Urewera, mana motuhake, and quantum. On the surface of it, it appears to be relatively easy, but of course the substance of trying to negotiate these components of a settlement package certainly tested us as Trustees but also as an *iwi*. As anyone who has been part of Treaty of Waitangi negotiations will know, nothing is relatively easy. However, what I did learn from my experience is just how much mana motuhake is part of Tūhoe identity, just like Te Urewera is part of our identity. This is confirmed in the tribe's vision: 'Tūhoetanga' and its mission 'Te Mana Motuhake o Tūhoe':[13]

> Tūhoetanga occurs by the will and want of Ngāi Tūhoe. Mana Motuhake is the acceptance of obligations, duty and responsibility to the full, in order to be deserving of all the rights, entitlements and privileges that ensue. Mana

> Motuhake is a 'collective action' grounded mechanism, not individual, therefore it comes in to view with hapū and their whānau (family) behaviour, attitude and actions.
>
> Mana Motuhake is the politics of being Tūhoe. The integrity of Tūhoetanga relies upon the dedication of Tūhoe people to be self-governing, paying and earning their own way, not beholden to others, and not enslaved by another ideology. The raising of whānau – hapū stature strengthens the iwi. The tribal authority will be the conduit by which the ideology and principles are restored to whānau and hapū.

In the lead up to the establishment of a post-Treaty settlement phase, Te Kotahi a Tūhoe undertook to develop a blueprint for the future. Mana motuhake didn't allow for a carbon-copy approach to a governance entity, and we knew that if it did not reflect organically a Tūhoe mindset or paradigm, then it would never stand a chance of succeeding. The Tūhoe Establishment Trust undertook research in to other *iwi* structures, but also went beyond to global examples and confirmed that we needed to ensure that any *iwi* governance structure must uphold mana motuhake. From our analysis of structures, there was an overwhelming prevalence to focus more on economic wealth generation versus preservation of identity and that this often promoted an individual rather than collective consensus voting system.

Whānau and more specifically *hapū* identities are prevalent in Te Urewera. This is not to suggest that these fundamental social structures and institutions are not quite so in other *iwi*, but in Tūhoe, governance and political power structures have always been and remain within the *hapū*. Individual personality traits are attributed to *whānau* and *hapū* and sometimes people are excused because they have a particular *hapū* affiliation. For example, I see this when comparing my grandmother's *hapū* that is literally next door to my grandfather's *hapū*. Although literally only a short distance away from each other, there are some very stark personalities and identities. Different *whānau* traits and dynamics influence personalities and politics, and therefore developing a PSGE needed to be conscious of all of this. Furthermore, *hapū* have maintained the political power within each of the key settlement areas of Te Urewera. 'Tribals' as they are called are *hapū* collectives located in Waimana, Ruatoki, Waikaremoana, and Ruatāhuna. These have been the main polities that have determined the management and organisation of Tūhoe for generations. Tribals are for the collective benefit of the people and allow them to make decisions based on the specific needs of those areas. As noted in the Blueprint:[14]

> Representation in a Tūhoe context is all about the credible presentation of Tūhoetanga; people, the land, the assets; these things give form, longevity and force. . . . The principle is collective identity, communal values being superior to the individual.

Therefore, the process to be part of the tribal governance structure is determined by the *hapū*. *Whānau* must put forward their nomination to the *hapū*, and the *hapū* determine who will be the best person to represent them. The *hapū* take their nominations to the Tribals, and each *hapū* has the opportunity to vote for their representatives. The *hapū* only have the number of votes as per their regions' number of seats, that is, two votes for Waimana, Ruatoki, and Ruatāhuna and one for Waikaremoana. This system prevents block voting in an individual vote system, and it also means that candidates must actively engage with all the *hapū* in the region if they are serious contenders. As the Blueprint for the *iwi* goes on to state:[15]

> The new board operates by the directive that Tūhoetanga must continue and prosper to accomplish the means of strengthening self-government by direct connection to collective hapū leadership. This is representation by kinship and culture, real things of innate and greater value, held in common and holding us together. This preference is about affirming Tūhoe values, beliefs and way of life as vital to the individual and family sense of well-being. Our Tūhoetanga is how we choose to be known and work for a secure future.
>
> Mana motuhake is a political stance that supports the retention and restoration of power and control by Tūhoe over all matters pertaining to Tūhoe. This confirms the validity of hapū political systems and rights to exercise leadership authority pertinent to decision-making that is based on Tūhoetanga. The freedom to determine how Tūhoe will live, how they will raise their children and mokopuna, how they will keep traditions alive, how they will celebrate who they are, how they will preserve and maintain their language and cultural values and ultimately how they will prosper and continue.

In preparing a PSGE that would realise and reflect Tūhoe mana motuhake, issues arose that led to a perception that negotiating Te Urewera and mana motuhake would lead to Tūhoe creating a separate nation and closing borders and access to Te Urewera, which was still a National Park at the time. This sensationalism led to the Prime Minister removing Te Urewera from the negotiation table at the eleventh hour before the signing of the Agreement in Principle between the Crown and Tūhoe. This halted the negotiations, as Te Urewera and mana motuhake are inextricably linked and as Te Urewera was a non-negotiable item for Tūhoe. To achieve 'full and final' settlement, the Crown was forced to return Te Urewera to the table in order to complete the settlement. Although at the time this was seen as a significant setback to the negotiations, it also paved the way for the introduction of the first geographic area to be given a legal personality. This world-leading piece of legislation helped to reframe our social relationship with the land and states, and in the background to this legislation explains Te Urewera and its multiple relationships:[16]

Te Urewera

(1) Te Urewera is ancient and enduring, a fortress of nature, alive with history; its scenery is abundant with mystery, adventure, and remote beauty.
(2) Te Urewera is a place of spiritual value, with its own mana and mauri.
(3) Te Urewera has an identity in and of itself, inspiring people to commit to its care.

Te Urewera and Tūhoe

(4) For Tūhoe, Te Urewera is Te Manawa o te Ika a Māui; it is the heart of the great fish of Maui, its name being derived from Murakareke, the son of the ancestor Tūhoe.
(5) For Tūhoe, Te Urewera is their ewe whenua, their place of origin and return, their homeland.
(6) Te Urewera expresses and gives meaning to Tūhoe culture, language, customs, and identity. There Tūhoe hold mana by ahikāroa; they are tangata whenua and kaitiaki of Te Urewera.

Te Urewera and all New Zealanders

(7) Te Urewera is prized by other iwi and hapū who have acknowledged special associations with, and customary interests in, parts of Te Urewera.
(8) Te Urewera is also prized by all New Zealanders as a place of outstanding national value and intrinsic worth; it is treasured by all for the distinctive natural values of its vast and rugged primeval forest, and for the integrity of those values; for its indigenous ecological systems and biodiversity, its historical and cultural heritage, its scientific importance, and as a place for outdoor recreation and spiritual reflection.

Tūhoe and the Crown: shared views and intentions

(9) Tūhoe and the Crown share the view that Te Urewera should have legal recognition in its own right, with the responsibilities for its care and conservation set out in the law of New Zealand. To this end, Tūhoe and the Crown have together taken a unique approach, as set out in this Act, to protecting Te Urewera in a way that reflects New Zealand's culture and values.
(10) The Crown and Tūhoe intend this Act to contribute to resolving the grief of Tūhoe and to strengthening and maintaining the connection between Tūhoe and Te Urewera.

Prior to this, symbolic gestures of returning iconic geographical landmarks were included in settlements on the provision that they were re-gifted back to the nation; such was the case with Ngāi Tahu's settlement with respect to Aoraki (Mount Cook). This underscores Belgrave's comments around negotiation processes continuing to evolve over time, and the potential for new, innovative forms of settlements is still to be discovered. However, in the Tūhoe context, the legal personality provision provided another platform to entrench Tūhoe mana motuhake within Te Urewera and ensure that our own values and aspirations for Te Urewera are maintained. These are best expressed in the principles of that legislation which states:[17]

(1) In achieving the purpose of this Act, all persons performing functions and exercising powers under this Act must act so that, as far as possible, –

(a) Te Urewera is preserved in its natural state:
(b) the indigenous ecological systems and biodiversity of Te Urewera are preserved, and introduced plants and animals are exterminated:
(c) Tūhoetanga, which gives expression to Te Urewera, is valued and respected:
(d) the relationship of other iwi and hapū with parts of Te Urewera is recognised, valued, and respected:
(e) the historical and cultural heritage of Te Urewera is preserved:
(f) the value of Te Urewera for soil, water, and forest conservation is maintained:
(g) the contribution that Te Urewera can make to conservation nationally is recognised.

(2) In achieving the purpose of this Act, all persons performing functions and exercising powers under this Act must act so that the public has freedom of entry and access to Te Urewera, subject to any conditions and restrictions that may be necessary to achieve the purpose of this Act or for public safety.

The Te Urewera Act sits alongside the Tūhoe Claims Settlement Act 2014. In the Acknowledgements section of this legislation are over 40 clauses and subclauses identifying the breaches to the Treaty of Waitangi. It also acknowledges that, although Tūhoe did not sign the Treaty of Waitangi, "The Crown's authority over New Zealand rested in part on the Treaty, and Crown's Treaty obligations, including it protective guarantees, applied to Tūhoe".[18] Many of the comprehensive acknowledgement clauses outline the historical injustices predicted by Te Kooti in his *waiata* included in this chapter. These were the discussions held by Tūhoe elders that ensured that my understanding of mana motuhake was built not only on this legacy of struggle for the recognition of ana motuhake but had endured throughout many generations. This is further recognised in the Crown apology which states:[19]

> The Crown unreservedly apologises for not having honoured its obligations to Tūhoe under te Tiriti o Waitangi (the Treaty of Waitangi) and profoundly regrets its failure to appropriately acknowledge and respect te mana motuhake o Tūhoe for many generations.

The signing of the 2013 Deed of Settlement in Wellington signalled the end of the negotiations between Tūhoe and the Crown for these comprehensive historical grievances. Tūhoe arrived en mass to participate in this historic event and realised yet again Te Kooti's prophecy contained in the opening song 'pūkohu tairi ki Pōneke rā, ki te kāinga i noho ai te Minita' (The mist hangs over Wellington, the home of the Minister). As the 'children of the mist'[20] converged on to Parliament, there were mixed emotions, relief, sadness, anxiety, animosity, restraint, and joy. So, has this new phase changed Tūhoe perceptions of the Treaty of Waitangi? Probably not. The Treaty of Waitangi Settlement process enabled Tūhoe to continue and realise the potential for mana motuhake.

Since the settlement, Tūhoe have set to work to realise the potential of mana motuhake and Te Urewera. The Tribals have been active in making changes in

Te Urewera that give expression to the settlement process. The creation of the PSGE, or as we described during the settlement process, 'Te Whare Hou o Tūhoe', involved directly and indirectly countless numbers of people. In the National Radio Constitutional Debate series,[21] I described the Treaty of Waitangi Settlement process for Tūhoe using the analogy of the cumulative tale 'This is the House that Jack built.' This provided a good analogy from which to describe the negotiation process and the creation of the PSGE. It also highlighted that mana motuhake for Tūhoe is not about separatism or anarchy against the State, but rather our interdependence with others. Relationships with people and the land continue to be fundamental in expressing our Tūhoetanga, and realising our *mana motuhake.*

The creation of the living building, Te Kura Whare in Tāneatua, came with a lot of criticism as to whether it was a good use of money. Personally, the Kura Whare is one symbol of actualising *mana motuhake*. It was a house that Tūhoe physically and mentally built together, from materials located in Te Urewera, and it represents a chapter in our history where we are able to close the door on the past and open a new door to our future. Furthermore, as hoped, this *whare* has become a blueprint for Tribals to adopt and create their own *whare* that meet their specific needs because it is a living building sourced from Te Urewera, creates its own power and water, and treats its sewerage, making it sustainable for future generations. Waikaremoana has subsequently also designed their own building for their community needs and plans are underway for other Tribals to adopt this same approach.

The Te Urewera Board responsible for looking after Te Urewera have recently released their draft 'Te Kawa o Te Urewera', the Te Urewera Management Plan, and unapologetically states that "Te Kawa is about the management of people for the benefit of the land – it is not about land management."[22] This value-based plan is premised on the principles of the legislation and pioneers approaches to management that are firmly located in the principles of mana motuhake that change the focus on the land from being a commodity to a personality that has its own *mana*. As Te Kawa states:[23]

> Humanity has much to gain from reigniting a responsibility to Te Urewera for within these customs and behaviours lies the answers to our resilience, to meet a forever changing climate. Through committing to Te Urewera values, we are innovating our instincts and adjusting our behaviour to ensure a prosperous future that is secure.

This approach, albeit in a draft form, demonstrates a new perspective on our interdependent relationships with people and our natural environment. It also highlights how a shift in focus from assuming control over the uncontrollable environment to managing people instead is a change in the paradigm that recognises Māori customary authority as indicated by the *whakataukī* (proverb): '*whatu ngarongaro he tangata, toitu te whenua*' (people will perish but the land remains). The sustainability and longevity of Te Urewera is fundamental to the survival of Tūhoe. For Tūhoe, mana motuhake is also a fundamental part of our identity; it is more than just our mission. It is a state of mind, and we are hard wired like this. But the realisation of mana motuhake comes with a lot of obligation and commitment to the collective and to maintaining the relationships that give expression to our overall vision: Tūhoetanga. So, although Te Kooti referred to mana motuhake as the third *mana* in his song, this chapter has highlighted some of the reasons why that particular line in the song is emphasised by Tūhoe.

Notes

1 Waiata 'Kāore te pō nei mōrikarika noa' composed by Te Kooti Rikirangi Te Turuki as a *waiata tohutohu to Tūhoe*. Author's personal collection and emphasis.
2 Judith Binney "Te Mana Tuatoru: Te Rohe Potae of Tuhoe" (2004) 38(2) *New Zealand Journal of History* 242.
3 Mason Durie *Te Mana, Te Kāwanatanga: The Politics of Māori Self-Determination* (Oxford University Press, Auckland, 1998) at 220.
4 Richard Boast *Buying the Land, Selling the Land – Governments and Māori Land in the North Island 1865–1921* (Victoria University Press, Wellington, 2008) at 202.
5 Durie, above n 3, at 220.
6 Michael Belgrave *Historical Frictions – Māori Claims and Reinvented Histories* (Auckland University Press, Auckland, 2005) at 318.
7 David Ritter *Contesting Native Title – From Controversy to Consensus in the Struggle over Indigenous Land Rights* (Allen & Unwin, Sydney, 2009) at 174.
8 Durie, above n 3, at 220.
9 Judith Binney *Stories Without End – Essays 1975–2010* (Bridget Williams Books, Wellington, 2010) at 364.
10 There are four 'Tribal executives' (Tribal), which represent the four primary regions of Te Urewera: Ruatoki, Ruatāhuna, Waimana, and Waikaremoana. These are explained later in this chapter.
11 Nicholas Abercrombie, Stephen Hill and Bryan S. Turner *The Penguin Dictionary of Sociology* (Penguin, London, 1984) at 18–19.
12 Te Whenuanui and others to Government (9 June 1872) AJHR, 1872, F-3A, at 29.
13 Tūhoe Establishment Trust "The Blueprint – New Generation Tūhoe Authority" (2011) <http://issuu.com/teurutaumatua/docs/the_blue_print_-_new_generation_tuh?e=18309847/15178257> at 12.
14 At 6.
15 At 12.
16 Parliamentary Counsel Office "Te Urewera Act 2014: Background to This Act" <www.legislation.govt.nz/act/public/2014/0051/latest/DLM6183606.html>.
17 Parliamentary Counsel Office "Te Urewera Act 2014: Principles for Implementing This Act" <www.legislation.govt.nz/act/public/2014/0051/latest/DLM6183611.html>.
18 Parliamentary Counsel Office "Tūhoe Claims Settlements Act 2014: Acknowledgements" <www.legislation.govt.nz/act/public/2014/0050/latest/DLM5481244.html>.
19 Parliamentary Counsel Office "Tūhoe Claims Settlements Act 2014: Apology" <www.legislation.govt.nz/act/public/2014/0050/latest/DLM5481246.html>.
20 Tūhoe are referred to as '*ngā tamariki o te kohu*' (the children of the mist) due to the genealogical connection to Hinepūkohurangi, the mist maiden.
21 Radio New Zealand "Debating the Constitution 3: Māori Aspirations" (2013) <www.radionz.co.nz/national/programmes/constitutional-review/audio/2552995/debating-the-constitution-3-maori-aspirations>.
22 Te Urewera Board "Te Kawa o Te Urewera Draft" (2017) <www.ngaituhoe.iwi.nz/Te-Kawa-o-Te-Urewera>.
23 Above n 22.

8 Reflecting on the Treaty of Waitangi and its constitutional dimensions

A case for a research agenda

Mark Hickford

Grasping the actual practices of the concrete and the particular is in keeping with getting at what I would characterise as a political constitution – importantly, what I have referred to as a historical-political constitution, allows access to a synchronic analysis sensitively attuned to diverse phenomena other than (and in addition to) legally meaningful or formalistic utterances or texts. Such a framing is undeniably legalistic in parts and, as I have contended elsewhere in 2011 and 2013, possesses, has developed and continues to develop an accent peculiar to these islands and seas in which we co-exist complicatedly and which we share, an accent comprising various ways of seeing and speaking drawn from across the seas and from those places in which we live.[1] As a frame of reference, however, it supplies us with a wider angle or lens of analytical vision, encompassing additional phenomena, not all of which may be legalistic or completely so, but which possess constitutional value or significance (or may do so from time to time). A specific mention of 'historical' within the concept permits us to examine complicated strains of change and development, episodes of discontinuity or disruption, whether creative, discomforting, or destructive.[2] The treaty initially marked at Waitangi in February 1840 ought not to be seen as an exhaustive representative or marker of the constitutional and political dimensions of Crown–*iwi–hapū* (Crown–tribal federation–tribe) relations.[3] Indeed, other registers or vocabularies, and other concepts were in play from complex Indigenous perspectives and remain so, adapting or changing as time proceeds.[4] The Treaty may be analysed agonistically in and through time, as a site for deliberation and contest, as an exemplary signpost of historical-political constitutionalism. Unlike Matthew Palmer, I do not see this as weakening or undermining our various political communities, together comprising a complex *dēmos*, but as strengthening them overall, notwithstanding points of disruption and grievous discomfort.[5]

Vitally, however, we ought to consider a range of moments and practices, including the conference of chieftains at Kohimarama in 1860, the deliberations on various *rūnanga* or councils, the comparatively recent phenomena of the Iwi Chairs Forum and *iwi* advisory groups engaging with cabinet members or senior officials. Through engaging with the historicity of multiple interpretations in practice as they were discarded, changed, or adapted, we may, as Quentin Skinner has recognised, appreciate:[6]

> how far the values embodied in our present way of life, and our present ways of thinking about those values, reflect a series of choices made at different times between different possible worlds.

The thrust of this chapter, albeit brief, will be to reflect on possible ways of approaching the constitutional dimensions of the Treaty from a historical lens that considers its contested place in reflecting the presence of Indigenous communities and a Crown that co-exist and associate in an archipelago.

While historical in its sensitivities, the argument will also advert to various ways in which getting at the conception of political activity and the political – seemingly ordinary as it might appear to scholarly commentators valorising legal doctrinal analyses on public or constitutional law or abstract jurisprudential views – is of considerable use in understanding the remit of constitutionalism beyond positive legal expressions. It will contend that the Treaty of Waitangi ought to be seen as a set of texts – English and Māori – instantiating contested and contestable, negotiated and negotiating communities of practice and interpretation. Vitally, though, the Treaty does not exhaustively account for, let alone explain, the range of politically salient or constitutionally material Crown–*iwi*–*hapū* relations. This view is aligned with how I have previously engaged with the placing of the Treaty texts relative to other aspects of authority or power relations in territories where Indigenous sources of governance and rights-talk interact with introduced imperial anglophone vocabularies or idioms of constitutional thought.[7] From different perspectives, I see the approach signalled here as allied to those of Carrie Stoddart-Smith[8] and, in certain respects, Nicole Roughan, who has also stated, albeit from a contemporary jurisprudential and philosophical way of speaking, that 'legal association' might capture the intersections between two or more systems of law.[9] More appositely for my purposes, Roughan acknowledges that "the totality of the relationship between Crown and Māori authorities [is one] that includes but is not limited to what has been established by the Treaty."[10]

I. The salience of politics

Hannah Arendt recognised the invariable interdependence of action given the "frailty of human affairs" insofar as activity, whether political or non-political was engaged.[11] She wrote:[12]

> Because the actor always moves among and in relation to other acting beings, he [or she] is never merely a 'doer' but always and at the same time a sufferer [indeed boundlessly].

As communities enlarge and diversify in scale, these challenges not only persist, but are also magnified and exacerbated. The political, truly appreciated, was an 'in-between' – sites of 'in-betweenness' – emerging with diverse, unique actors interacting with one another, setting activities into motion.[13] What Arendt characterised as 'the political realm' arose directly out of this dynamic co-existence consisting of interdependencies in action, exhibiting the "sharing of words and deeds" (after Aristotle) and giving rise to a *polis*, understood as an organisation or community of people or peoples: "Wherever you go, you will be a *polis*."[14] As a stressing and oft-discomforting place for activity and reflection, it has an undeniable albeit demanding and exhausting normative value, although it is fashionable to forget or to dismiss such a perspective. It reserves places for the creative articulation of rights and interests or policy proposals, but in ways that nevertheless preserve ongoing conversational spaces, the polishing and re-polishing of relationships and understandings, amendment through time and incompleteness – the work is never complete. What Cass Sunstein has called "incompletely theorized agreements" may emerge in such contexts; the rationale underlying an outward display of concurrence might not be one that is ***ad idem*** such that diverse narratives or explanations might underpin a seemingly agreed outcome.[15] Such a perspective aligns with a notion of an *agōn*.[16] Raymond Geuss notes that politics "is more like the exercise of a craft or art":[17]

> [i]t requires the deployment of skills and forms of judgment that cannot easily be imparted by simple speech, that cannot be reliably codified or routinised, and that do not come automatically with the mastery of certain theories.

Technique and skill-craft may be tactical or transactional but also generate norms in the turbulence or discomfort of needing to work with or through others; to build consensus or coalitions of opinion (even if temporary or impermanent), to attain decisions as to what is to be pursued socially or not, case by case. Furthermore, it is a place for diverse ways in which relations might be narrated and re-narrated:[18]

> There is a plurality of narratives because politics is a contested activity, in which actors [or teams or clusters of actors] have diverse goals, tell different stories and, to some degree, live in the narratives they succeed in relating.

Plurality is an abiding feature, certainly in those histories peculiar to New Zealand, as much as it became fashionable to elide such a characteristic or to speak in terms of binaries. At its simplest, politics implies ways of interacting in the face of difference and disagreement, occasionally unpleasant, rarely restful. Its organicity and fluid qualities resonate with Indigenous political efforts to resist the colonial assumptions of settler states, as well as to re-visit and to modify those assumptions.[19]

Unlike a legalistic constitution, conventionally understood as comprising the operations of the introduced courts and legislature, as well as their outputs in statutory and common law, the gaze of a historical–political constitution or, to pluralise, constitutions is cast more broadly.[20] It encompasses behaviours and practices that narrower legal understandings do not necessarily regard as worthy of attention or privileging. It is an approach that permits one to analyse and to theorise about the material or customary constitution, including assorted non-state actors and institutions as well as engaging a searching examination of the executive branch of government.[21] The ordinary courts, representing the adjudicative dimension of the Crown ("Her Majesty's judges"), whereby the Crown permits itself to be critiqued in contained, narrowly ritualistic ways, are implicated *within* a colonial legal order as it is understood, interacting with a broader political constitutional setting, as in recent cases, such as *New Zealand Māori Council v Attorney-General* (2013), that they have little eyesight upon or operative status within.[22] Herein, too, lies the spectre of what might be construed as 'framing' judgments on the part of jurists. Such decisions frame, from one standpoint, the particular processes and relevant considerations which political engagements (such as negotiations on policies) ought to factor in while avoiding any direct intervention in the political heat of an emergent issue or resolving the content of specific rights and interests in a specific circumstance. In this sort of vein I suggest, Matthew Palmer has understood the *New Zealand Māori Council* decision in the Supreme Court as an exemplar of "judicial statecraft" in relying on the ongoing negotiations concerning Indigenous "rights and interests" in freshwater and geothermal resources and the good faith representations in ministerial affidavits.[23] In the executive's engagements with *iwi* leaders and their advisors, those discussions continue, with the government appreciating that a plurality of interests is involved, not merely Indigenous, but also others, including local government, non-governmental organisations, economic concerns, and urban populations. Politics and law will continue to intermesh in coordinating how these interests interact.

Again, as I have said previously, the concept of a historical–political constitution is not merely a heuristic device – one that permits us to stand back somewhat and analyse afresh through a speculative formulation. It is also a terminology that aligns with a broader, more nuanced sense of lived constitutional practices and communities evident in the nineteenth-century reflections on constitutional formation and change. These we have inherited, although they are at risk of being forgotten in the tendency of some anglophone officials to ascribe legalism of a northern American or European Union sort as the evolving tendency as at 2016 or to resort to calculations of economic logic. In 1864, the historian Edward Augustus Freeman invoked the concept of a 'political constitution' as a generic one able to encompass any variety or combination of a partition of powers within a community. Freeman also spoke with ease of the practice-informed and customary aspects of an inherited, organic British political constitution. "[A]ll these doctrines", he said, "are mere customs which have gradually, and some of them very recently, grown up, and of which the law of England knows nothing".[24] Elsewhere he referred to a "kind of silent, I might say stealthy, growth", which had produced "without the help of any legislative enactment . . . the unwritten and conventional code of political rules which we speak of as the Constitution".[25] It was in this vein he commented on how the term 'government' had come to be applied to what he called "this extra-legal body", a "certain knot of [privy councillors or ministers]".[26] Likewise, Thomas Babington Macaulay had earlier remarked on the failure of two legal writers, William Blackstone and Jean-Louis De Lolme, to notice its existence.[27] We should all know this, but it is a point that bears repeating. A political constitution that is prominently legal in parts may engage with a host of languages or conceptual resources. Its engine is predominantly political although it is juris-generative – for one thing, it may generate laws whether through enacted legislation or judicial law-making, but also through Indigenous communities.[28] Such a perspective contemplates a constitution as a place of interdependencies between law and politics, with each acting dynamically relative to the other, intermeshing strands of legalism and politics relationally; that is, an "and–and" proposition rather than an "either–or". Legal sources and ways of speaking are used as a resource and are important, but cannot be seen as exhaustive or determinative of everything that is 'constitutional'. Māmari Stephens, in reviewing my book *Lords of the Land*, observed, "From the perspective of political constitutionalism the Treaty of Waitangi generates a kind of positive uncertainty."[29] The most salient aspect of historical-political constitutionalism was that it beget conversations without end, such that relations of Indigenous communities with the Crown might be seen as exercises in complex mutual co-existence, incompletely theorised, and in pursuit of or striving towards better conditionalities in the relationship.[30] Here, in my view, lies its usefulness in examining Indigenous constitutionalism, allowing a broader set or series of episodes, moments, continuities, and discontinuities to be analysed as illuminating a sense of power and authority relative to others, its distribution and conditionalities, the possibilities of change and disruption, neglect, and forgetfulness. In this manner, we can distance ourselves from a claim expressed by Andrew Sharp in 2001 that Māori constitutional histories are relatively recent innovations, "better thought of as *constitutive* rather than constitutional".[31] In elaborating this observation, he surmised that, "They seek to create a constitution in the present," as opposed to recording "the attainment of one in the past – for there was no such attainment".[32] Such a perspective is problematic if by 'Māori', one intends to signify hapū or clusters of these collectives, and yet that appears to be what is intended to be caught, with reference to assertions of "separate mana (mana motuhake), autonomy, rangatiratanga (chieftainship), sovereignty and right to self-government" on the part of "groupings such as hapu and iwi".[33] If anything, the very plurality of normative relations on the ground historically, often expressed through complicated political diplomacy or Indigenous 'custom' or laws, implied understandings of the constitution and distribution of relative authorities and their interactions over time.[34]

II. Not merely "pragmatic" – further interrogating is required . . .

This is not simply 'pragmatic', whether of a corrosive sort or otherwise. Matthew Palmer has referred to pragmatism as one of the underpinning cultural attitudes of New Zealand's contemporary constitutional order in the sense of it being adaptable to issues as they arise.[35] As I have commented in other places, pragmatism, as understood by constitutional scholars within legalistic frames of reference, such as Palmer, diminishes or denudes what is happening and has happened of much of its richness and normative content or implication. For many such commentators, it leads them to route right back to the value of 'legality' as a doctrine to underpin, and indeed authorise, constitutional action and design, all with a view to disciplining politics and its perceived weaknesses. Indeed, a consequence is that legalistic norms are resorted to in order to supplant or overtake political realms, these realms having been adjudged in some fashion as tarnished, unpleasant, or incapable of generating creative possibilities. In my view, lived practices within historical – political constitutional settings neither eschew nor preclude evaluative assessments or normative judgments, as I would understand from my own readings of the literature associated with James Tully, Bernard Williams, Duncan Ivison, or John Borrows.[36] Rainer Forst, for one, has said:[37]

> For we always live in both worlds, the realm of practice and of reasons, which in fact are not two realms but just two aspects of social reality, and with Wittgenstein we should rid ourselves of the habit of only seeing one aspect at a time.

He concluded, "We are, as Tully rightly says, 'transcending' beings as well as social beings, when we criticize our practices."[38] To resort to pragmatism as a term or conception, unless further interrogated with care, also rubs out or at least obscures much that is tacit or unsaid, which I consider to be of immense value. A historical–political constitution serves to direct attentions to phenomena beyond the courts and any legislature. Its jostling inhabitants are varied. It is multi-directional in its diverse interactions and sources. There is also an outside to it (*exteriority*), by which I mean not only a 'constitutive outside' (separate from or even anterior to the constitutional setting) but also conditions of exteriority or worlds beyond its purview or scope from which it might be evaluated and critiqued – here we may find ontologies, dimensions of things, or ways of seeing withheld from engagement, some spiritual or theological – others with an eye towards more propitious times or future possibilities (which may never materialise). That is, these rich understandings, circumstances, and situations were either not necessarily or even able to be embraced within the colonial suppositions that were freighted in formally from 1840 – there may come a time, but there is a live question as to whether one would wish to expose such understandings to the risks of maladroit recognition. There is a persisting political and constitutional significance to silence, to things left unsaid or kept in reserve.

Let me elaborate a little further, at a somewhat concrete level. As the Indigenous activist Noel Pearson has suggested from the viewpoint of Australia,[39]

> indigenous people are effectively engaged in a double game – non-Aboriginal and Aboriginal – in which one of the main drivers for participation in the former is the desire to bolster and create more autonomy in the latter.

Indigenous communities may engage agonistically with the game with a view to re-calibrating relations, whether "in order to expand and protect indigenous-specific rights"[40] of governmentality or to natural resources or otherwise. If certain rights or interests are not yet fully recognised in a territory populated with strangers, the possibility of their communities' ongoing, *incomplete* normative accommodation within or reconciliation is not foreclosed. No system is completely open to pluralistic influences. But, "[a]t the same time", as the philosopher Paul Muldoon has stated:[41]

> the ongoing precariousness of those rights, their susceptibility to extinguishment at the hands of the colonial sovereign, makes it necessary to continually call into question the legitimacy of the legal framework itself.

A creative (sometimes destructive) tension persists. In 1999 and subsequently, much of my research interest has been on how abstract assumptions, to the extent they were formed, were refined or changed as they were stress-tested through engaging with lived, messy circumstances on the ground. Various, often nebulous or vague sentiments or labels, such as 'humanitarianism' (actually referred to most often as 'philanthropic' or 'humane' in the contemporary nineteeth-century commentaries),[42] needed to be interrogated as to how they were to be implemented or operationalised through policy or *institutional* design in *practice*. Here, Tully's views are apposite once more. Case studies ought not to ignore the "entire field of implementation and review to empirical social sciences" alone, but also welcome normative analysis as to legitimacy and justificatory arguments, as there are "numerous ways actors can interpret and act in accord with an agreement once it is implemented".[43] Disputes may emerge, as well as rivalrous interpretations. Bernard Williams's salutary characterisation as to how politics ought to be approached on the part of scholars is a caution to the totalising vanities of philosophers, legal academics, and certain sorts of historian alike but, regrettably, it appears to be forgotten or all too often neglected. Bernard Williams wrote in 1973 that "The significance of the immediate should not be underestimated."[44] While "philosophers" and, I would suggest, certain jurists, "repeatedly urge one to view the world *sub specie aeternitatis*, . . . for most human purposes that is not a good species to view it under". Williams continued:[45]

> If we are not agents of the universal satisfaction system, we are not primarily janitors of any system of values, even our own: very often, we just act, as a possibly confused result of the situation in which we are engaged.

He suspected that sort of immediacy and contingency was "very often an exceedingly good thing".[46]

It is a basis for humility and self-awareness. Officials, as with politicians, confronted with a voluminous range of demands for attention, tend to satisfice or, in other words, to pursue the minimum activities deemed necessary to attain an objective or performance. I find echoes of these sensibilities in the ways of human life, as it is lived and practised. I am not comfortable with seeking what Matthew Palmer has characterised as "stable meanings" of the Treaty, to codify or to make express that which is tacit and indeterminate or uncertain, requiring working out and working through. If there are to be stable meanings, then such meanings should remain open to critique and challenge, to different interpretations and to complete unseating or replacement.

The Treaty may be seen as a normative political instrument occasioning an interpretative 'custom' as well as an instrument of cession at *ius gentium* (a law of nations), as élite policy-makers understood it to be in the first decade of Crown colony administration from 1840. Frail, yes, and undeniably vulnerable to interpretative risks, as its histories demonstrate,[47] but also resilient as a textual resource in and through time. As such, it could also be enlisted as a marker of a constructed or constituted community at places of meeting and discourse, of advocacy and persuasion, for at least certain interlocutors and at points in time. It may be invested with sacred qualities on the part of some, while others denigrate it or view it with suspicion. We find all of these possibilities present. As is well-trodden in the secondary literature, the first article of that treaty in Māori referred to *kāwanatanga* or 'governorship' as being conferred upon the crown ('*te Kuini o Ingarani*' or the monarch of 'England') as opposed to 'sovereignty', which was deployed in the English document.[48] '*Te tino rangatiratanga*' or 'the full, eminent chieftainship' relative to '*o ratou w[h]enua o ratou kainga me o ratou taonga katoa*' ('lands', 'settlements', and 'treasures') was to be retained on the part of the Indigenous parties pursuant to the second article. Did deliberating upon the Treaty shape and influence the design of policies and legal instruments, such as ordinances and statutes? Most assuredly. How these assorted engaged the Treaty involves specific histories and discourses, often particular to a prescribed forum, such as a commissioner's inquiry into land purchase claims, or a dispute resolution process assisted by an Indigenous leader, protector of aborigines, or magistrate. Of late, we see it being invoked as a foundation for identity or nation-building, even in historical works of recent vintage, as well as in official documentation. As recently as 2014, with the publication of *Tangata Whenua*, 'nation-building' is referred to swiftly and unproblematically:[49]

> In recognising their rangatiratanga, the Treaty appeared to offer a partnership in which the rangatira and the Crown would govern in cooperation, continuing the work of nation-building and deepening the long history of friendship and alliance between northern Māori and the Crown.

So-called Crown–Māori relationship instruments or 'CMRIs', containing approved statements for the executive as to how the Treaty might be characterised or understood, were set out in 2006 during the Helen Clark-led government and published.[50] Even the indefinite article '*a*' as opposed to '*the*' as a way of qualifying the term 'founding' appears to be insisted upon less and less in published domains, despite the caution of courts as to its status and the guidance to state officials in the cabinet-approved *Crown–Māori Relationship Instruments: Guidelines and Advice for Government and State Sector Agencies*.[51]

This chapter's aim is not to decry such efforts in the here and now – it is simply to say that scholars ought to take care not to be ensnared themselves in these smooth even if troubled narratives of nation-building, to stand back and to reflect on such performances and interventions: what they signify and whether they do indeed capture the range of possible meanings or perceptions uttered and given expression to through practice. Andrew Sharp noted how the Treaty became the centrepiece for talking about justice and claiming redress for unresolved grievances, particularly with the encouragement of the New Zealand Māori Council in the period from 1983.[52] Examining rather more closely for a moment some of the processes illustrating this trend, one sees how the Treaty was indeed a subject of extensive deliberation and interpretative varieties. A national *hui* (meeting or gathering) on the status of the Treaty confirmed using it as a basis for "claims in respect to the land, forests, water, fisheries and Human rights of Māori people".[53] Moreover, the Treaty was seen as "a symbol which *reflects*" but, importantly, it was declared that "our Mana Tangata, Mana Wairua, Mana Whenua, supersedes the Treaty of Waitangi".[54] The *hui* was convened at *Turangawaewae marae* (courtyard or spiritual and symbolic centre of community affairs) in Ngāruawāhia from 14 until 16 September 1984, with formal resolutions emanating on the final day. Keynote addresses were given, papers introduced, and workshops held. While the *mana*[55] of the Treaty compact was noted, as Sharp has written, the "ancestral signatories had not created the primordial existence of mana Māori; they simply confirmed and registered it [reflectively] in the Treaty".[56] Dynamism or change in how these points might be operationalised most effectively for the time being was in evidence at the *Ngāruawāhia hui*, as was debate on such questions. Its record of proceedings remains an important, composite source for deliberating upon, as it displays forms of agreement and debate or discord. Ranginui Walker, for instance, disputed the significance of the Treaty saying it was a "flawed document" as the "cornerstone of the nation", adding its "inaccurate use of language and translation disguised its meaning so that the chiefs were misled into signing away their mana."[57] In 1985, Shane Jones, then of the Maungarongo Centre, Te Kopuru, advocated reference to the *hui* to locate ways to implement the Treaty of Waitangi in practice alternatively to the fourth Labour government's proposals under a White Paper, *A Bill of Rights for New Zealand*.[58] That White Paper suggested the entrenchment of the Treaty of Waitangi (to be "applied to circumstances as they arise so that effect may be given to its spirit and true intent") and the "rights of Māori" under it through article 4 in a Bill of Rights that would become "supreme law".[59] Jones was not supportive at this time and, in any event, the Bill of Rights was never enacted in its proposed entrenched form under the White Paper. Some two decades later, however, Jones would assume a different viewpoint, reflecting that rendering the Treaty of Waitangi justiciable would have generated constitutional change, personifying the deliberative dynamism within the complexities of a single human life.[60] Separately, Matthew Palmer has observed how the then cabinet received accounts from the *Ngāruawāhia hui* by way of noting.[61]

Palmer's work in 2008 was an important exercise in understanding how, from what he called a 'realist' perspective as to constitutional settings (that is, one that ventures to engage with constitutional arrangements as they function, operate, or perform in practice – emphasising "substance over form and context over text"), the executive interacted with the Treaty of Waitangi in and through policy developments, including enactments it promoted in the legislature.[62] In approaching the living as opposed to the lawyerly constitution in this fashion (a stance with which I sympathise and support), Palmer's contribution considered a host of cabinet processes and decisions concerning how the Treaty might be interpreted, accorded recognition or accommodated in part.[63] Indeed, he identified the extent to which cabinet decisions, particularly throughout the period of the fourth Labour government and beyond, have wrestled with ways in which policy might navigate relations with *iwi–hapū–*Māori with varying degrees of sophistication. These moments of cabinet decision or pronouncement are certainly important. More uncovering remains to be pursued across a series of governments. Yet to focus on such formal points is simply a starting point in the absence of tracing the interior calculations and advice on the part of officials or ministers in assorted papers and meetings.

III. Histories illuminating complexities of co-existence

One consequence of focusing on the Treaty of Waitangi at the analytical centre has been to ensnare narrative and commentary as to how we might analyse historical experiences since 1840. Simplicities are too often welcomed. Rhetorically, and as a matter of political constitutionalism, the Treaty at the centre of a narrative of identity-forming for New Zealand could be ventured as creating or as having created (in the past tense) an imagined or refashioned community that could be riven through civil war, grievance, and grave disappointment. Hence, in 1879, casting eyes and thoughts back, Wahanui Huatare of Ngāti Maniapoto posed the query, "but, I ask, is the Treaty of Waitangi mine? All that I have done is seek for a post to tie the canoe to," specifically the Kīngitanga.[64] The archive toys with us. It should be evident that fragments on the folio leaf can be as tone-deaf to irony as written words are to this day. The Treaty could be objected to or distanced as speaking to different communities of interpretation entirely (even if only for a time). Paora Tuhaere of Ngāti Whātua reportedly said at Kohimarama in 1860, "As to the talk about Waitangi (treaty), that is Ngapuhi's matter."[65] The English text may be seen as a 'monster' or *taniwha* in terms of those manifold interpretative risks it has posed to relations with strangers and normative understandings voyaging from across the seas, as a 2014 Ngā Puhi text makes clear in characterising it from the vantage point of the twenty-first century.[66] Of course, these contested points could be inter-*hapū* or intra-*hapū*. How communities might be understood through ties of place and genealogy or constructed or imagined in a way that it makes sense to speak of civil dissension or war or, as David Armitage reminds us relative to its ancient Roman lineage, *bellum civile*, remains a significant challenge.[67] This is why Michael Belgrave's historical project on the analytical utility of the concept of 'civil war' in colonial New Zealand contexts is to be welcomed.[68] Belgrave's research potentially supplies different ways of thinking about and narrating politically and spiritually mindful communities in these islands. Histories complicate, often illuminating the melange of factors at play, their contingency, and *sui generis* characteristics, points to be welcomed if we are to examine and evaluate our contemporary notions – critical friends unto ourselves – with the requisite care and rigour. If they bequeath anything, it ought to be a sense of humility rather than condescension, as we survey and consider the unruly richness of inhabited pasts.

Importantly, understandings or thoughts associated with a treaty were refined and adjusted as novel or different circumstances emerged or played out. Not long after Treaty texts voyaged to different signing sites throughout Indigenous territories it came to disconnect from those who drafted it and was authored by commentators and interpreters of it. It became a subject of deliberation. Its meaning and application, its relative place were subject to debate and discussion. Yet it is important *not* to see it as the exclusive driver or narrative underpinning of *iwi–hapū* Indigenous relations with the incoming Crown, although among certain commentariats, it is treated in such a way. As with the *arriviste* Crown in 1840 and since, *iwi–hapū* communities and politics cultivated different interpretative approaches and understandings distinct or apart from and prior to any Treaty texts. This lent an idiosyncratic and bespoke approach to how those relations might be played out and thought about on the ground. The materiality of *hapū* power, their plurality, their normative presence as generators of legal understandings and customs, was critical. Having said that, arriving Europeans posed undeniable managerial challenges to *hapū*. This was acknowledged rhetorically in advance of 1840, with a dialogue in 1820 capturing the implicit risks to *hapū* norms of governance relative to the presence of missionaries.[69] Here, we may see the early implicit musings on whether the European visitors might linger beyond welcome.

Moreover, with the formal advent of the Crown from 1840, the precariousness of effective or tangibly embedded legal claims on the part of Britain was well appreciated within élite official circles. Both context and the anxieties of historical actors tell us much. James Stephen, the permanent Under-Secretary at the Colonial Office, in writing to his counterpart at the Foreign Office in December 1840, supposed on behalf of Lord John Russell, the principal secretary of state, that the "law of nations" supposed:[70]

> no Alien has a right to Fish in land-locked waters such, for example, as Portsmouth Harbour, or the Chesapeake; but that all mankind have a right to fish on the open Sea, and even close on shore in any territory under the State to which that territory belongs.

There was no thought on Stephen's part as to what Indigenous custom might hold even if deemed relevant to a question as to admitting strangers or others into waters – he resorted to the contemplations of a European law of nations (*ius gentium*). Closer examination reveals the contingencies in play, as legal advice received in London observed that the colonising state had effective legal ability to exclude foreign fishers over those seas adjacent to coastal areas in its settlers' *actual* 'occupation'.[71]

Much is masked or omitted then if one focuses on the Treaty per se. Daniel Keenan acknowledged this in reflecting on DF McKenzie's innovative contributions on orality and literacy relative to the process of garnering Indigenous assent to Treaty texts in 1840. Despite acknowledging the undoubted import of the negotiations concerning the Treaty 'for' Māori, he proposed, appropriately, how[72]

> it might be argued that the Treaty signing process was in fact of secondary importance as a context for such a critical contest, or for judgments as to the real power of the written word over the spoken word.

He cautioned that words expressed on the locationally specific *paepae* (orator's bench) possessed power in ways that were different from the Treaty signing events. To the extent the Treaty's status has not been completely marginalised or treated as irrelevant,[73] anglophone commentators historically assumed its efficacy as a conveyor to the Crown of entitlements to govern territorial space and to enjoy exclusive jurisdiction to relate diplomatically with non-British polities, such as France, let alone Indigenous polities scattered throughout the archipelago. Recently, the Treaty has been referred to a 'founding' instrument or artefact. What this behoves us to understand, it is argued, is that Treaty texts and their signification need to be analysed historically – this seeing the Treaty as an interpretative custom or a custom of interpretation potentially gets us into tricky places, as it swiftly can be seen to be less than historical inquiry or recovery of messy pasts and something approaching what John Pocock characterised as 'historiosophy'. As he used the term, it referred to attempts to use histories in order to yield varied, contested insights as to how we might understand or critique contemporary circumstances and climes.[74] I believe one can do that provided it is done consciously with self-awareness. As Pocock also said, "It is also possible that the formation of these perceptions of history will itself have a history, part of the subject matter the historian studies."[75] In a number of places, Sharp ventured scholarly efforts in elaborating a variety of constitutional histories in play, an important contribution that envisages the need (correctly in my view) to trace differing historical accounts of the Treaty and how its meanings might be constructed and practised (although it does not do to treat such accounts schematically or simply).[76]

In the sketch presented here, I cannot do full justice to such a project. I do believe, however, that the discourses in these islands are of such a pitch and level that we can begin to interrogate how these varied ways of seeing have been deployed, played with, disrupted and confounded. It suggests a research agenda for further, exacting efforts. Here, the philosopher Ivison is helpful. He has remarked how the[77]

> normative power of critique is tied not to general principles or norms imposed on particular experiences, but rather arises through a genealogical unmasking of historically and socially contingent social and political arrangements.

Tony Ballantyne rightly warns about us conceiving of 'New Zealand' as anything other than a construct, which altered in and through time, contingent on specific audiences and registers or ways of speaking (including legal definitions through proclamations, letters patent or legislation).[78] Likewise with the Treaty compact, we see texts that were deliberated upon and debated. In anglophone legal comprehension, it was an important, but not sole basis for grounding Britain's claim to sovereignty such that it could exclusively conduct foreign relations with other powers, including the United States and France, relative to those areas specified to be subject to its claim as set out in the letters patent. The picture was much more complex, as interlocutors appreciated at the time. As I have noted previously, this extended imagination of *the* Treaty (with use of the definite article 'the' before the term 'treaty') was drawn upon to discipline executive conduct and judicial interpretations not always efficaciously. Certain anglophone participants in early colonial New Zealand were swift to enlarge its possibilities both in northern parts of the North Island and towards the south in Port Nicholson while others might resist. By 1845 Viscount Stanley, then the secretary of state for colonies, commented with some ease that the Treaty applied across colonial New Zealand notwithstanding continuing claims to the contrary. This enlargement or extension of the imaginative reach of the Treaty in a range of anglophone political and juristic discourses is a process that deserves its own histories, which I have tried to pursue in part both with reference to the mid-nineteenth century and the early twentieth century. So, too, have Belgrave and Sharp. It has travelled or voyaged to become a symbol or metaphor – persisting *mythopoeisis* even – for I see Alfred Gell's ruminations on the agency of texts or artefacts as helpful. In this manner, the treaty texts become a "movement of thought, a movement of memory reaching down into the past and a movement of aspiration, probing towards an unrealized, and perhaps unrealizable futurity".[79] This process comprises an interesting set of journeys and one that is not yet really told except in bits, as Claudia Orange's narrative still holds fast on the historical and official imagination – to speak of a totalising treaty across the archipelago known as New Zealand has an undeniable ease and tidiness if it remains unproblematically at the controlling centre of the 'nation-building' ethos.

An idiosyncratic New Zealand accent is desirable here, albeit one mindful of an empire of variations throughout the globe. Andrew Sharp alluded to as much in his own reflections in 1997 on James Tully's important work *Strange Multiplicity*, where, to quote Sharp, Tully admitted that he "sometimes talks as if 'all the world is America' [or, I might say, Canada]" in regarding constitutions as frameworks which "ought to be complexly-federal and never unitary in form".[80] At that time, Sharp wryly confessed to "harbouring a tendency to think all the world in New Zealand".[81] Here we may discern an admission or at least an observation that the seeming curiosities of New Zealand's unitary constitutional setting enable us to look beyond or behind the distraction of architecture or the edifice of formalistic legal structure and to gaze more deeply into the less express understandings, the warp and woof of political activities, currents of discourse and thought. There is certainly an important point to be made here and one with which this essay concurs completely. That is, we should not casually assume that some form of federalism supplies an answer to the challenges of accommodating pluralities of power and authority; behaviours and thought in practice matter, and not merely structure. All must be factored in. Sharp's adroit comparison with Tully is slightly misleading, however, as the histories with which we ought to be concerned illustrate considerable variety, including experiments with federalism in these islands. I have contended that interpretations of consociation have been evident.[82] Again, appreciating historicity permits one to survey and analyse a variety of possibilities, reflecting as to how ancestors might have opted for different paths under pressed human circumstances. Disagreements about participation in various forms of civil governance were in the offing from 1840 although, as I have noted elsewhere, these disputes were proxied through vexed questions as to authority or an ability to influence third parties' conduct relative to territorial space – entitlements to, say, oppose the approval of strangers to occupy or use space – or the identities of those with decision-making rights. These aspects, among others, were riven with subtleties peculiar to time and place, as well as to those persons engaged, but illustrate the complicated, stressed nature of co-existence and options as to how one might engage with guests or strangers who remained in numbers.

Constitutional communities comprising a plurality of powers were in evidence. Ideally, these traversed grounds ought not to be interrogated or rehearsed anew as if one were approaching a *tabula rasa*, but engaged with a respect for the historical analyses previously pursued. Still, it would appear that not all that is published is read with care, if read at all. As long ago as 1973, the late Alan Ward identified Stephen's musings on the survival or continuities of Indigenous customary law.[83] Recent scholars such as Damen Ward and Damon Salesa, to name only two, have worked with these understandings, citing them and the relevant secondary literature.[84] The debates engaging William Swainson and Stephen reveal an awareness of legal and political pluralities.[85] Of course, these very comments or interventions were expressed with full appreciation of the Treaty texts, including the English language articles. There is nothing new, original or unstartling here, despite some who might claim there is.[86] It is all there to be read. Theoretically it is also unsurprising if one draws a longer bow back in time. Jean Bodin, for one, set out that sovereignty or overall territorial jurisdiction and administration on the ground need not be in the same hands.[87] Indigenous territorial rights themselves implied the existence of norms and legal regimes to construct or to set out such claims or entitlements. Customary laws were seen as shaping or informing Indigenous communities and their interactions with each other irrespective of the Treaty compact (which certain groups had not signed or acceded to). How they were adapted and modified so that they are not treated as some ahistorical corpus requires careful examination and analytical debate.[88]

As such, it is unstartling to say that custom was recognised as a matter of abstraction and policy. A serious question emerges as to institutional recognition and the infrastructure giving such abstract acknowledgement operational functionality – to whom and on what terms was such decision-making influence given? How, if at all, did such a configuration change across time?[89] Anyone among Pākehā academic or judicial commentators who consider officials and courts were somehow "benign" or presumes they would have been if only a certain case on the legal status of a treaty marked at Waitangi came before them – interpreting the silences of the courts optimistically – is ignoring the realities of how the courts, the chief justice, and others at that time actually engaged with customary law and the Treaty texts.[90] It is not sufficient to simply identify isolated, even if repeated, instances of the sayings of certain officials or jurists, particularly when those utterances might be seen as congenial to the preferences or views of the latter-day legal scholar. That sort of practice towards various pasts is akin to legal advocacy, stringing oft-dispersed textual references to formulate a persuasive interpretative stance. Yet, as Peter Mandler reminded audiences some time ago, when pursuing historical analyses, one must also critically ascertain the efficacy of such statements beyond discursive fields. "Plunging deep into a text" or into patterns of utterance on the part of an individual author of policy thought, for instance[91]

> can distract us from other responsibilities, to evaluate not only the meanings of a text but also its relations to other texts, its significance in wider discursive fields, its 'throw', its dissemination and influence; that is, the conditions not only of its production but also of its distribution and reception.

Making sense of what actors thought they were doing and why requires a recovery of moments and utterances sensitive to differences in understanding or approach (occasionally in the same person) across a range of circumstances and the myriad ways in which they might be implemented or executed in practice.

IV. Bridges, intermediaries, relationships, associations, and . . . Indigenous governance – the continuing, albeit neglected importance of political and institutional design in constitutional thought

Why historicity is important is that it permits us to examine phenomena that are not the subject of court litigation, but may influence thought, practices, and configurations of personnel engaging with the Treaty of Waitangi and construing its constitutional materiality across time. A distant mirror, then, allows us to see a variety of things otherwise concealed or assumed casually in contemporary twenty-first century climes as unchallengeable or unassailable. As a method, it assists us with the twenty-first century approaches, although, as a caveat, much is concealed or hidden from the archive to date. More remains to be uncovered, although it is a laborious and demanding task methodologically.[92] The Iwi Chairs Forum and the associated clusters of *iwi* advisors engaging with officials or non-state actors in various *fora* is a constitutional adjustment in progress barely understood or evaluated. Different commentators such as Justice Joseph Williams have noted the salience of this development to constitutional change.[93] The Iwi Chairs Forum was initially convened in 2005 at Takahanga Marae in

Kaikōura. We do not yet have studies of its interactions with the executive dimension of the Crown, but it reflects a conception of Indigenous engagement in policy development accompanied by participation in scheduled meetings with cabinet ministers. This shift has become particularly pronounced since 2009. By February 2016, some 13 or so ministers attended the meeting with *iwi* chairs at Waitangi along with approximately 30 crown officials. In different subject areas of policy development, such as freshwater resources reform, sub-groups of the Iwi Chairs Forum, overseen by a nominated *iwi* leader as chair,[94] may liaise with and challenge ministers and senior officials directly. Yet it has not received scholarly attention of a sustained, inquiring sort.

Roughan offers us a glimpse into how we might narrate these relations in contemporary, twenty-first-century settings. As she notes, her model assumes a State system setting up a supervisory hierarchical relationship with Indigenous laws and authorities, meaning that colonial assumptions are very much in play.[95] Following Pocock, she suggests a negotiated set of arrangements might be a better way of dynamically addressing the terms of legitimacy and justice in co-existence between an introduced political – legal regime and ongoing albeit changing Indigenous norms.[96] That is a worthy point. The practicalities of negotiation where asymmetries in bargaining power or resources operate is that we tend to witness incremental modifications rather than transformative moments. Taken together, they may have a cumulatively transforming effect. Yet it is difficult to be certain while one is in the process.[97] It is notable that I have likewise commented on these same possibilities with reference to Pocock, although having done so from a historical-political constitutional angle.[98] Roughan's approach, offered from a contemporary philosophical vantage point, poses 'relative authority' and 'association' as organising concepts.[99] Elsewhere, from a historical perspective, I have separately used 'associative relations', 'occasional association', and in specific circumstances, 'consociation' (connoting parallel or shared authorities in a single territory).[100] In this fashion, her proposition aligns broadly with a conception that I have used for historical assessments in other places. In what follows, brief as it is, I wish to be clear that this writer does not disagree with Palmer's views as to 'relationships' or 'realism'. Rather, the angle of vision and analysis differs (although not inconsistently) in commencing with a steadfastly historical, archival-based outlook, engaging with the often fraught contestability as to constitutional arrangements or ways of framing and narrating relations of relative authority and power in the body politic.

Justice Joseph Williams has concurred with Matthew Palmer in seeing the significance of the treaty Texts as 'relational'. This trope has much behind it with Paul McHugh and others cleaving to it for some time. It is consistent with the notion of relations akin to a 'partnership' and the possibilities of a "Treaty relationship *after* grievance", as Williams expressed it in his letter of transmission dated 28 June 2011 for the *Ko Aotearoa Tēnei* first-level report (*Te Taumata Tuatahi*).[101] With a foundational role for the Treaty compact, a platform bringing strands together for "nation-building" in these early decades of the twenty-first century and crafting "national identity", having as its "solid core" what is presented as "bicultural fusion".[102] The undeniable importance of this framing is that it squarely acknowledges the point that the relationship is ongoing and will pose enduring challenges. Different perspectives as to how the interaction might be understood come to the fore, while only a few illustrations might be reproduced here. In the view of Hōne Sadler of Ngā Puhi, Te Tiriti o Waitangi (in Māori) rather than the English text Treaty is to be resorted to in order to shape the configuration or design of relationships as a 'covenant' or '*kawenata*'. It was an admission point or concession to strangers to enter territories and an 'intermediary' for conditional co-existence, permitting "entry, and that is all, nothing more, nothing less, except to agree that you can come here and we can live harmoniously together".[103] It enabled the Crown to discipline and manage its own "wayward people".[104] Underlying these characterisations is still a theme of Treaty texts interweaving relations between Indigenous and introduced, settler norms. For Williams, *lex Aotearoa* represents one avenue for operationalising this trope in legal terms. But it is consciously predicated on crafting a 'nation' and 'national identity' with or through streams of Indigenous and anglophone law.[105] It implicitly leverages off the metaphor of a 'bridge', a crossing that enables a mingling of diverse legal norms.[106] Similarly, with the Waitangi Tribunal report in *Ko Aotearoa Tēnei* (2011) too, we perceive a tidying analytical narrative (perhaps comforting as much as optimistic) that seeks to bridge or entwine Indigenous and settler–State streams of legal reasoning or thought – peoples of Kupe and James Cook coming together, as it was expressed. As a programme for action and rhetorical style, that sort of approach to reconciling different pasts or ways of seeing is understood, but it is uncertain whether it assists critical analysis as to the variety of interpretative pathways and communities scattered throughout New Zealand and its pasts, their shifts across time, how these variations might discomfort or disrupt, and what these might illuminate. That is, we can stand apart from it as scholars and examine this conception of a bridging or an entwining as one way to construct communities of interpretation and action (or inaction) within these islands. As a metaphor, it is not unusual in examining State–Indigenous relations elsewhere. The point is that the propositions put forward in Williams' stance on *lex Aotearoa* is another slant on this technique.

Nevertheless, it poses difficulties depending on the vantage of one's perspective. Without institutional change, it still tends to assume the overarching supervisory jurisdiction of the colonial polity rather than necessarily re-calibrating power relations effectively within that interpretative political community. It suffers from the inevitabilities of compromise in political life. As stated in this chapter, that is no negative course to pursue, but it does illustrate the difficulties of de-colonising introduced legal norms beyond anything more than incremental modification. Further, there are no isolated capsules of untrammelled *tikanga* (a customary system of values and norms, embedded in social contexts)[107] untouched by introduced, previously exogenous influences. The ways of politics in plural situations are such as to encourage or to enable a resort to multiple sources from an array of inheritances or communities located elsewhere. One consequence for Indigenous polities, then, is to reserve the possibilities for re-visiting these moments of law-making on the understanding that these very human compromises may be temporary and incomplete and, as a work-in-progress engaging many minds and hands, may contrive or create something unheralded and unexpected. Against this broad background, Carwyn Jones' exploration of Indigenous legal inheritances and norms as to peace and resolving disagreement through investigating *tikanga*-grounded laws demonstrates the comparatively untapped seams of this thinking and its part to play in constitutional thought.[108] It is also plausible that ordinary courts might draw upon international instruments and sources of law, effectively supplying further interpretative buttressing for Indigenous norms.[109]

Institutional or structural design, and an unremitting focus on it, as well as what behaviours certain configurations of human structure or contrivance might incentivise or encourage, is a vital part of constitutional thought, as early and mid-nineteenth century anglophone commentators on constitutional histories and thought, such as Freeman, Macaulay, the third Earl Grey, or Walter Bagehot, well appreciated.[110] For them, there was no hurried leaping to a particular structure or textual innovation – such as a codified constitutional text – without at least engaging with the possible outcomes that were sought. This feature of reflection is pronounced in Indigenous approaches evidenced in the independent working group on constitutional transformation dated February 2016.[111] It develops, for instance, indicative constitutional models with a marked slant on institutional configurations, such as having under the first model a tricameral or three-sphere model consisting of an *iwi–hapū* assembly (the *rangatiratanga* or autonomous Indigenous sphere), the Crown-in-Parliament (the *kāwanatanga* or government sphere) and a joint deliberative body (the relational sphere).[112] Whatarangi Winiata has also expressed institutional analyses in his own well-known interventions.[113] The juristic focus on legal texts per se can often neglect the significance of this sort of thought. Recently and from his own perspective, Waldron has recognised that legal scholars need to be reacquainted with the profound significance of political institutions.[114] Legal and political historians have appreciated this factor for some time.

Certain settlements of historical grievances in the past two decades are re-calibrating by degrees relative power relations and authorities.[115] Te Awa Tupua is one recent illustration concerning a natural resource, specifically the catchment of the Whanganui River. Te Awa Tupua (Whanganui River Claims Settlement) Act 2017 vests the Crown-owned parts of Whanganui River and its catchment tributaries in a separate legal person named "Te Awa Tupua" – a natural resource construed as a legal person (section 14), "an indivisible and living whole, comprising the Whanganui River from the mountains to the sea, incorporating all its physical and metaphysical elements" (section 12). The fee simple estate in the Crown-owned parts of the Whanganui River vest in Te Awa Tupua on settlement date (30 days after the enactment comes into force). The vesting does not create a proprietary interest in the water itself, but will give such rights to Te Awa Tupua in relation to the relevant space occupied by water. The human face of Te Awa Tupua is the office of Te Pou Tupua (with specified exceptions set out under section 42). As with other settlements, such as the Te Arawa Lakes Settlement

Act 2006 or Te Urewera Act 2014, it poses novel questions of landscapes or queries at least that might not have been posed for some time through adjusting relations of power concerning a particular landscape and resources within it. It may be re-adjusted again. Such a possibility cannot be discounted, even though it might lie well beyond the horizon of one's gaze. As with any enactment, there is every possibility that a better conditionality in the relationships might be sought through politics.[116] The resolution of claims is not necessarily final across the broad compass of possibilities given the insights of inexorably unpredictable historical change.

Conclusions

I have outlined a research agenda and an orientation with which to approach the Treaty of Waitangi and its constitutional dimensions. Pocock, Sharp, and McHugh augur a tendency to examine varied, often vying accounts of constitutional histories, displaying the differing, contested, and negotiated ways in which a narrative of political and legal constitutionality is shaped and told. That work needs to be continued. It is timely to grasp such a challenge anew with a view to situating the constitutional dimensions of the Treaty of Waitangi in contingent pasts and presents. Scholarship does these lived complexities a disservice if it arcs teleologically towards the soothing simplicities or comforts of "nation-building" or "national identity", even while pointing out periods of turbulence along the path (grievance, warfare, protest). These may be programmatic labels for policy ends or imaginings, but they should not allow the obscuring of the complicated co-existence negotiated behind the mask of a unitary, legal setting. In the foregoing argument I have aimed to supply an account of how one might approach the constitutional dimensions of the Treaty of Waitangi that resonates with lived practice. It is sympathetic to Matthew Palmer's efforts in his important work on placing the Treaty of Waitangi in New Zealand's law and constitution. Yet my stance is historical-political, focusing on the interior lives of disputes. While that comports with Palmer's "realist" perspective, it is predicated on engaging deeply with the contingencies and untidiness of the historical record, oral and textual, beyond cabinet or legislative outputs alone. Second, the approach is mindful of where the various trajectories of thought and practice might head while being cautious, as anticipation can be little more than vain expectation. The point is to reveal what in current practice might discomfort a hegemonic, self-referential, formalistic legal view. Ultimately, recovering histories and narratives in contention and critique allows one to do just that.

Notes

1 Mark Hickford *Lords of the Land: Indigenous Property Rights and the Jurisprudence of Empire* (Oxford University Press, Oxford, 2011) at 2–3, 10–39, 247–266; Mark Hickford "The Historical, Political Constitution – Some Reflections on Political Constitutionalism in New Zealand's History and Its Possible Normative Qualities" (2013) 4 *New Zealand Law Review* 585.

2 Above n 1.

3 *Hapū* (literally "pregnant") signifies genealogically affiliated and fluid clans (tribes or sub-tribes), the principal political collective. *Iwi* ("peoples", "bones") are composed of *hapū* and conventionally translated as "tribe" (Angela Ballara *Iwi: The Dynamics of Māori Tribal Organisation From c.1769 to c.1945* (Victoria University Press, Wellington, 1998) generally), or tribal federation. Although deployed in this chapter for terminological convenience, the concept of "Crown" ought to be disaggregated and complicated: Mark Hickford, "Strands From the Afterlife of Confiscation: Property Rights, Constitutional Histories and the Political Incorporation of Māori, 1920s" in Richard Boast and Richard Hill (eds) *Raupatu: The Confiscation of Māori Land* (Victoria University Press, Wellington, 2009) at 169–204, 171–174, 204.

4 As exemplified in Rawinia Higgins's chapter in this volume concerning *mana motuhake* (self-determination or self-government).

5 Matthew Palmer "Resolving the Foreshore and Seabed Dispute" in Raymond Miller and Michael Mintrom (eds) *Political Leadership in New Zealand* (Auckland University Press, Auckland, 2006) at 197–214.

6 Quentin Skinner *Visions of Politics: Volume I: Regarding Method* (Cambridge University Press, Cambridge, 2002) at 6.

7 Hickford *Lords of the Land*, above n 1, at 273–299, 390–407.

8 Carrie Stoddart-Smith "Radical Kaupapa Māori Politics" in Morgan Godfery (ed) *Interregnum: Rethinking New Zealand* (Bridget William Books, Wellington, 2016) at 80–96, 83–84, 95.

9 Nicole Roughan "The Association of State and Indigenous Law: A Case Study in 'Legal Association'" (2009) 59 *University of Toronto Law Journal* 135.

10 Nicole Roughan *Authorities: Conflicts, Cooperation, and Transnational Legal Theory* (Oxford University Press, Oxford, 2013) at 218.

11 Hannah Arendt *The Human Condition* (2nd ed, Chicago University Press, Chicago, IL, 1998) at 188–189.

12 At 190.

13 Hannah Arendt *The Promise of Politics* (Schocken Books, New York, NY, 2005) at 190.

14 Arendt, above n 11, at 198.

15 Cass Sunstein "Incompletely Theorized Agreements" (1995) 108 *Harvard Law Review* 1733.

16 Mark Hickford "Framing and Reframing the *Agōn*: Contesting Narratives and Counter-Narratives on Māori Property Rights and Political Constitutionalism, 1840–1861" in Saliha Belmessous (ed) *Native Claims: Indigenous Law Against Empire, 1500–1920* (Oxford University Press, New York, NY, 2011) at 152–181. See also, Christa Davis Acampora "Demos Agonistes Redux: Reflections on the *Streit* of Political Agonism" (2003) 32 *Nietzsche-Studien* 374. I have adapted what I discern to be useful aspects of what scholars like Acampora have said with a view to getting at what occurs in contested politics and its possible normative value while being mindful of not mimicking, or being tethered to, any existing, singular account they have supplied themselves, let alone erecting a novel edifice of abstraction, less than able to speak eloquently to what happens in lived or inhabited practice.

17 Raymond Geuss *Philosophy and Real Politics* (Princeton University Press, Princeton, NJ, 2008) at 15.

18 J.G.A. Pocock *Political Thought and History: Essays on Theory and Method* (Cambridge University Press, Cambridge, 2009) at 266.

19 Audra Simpson *Mohawk Interruptus: Political Life Across the Borders of Settler States* (Duke University Press, Durham, NC, 2014).

20 A "legalistic constitution" is effectively a starting point for analytical focus, as it is appreciated that codified legal constitutions also encompass non-legal political norms and conventions: refer to Mark Tushnet "Constitution" in Michel

Rosenfeld and András Sajó (eds) *The Oxford Handbook of Comparative Constitutional Law* (Oxford University Press, Oxford, 2012) at 217–232, 222–226.

21 This approach resonates with Marco Goldoni's conception of a 'material constitution', although Goldoni arrives at his analysis largely through continental European philosophy, whereas my own stance is grounded in *historical* analyses and tropes tied to anglophone imperial-colonial and Indigenous histories.

22 *New Zealand Māori Council v Attorney-General* [2013] NZSC 6.

23 M.S.R. Palmer "Judicial Review" in Mary-Rose Russell and Matthew Barber (eds) *The Supreme Court of New Zealand 2004–2013* (Thomson Reuters, Wellington, 2015) at 158–170, 169–170.

24 E. A. Freeman "Presidential Government" in *Historical Essays* (Macmillan, London, 1871) at 384.

25 Edward Augustus Freeman *The Growth of the English Constitution From the Earliest Times* (Macmillan, London, 1872) at 118.

26 Freeman, above n 24, at 384.

27 T. B. Macaulay *The History of England From the Accession of James II* Vol IV (Longman, Brown, Green and Longmans, London, 1855) at 435 (in this passage, he uses the term 'ministry' as an alternative to 'cabinet').

28 On the adjudicative process as law-making, see Jeremy Waldron *The Rule of Law and the Measure of Property* (Cambridge University Press, Cambridge, 2012) at 95.

29 Māmari Stephens "Māori Constitutionality (and the Treaty of Waitangi)" (2013) *Māori Law Review* <http://maorilawreview.co.nz/2013/06/maori-constitutionality-and-the-treaty-of-waitangi/>.

30 Hickford *Lords of the Land*, above n 1, at 9, 37–39, 457.

31 Andrew Sharp "Recent Juridical and Constitutional Histories of Māori" in Andrew Sharp and Paul McHugh (eds) *Histories, Power and Loss: Uses of the Past – A New Zealand Commentary* (Bridget Williams Books, Wellington, 2001) at 31–60, 36 (emphasis in original).

32 Sharp, above n 31.

33 Sharp, above n 31.

34 Hickford *Lords of the Land*, above n 1, at 37–39, 388, 398; Hickford, "Interpreting the Treaty: Questions of Native Title, Territorial Government and Searching for Constitutional Histories" in Richard Hill, Brad Patterson and Kathryn Patterson (eds) *After the Treaty: The Settler State, Race Relations and Power in Colonial New Zealand* (Steele Roberts, Wellington, 2016) at 92–131.

35 Matthew S. R. Palmer *The Treaty of Waitangi in New Zealand's Law and Constitution* (Victoria University Press, Wellington, 2008) at 281.

36 James Tully *Strange Multiplicity: Constitutionalism in an Age of Diversity* (Cambridge University Press, Cambridge, 1995); Bernard Williams *In the Beginning Was the Deed: Realism and Moralism in Political Argument* (Princeton University Press, Princeton, NJ, 2005); Duncan Ivison *Postcolonial Liberalism* (Cambridge University Press, Cambridge, 2002); John Borrows *Canada's Indigenous Constitution* (University of Toronto Press, Toronto, 2010).

37 Rainer Forst "The Power of Critique" (2011) 39 *Political Theory* 118 at 122.

38 Forst, above n 37, citing James Tully *Public Philosophy in a New Key: Volume I: Democracy and Civic Freedom* (Cambridge University Press, Cambridge, 2008) at 35.

39 Paul Muldoon "'The Very Basis of Civility': On Agonism, Conquest, and Reconciliation" in Will Kymlicka and Bashir Bashir (eds) *The Politics of Reconciliation in Multicultural Societies* (Oxford University Press, Oxford, 2008) at 114–135, 134. See Noel Pearson, "*Mabo*: Towards Respecting Equality and Difference", as reprinted in Noel Pearson *Up From the Mission: Selected Writings* (Black Inc, Melbourne, 2009) at 31–40, 39–40.

40 At 134.
41 Muldoon, above n 39.
42 Hickford *Lords of the Land*, above n 1, at 227–228, 245.
43 James Tully *Public Philosophy in a New Key: Volume II, Imperialism and Civic Freedom* (Cambridge University Press, Cambridge, 2008) at 122.
44 Bernard Williams "A Critique of Utilitarianism" in J. C. Smart and Bernard Williams (eds) *Utilitarianism: For and Against* (Cambridge University Press, Cambridge, 1973) at 118.
45 At 118.
46 At 118. For an instructive discussion, refer to Melissa Lane "Constraint, Freedom, and Exemplar: History and Theory Without Teleology" in Jonathan Floyd and Marc Stears (eds) *Political Philosophy Versus History? Contextualism and Real Politics in Contemporary Political Thought* (Cambridge University Press, Cambridge, 2011) at 128–150.
47 For illustrations, see David Williams *A Simple Nullity? The Wi Parata Case in New Zealand Law and History* (Auckland University Press, Auckland, 2011); Mark Hickford "John Salmond and Native Title in New Zealand: Developing a Crown Theory on the Treaty of Waitangi, 1910–1920" (2008) 38 *Victoria University of Wellington Law Review* 853.
48 'Treaty', CO209/7, fo.104 (National Archives, Kew, London (TNA)). At Waikato and Manukau, there were merely 39 signatories to the English text out of a total of some 540 signatories across all signing sites. The historiographical and legal literature is extensive. Illustrations include, Judith Binney "The Māori and the Signing of the Treaty of Waitangi" in Judith Binney and others (eds) *Towards 1990: Seven Leading Historians Examine Significant Aspects of New Zealand History* (GP Publications, Wellington 1989) at 20–29; Claudia Orange *The Treaty of Waitangi* (Bridget Williams Books, Wellington, 2011); Michael Belgrave *Historical Frictions: Māori Claims and Reinvented Histories* (Auckland University Press, Auckland, 2005). Also refer to the analysis of the Waitangi Tribunal in *He Whakaputanga Me te Tiriti – The Declaration and the Treaty: The Report on Stage 1 of the Te Paparahi o Te Raki Inquiry (Wai 1040)* (Legislation Direct, Wellington, 2014) at 526–529.
49 Judith Binney with Vincent O'Malley and Alan Ward "Part 2: Te Ao Hou: The New World" in Atholl Anderson, Judith Binney and Aroha Harris (eds) *Tangata Whenua: An Illustrated History* (Bridget Williams Books, Wellington, 2014) at 224.
50 Te Puni Kōkiri "Crown-Māori Relationship Instruments: Guidelines and Advice for Government and State Sector Agencies" (2006) <www.tpk.govt.nz/en/a-matou-mohiotanga/crownmaori-relations/crown-maori-relationship-instruments>. Regrettably understudied, Matthew Palmer usefully presents these in *The Treaty of Waitangi in New Zealand's Law and Constitution*, above n 35, at 378–382.
51 Te Puni Kōkiri, above n 50, at 42 ('*a* founding document of Aotearoa/New Zealand'). Also, 'a founding document of Government in Aotearoa/New Zealand', at 38.
52 Andrew Sharp *Justice and the Māori: The Philosophy and Practice of Māori Claims in New Zealand Since the 1970s* (2nd ed, Oxford University Press, Auckland, 1997) at 87–98. The role of the Waitangi Tribunal was also critical, as it is a specialist standing commission of inquiry, which is to inquire into claims to the effect that an individual claimant Māori, or any group of Māori of which he or she is a member, is or is likely to be prejudicially affected by, *inter alia*, an act or omission on or after 6 February 1840 by or on behalf of the crown, which "was or is inconsistent with the principles of the Treaty" (section 6 of the Treaty of Waitangi Act 1975, as amended in 1985).

53 Arapera Blank, Manuka Henare and Haare Williams (eds) *He Kōrero mo Waitangi, 1984* (Te Runanga o Waitangi, January 1985) at 2.
54 At 2.
55 *Mana* connotes spiritually sanctioned or immanent power (Joan Metge *Tuamaka: The Challenge of Difference in Aotearoa New Zealand* (Auckland University Press, Auckland, 2010) at 69–70, 126. See also Richard Benton, Alex Frame and Paul Meredith (eds) *Te Mātāpunenga: A Compendium of References to the Concepts and Institutions of Māori Customary Law* (Victoria University Press, Wellington, 2013) at 154–159.
56 Andrew Sharp "The Treaty of Waitangi: Reasoning and Social Justice in New Zealand?" in Paul Spoonley, David Pearson and Cluny Macpherson (eds) *Nga Take: Ethnic Relations and Racism in Aotearoa/New Zealand* (Dunmore, Palmerston North, 1991) at 131–147, 133.
57 Blank, Henare and Williams, above n 53, at 49.
58 Shane Jones "The Bill of Rights and Te Tiriti o Waitangi" in *A Bill of Rights for New Zealand* (Legal Research Foundation, Auckland, 1985) at 207–217, 216.
59 *A Bill of Rights for New Zealand – A White Paper* (Appendices to the Journals of the House of Representatives (AJHR) A6, 1985).
60 Shane Jones (based on an interview with Paul Diamond) "Cornerstone of the Nation" in Michael Belgrave, Merata Kawharu and David Williams (eds) *Waitangi Revisited: Perspectives on the Treaty of Waitangi* (Oxford University Press, Melbourne, 2005) at 20–34, 22.
61 Palmer, above n 35, at 135–136.
62 At 20.
63 At 130–151, 371–382.
64 "The Native Meeting" in *New Zealand Herald*, 12 May 1879, volume xvi, at 6.
65 Cited in Hickford *Lords of the Land*, above n 1, 395.
66 As characterised by Hōne Sadler *Ko Tautoro Te Pito o Tōku Ao: A Ngāpuhi Narrative* (Auckland University Press, Auckland, 2014) at 163.
67 David Armitage "What's the Big Idea? Intellectual History and the *longue durée*" (2012) 38 *History of European Ideas* 493.
68 For my own preliminary engagements with the issue, see Mark Hickford "Looking Back in Anxiety: Reflecting on New Zealand's Historical-Political Constitution and Laws' Histories in the Mid-Nineteenth Century" (2014) 48 *New Zealand Journal of History* 1 at 16–17; Hickford *Lords of the Land*, above n 1, at 274, 280–281, 327, 380, 404, 440. Samuel Carpenter is embarking on an important research effort on the question of "civil government" and the Treaty of Waitangi.
69 Tony Ballantyne *Entanglements of Empire: Missionaries, Māori, and the Question of the Body* (Auckland University Press, Auckland, 2014) at 248–249.
70 Stephen to Backhouse [8 or 6] December 1840, CO209/6, fos.207a–208, TNA.
71 Dodson to Le Marchant 25 January 1841 *Historical Records of Australia, Series I: Volume XXI*, (Library Committee of the Commonwealth Parliament, 1924) at 270.
72 D. Keenan "'Hear the Word, See the Word' – A Comment on *Oral Culture, Literacy & Print in Early New Zealand: The Treaty of Waitangi*" in J. Thomson (ed) *Books and Bibliography: Essays in Commemoration of Don McKenzie* (Victoria University Press, Wellington, 2002) at 57–68, 58.
73 See the account in Williams, above n 47. See also Hickford, above n 47.
74 J.G.A. Pocock "Quentin Skinner: The History of Politics and the Politics of History" (2004) 10 *Common Knowledge* 532 at 547–548.
75 At 548.
76 Andrew Sharp "The Treaty in the Real Life of the Constitution" in M. Belgave, M. Kawharu and David Williams (eds) *Waitangi Revisited: Perspectives on the Treaty of Waitangi* (Oxford University Press, Melbourne, 2005) at 308–329.

77 Duncan Ivison "Afterword: The Normative Force of the Past" in Saliha Belmessous (ed) *Native Claims: Indigenous Law Against Empire 1500–1920* (Oxford University Press, New York, NY, 2011) at 248–258, 251.

78 Tony Ballantyne "On Place, Space and Mobility in Nineteenth-Century New Zealand" (2011) 45 *New Zealand Journal of History* 50.

79 Alfred Gell *Art and Agency: An Anthropological Theory* (Clarendon Press, Oxford, 1998) at 258.

80 Andrew Sharp "What Is the Constitution of 'The Spirit of Haida Gwaii'? Reflections on James Tully's *Strange Multiplicity: Constitutionalism in an Age of Diversity*" (1997) 12 *History and Anthropology* 241 at 242.

81 At 242.

82 Hickford *Lords of the Land*, above n 1, at 273–276; Hickford "Looking Back in Anxiety", above n 68, at 7–8.

83 Alan Ward, *A Show of Justice: Racial 'Amalgamation' in Nineteenth Century New Zealand* (Auckland University Press, Auckland, 1995) at 61–63.

84 See Damen Ward "Constructing British Authority in Australasia: Charles Cooper and the Legal Status of Aborigines in the South Australian Supreme Court, c1840–60" (2006) 34 *Journal of Imperial and Commonwealth History* 483 at 489–490; Damon Salesa *Racial Crossings: Race, Intermarriage, and the Victorian British Empire* (Oxford University Press, Oxford, 2011) at 102–103 (referring to Swainson and Peter Adams), 109–110 (Alan Ward).

85 Stephen, minute, 28 December 1843, CO209/22, fos.252–253; Stephen, minute, 19 May 1843, CO209/16, fo.455; Stanley, minute, 23 August 1842, CO209/14, fo.202, TNA.

86 For instance, Edwin Fletcher *'A Praiseworthy Device for Amusing and Pacifying Savages'? What the Framers Meant by the English Text of the Treaty of Waitangi* (PhD Thesis, University of Auckland, 2014) at 1071–1075. Beyond the introductory chapter, there is little thoroughgoing reference to the important analyses of how 'custom' was both *intellectually* and *operationally* reconciled or not with English legal usages and institutions in practice (such as in the work of Alan Ward, Damen Ward, Shaunnagh Dorsett, and Richard Boast). Despite what Fletcher claims, Chief Justice Martin, for one, expressed a range of views, *including* that native title was not necessarily enforceable in the courts (although it could be recognised or noted legally) or that the stance was a contested one, and it is this range of actually expressed views (and not optimistically interpreted silences) that historical analyses must wrestle with: see Hickford *Lords of the Land*, above n 1, 10, 424–425, 427–428.

87 Richard Tuck *The Sleeping Sovereign: The Invention of Modern Democracy* (Cambridge University Press, Cambridge, 2015) at 21–22.

88 See, for instance, Martin Chanock *Law, Custom and Social Order: The Colonial Experience in Malawi and Zambia* (Cambridge University Press, Cambridge, 1985). Also, Terence Ranger "The Invention of Tradition Revisited: The Case of Africa" in Terence Ranger and Olufemi Vaughan (eds) *Legitimacy and the State in Twentieth Century Africa* (Macmillan, London, 1993) at 62–111.

89 Changes and adaptations to these norms within Indigenous communities were also in evidence: Angela Ballara *Taua: "Musket Wars", "Land Wars" or "Tikanga"? Warfare in Māori Society in the Early Nineteenth Century* (Penguin, Auckland, 2003) at 428–430, 437; Hickford, "Interpreting the Treaty", above n 34, 114–215.

90 This is a point of difference from Fletcher's thesis, above n 86, at 1063 *et seq*, although he does recognise at 1064 that practice on the ground had to be worked out (which is what Damen Ward, Dorsett, Boast and myself tease out).

91 Peter Mandler "The Problem With Cultural History" (2004) 1 *Cultural and Social History* 94 at 96.

92 Matthew Palmer's work on the *Treaty of Waitangi in New Zealand's Law and Constitution*, above n 35, is one instance of the painstaking labour required, although he would acknowledge that it is merely a beginning. Other examples include Carwyn Jones "Tāwhaki and Te Tiriti: A Principled Approach to the Constitutional Future of the Treaty of Waitangi" (2013) 25 *New Zealand Universities Law Review* 703; Hickford "The Historical, Political Constitution", above n 1; Mark Hickford "Quasi-constitutionality in a Political Constitution: The Case of the Treaty of Waitangi" in Richard Albert and Joel Colón-Ríos (eds) *Quasi-Constitutionality and Constitutional Statutes: Statutes, Forms, Functions, and Applications* (Routledge, 2018) [forthcoming].

93 Hon Justice Joseph Williams "Can You See the Island?" (2015) *Māori Law Review* 21 at 25–26.

94 Occasionally, two might be designated as "lead chair", as with the Freshwater Iwi Leaders Group, which had Tā Tumu Te Heuheu and Tā Mark Solomon listed for the Waitangi meeting in 2016, for instance.

95 Roughan, above n 9, at 177.

96 At 177.

97 On which, see James Tully "Dialogue" (2011) 39 *Political Theory* 145 at 155.

98 Hickford "The Historical, Political Constitution", above n 1, at 593–623.

99 Roughan, above n 9, at 236–237.

100 Hickford *Lords of the Land*, above n 1, at 37–38, 273–283, 330–332, 378–379, 399–401; Hickford "Looking Back in Anxiety", above n 68, at 7–8.

101 Justice Joseph Williams, letter of transmission, 28 June 2011, *Ko Aotearoa Tēnei: A Report Into Claims Concerning New Zealand Law and Policy Affecting Māori Culture and Identity – Te Taumata Tuatahi* (Waitangi Tribunal, Wellington, Wai 262, 2011), xviii (emphasis in original). Also, at xviii–xix: "It is in the fact that the agreement at Waitangi took the form of a treaty that we see mutual respect for each other's mana, and it is in the Treaty's words that we find the promise that this respect will last forever. That is the essential element of the Treaty partnership confirmed time and again in the courts and in this Tribunal. There are many reasons to take this partnership principle and build it into all of our national institutions. It gives us our sense of right and place, grounding us in the traditions of the Pacific and the West at the same time. It provides the centre of gravity around which our multicultural nation can coalesce."

102 At 16. For Paul McHugh refer to his "Law, History and the Treaty of Waitangi"(1997) 31 *New Zealand Journal of History* 38 at 39 and, more specifically, McHugh, "Aboriginal Identity and Relations in North America and Australasia" in Ken Coates and Paul McHugh (eds) *Living Relationships – Kōkiri Ngātahi: The Treaty of Waitangi in the New Millennium* (Victoria University Press, Wellington, 1998) 107.

103 Sadler, above n 66, at 167.

104 At 169.

105 Justice Joseph Williams "Lex Aotearoa: An Heroic Attempt to Map the Māori Dimension in Modern New Zealand Law" (2013) 21 *Waikato Law Review* 1 at 12.

106 At 22.

107 Refer to Benton, Frame and Meredith, above n 55, at 429–433. Carwyn Jones *New Treaty, New Tradition: Reconciling New Zealand and Māori Law* (University of British Columbia Press, Vancouver, 2016) at 23–24. Tikanga Māori is defined statutorily in section 4 of Te Ture Whenua Māori Act 1993 as meaning "Māori customary values and practices".

108 Carwyn Jones "A Māori Constitutional Tradition" (2014) 12 *New Zealand Journal of Public and International Law* 187. Also, Māmari Stephens, "A Loving Excavation: Uncovering the Constitutional Culture of the Māori Demos" (2013) 25 *New Zealand Universities Law Review* 820.

109 As with the *United Nations Declaration on the Rights of Indigenous Peoples* GA Res 61/295, A/Res/61/295 (2007), to take merely one illustration. For its deployment in court decisions to date, refer to *Paki v Attorney-General (No 2)* [2014] NZSC 118, [2015] 1 NZLR 67, at [158] and [164] per Elias CJ and [317] per Glazebrook J. There is insufficient space to examine this factor here, but readers could refer to Andrew Erueti (ed) *International Indigenous Rights in Aotearoa New Zealand* (Victoria University Press, Wellington, 2017).

110 On which see Mark Hickford "Considering the Historical-Political Constitution and the Imperial Inheritance in Mid-Nineteenth Century New Zealand: Balance, Diversity and Alternative Constitutions" (2014) 12 *New Zealand Journal of Public and International Law* 145.

111 *He Whakaaro Here Whakaumu mō Aotearoa – The Report of the Independent Working Group on Constitutional Transformation* (February 2016).

112 At 104. The '*rangatiratanga* sphere' is characterised as a sphere of "influence . . . where Māori make decisions for Māori", while the '*kāwanatanga* sphere' is where "the Crown will make decisions for its people" (at 9).

113 W. Winiata "How, Can or Should the Treaty Be Reflected in Institutional Design?" in C. James (ed) *Building the Constitution* (Institute of Policy Studies, Wellington, 2000) at 205–206.

114 Jeremy Waldron *Political Political Theory: Essays on Institutions* (Harvard University Press, Cambridge, MA, 2016).

115 Hickford "The Historical, Political Constitution", above n 1, at 619–621; Hickford "Quasi-constitutionality", above n 92.

116 I have commented on this previously in Hickford *Lords of the Land*, above n 1, at 9, 456–457. Also, Mark Hickford "A Commentary on the Problematics of 'Cultural' Property: *Modus Vivendi in New Zealand*" (2017) 21 Hors Serie: *Do Cultural and Property Combine to Make "Cultural Property"*? 101.

9 Future contexts for Treaty interpretation

Natalie Coates[1]

How Te Tiriti o Waitangi and the Treaty of Waitangi should be interpreted and applied has been contentious since it was signed in 1840.[2] It is coloured by context: who is interpreting it, when they are interpreting it, and for what purpose. This chapter aims to identify some of the trends that are apparent now and comment on how they might form part of the context in which the Treaty is interpreted in the future.

In particular, I examine some of the legacies of the Treaty of Waitangi settlement process on how the Crown–Māori Treaty relationship might practically manifest itself. This legacy includes ongoing relationship redress that has written Māori further into the fabric of decision-making and governance in New Zealand and that can act as a base on which to improve the Crown–Māori relationship. It also includes the emergence from Treaty settlements of centralised tribal groups that are better resourced, are building capacity, becoming more influential in their regions, and engaging in direct negotiations and discussions with the Crown. Although these developments come with their challenges, they may mean that Māori are in a stronger position to negotiate the Treaty relationship in the future.

The imminent end of the historic Treaty settlement process will inevitably entail a renewed forward-looking focus, including navigating the ways in which the Māori and Crown Treaty relationship should be reflected. I also discuss two areas that are likely to be particularly relevant going forward, including inequality and the disproportionate number of Māori that feature across negative statistics, and constitutional reform. There are indications that devolution of social services to Māori to address issues of inequality and poverty may become increasingly likely in the future and, although fundamental constitutional transformation would be difficult to achieve in the contemporary political climate, there is much work to be done to pave the way towards positive constitutional change in the future. Of course, the risk in undertaking any venture which purports to comment on current and potential future developments is that it becomes outdated very quickly. These comments therefore modestly represent a time and date relevant snapshot of thought as we move on to a new era in the Crown-Māori relationship.

I. Post-Treaty settlement context

On 22 May 1995, representatives of Waikato-Tainui and the Crown signed a Deed of Settlement that settled Waikato-Tainui's historic claims in respect of vast land confiscations by the Crown under the New Zealand Settlements Act 1863 that occurred after the Waikato wars. Waikato-Tainui was the first *iwi* (tribal federation) in Aotearoa to settle their historic Treaty claims against the Crown. The Deed of Settlement included an apology from the Crown, cash and land valued at a total of $170 million, rights of first refusal for certain Crown properties within the Waikato-Tainui *rohe* (region), and a relativity mechanism that ensured that the Crown would pay Waikato-Tainui additional monetary redress if they exceeded the Crown fiscal envelope policy that existed at the time that set a maximum cap of $1 billion for the settlement of all historical Treaty claims. The Waikato-Tainui settlement marked a momentous occasion in New Zealand history as it paved the way for hundreds of subsequent settlements.

In essence, Treaty settlements are an agreement between the Crown and a settling Māori group that the Crown breached the Treaty and that the settling group will receive redress in exchange for giving up all of the historic claims that they may have against the Crown.[3] The Treaty settlement process, however, has had its major challenges for Māori. The process pits neighbouring *iwi* and *hapū* (tribes) against each other and can further entrench divisions. It can result in the drawing of boundaries and lines where *rohe* and territories were generally traditionally more fluid and relational. It forces some *hapū* to be included in settling groups that they see as anything but 'natural' against their consent and wishes. It also requires settling groups to accept only a fraction of the true value of what they have unjustly lost. This is reflective of the negotiation disparity between the Crown and Māori in the settlement process. When making the difficult decision on whether to settle all historic claims that a settling group may have against the Crown (including those that arise from the Treaty of Waitangi, legislation, the common law, fiduciary duties, and otherwise), settlement groups have to weigh up whether to make the pragmatic decision to get what they can in the contemporary political climate or turn away from the negotiating table in the hope that a better option may be available in the future.

For all the challenges and difficulties that Treaty settlements pose, and although it may take a settling group many years to come to an agreement, Māori have ultimately been choosing the pragmatic route of settling their claims with the Crown. Since 1995, over 77 groups have settled their historic Treaty claims.[4] Further, the Office of Treaty Settlements indicated in a March 2017 report that there was only one area in South of the North Island in the *rohe* of Ngāti Toa that was "not in active engagement with the Crown".[5] Therefore while there are some major groups yet to settle their claims, including Ngāpuhi, Te Rūnanga o Ngāti Whātua, Whakatōhea, Te Whānau a Apanui, and the Moriori, almost all of the major *hapū* and *iwi* have either settled their historic Treaty claims or are in the process of doing so by negotiating with the Crown or preparing for negotiations.

The end of the historic Treaty claim settlement era is therefore nigh, and this important period of New Zealand history will soon come to an end. Treaty settlements, however, leave a footprint and lasting legacy on the Treaty landscape of New Zealand and how the Treaty relationship between Māori and the Crown will likely be manifested in the future.

i) Ongoing relationship redress

One of major ways in which Treaty settlements will have a long-term impact is that they provide for contemporary ongoing relationships between the settling group and the Crown beyond settlement date. The first Treaty settlement was primarily financial in nature. However, as settlements developed, relationship orientated redress was negotiated and included in settlement packages. It is now common for settlements to include redress such as protocols that set out how the Crown will interact with the governance entity in respect of particular matters such as Crown Minerals; statutory acknowledgements that provide for the recognition of a settling group's association with particular areas and for this to be relevant in authority decision-making; the establishment of advisory committees to Ministers; letters of recognition that require a Crown entity such as the Ministry for Primary Industries to outline how the settling group will have input into their processes and decisions; and letters of introduction whereby the Crown is required to introduce the governance entity to both Crown and non-Crown organisations (such as local government bodies and museums) and encourage the establishment or enhancement of an ongoing relationship between the entities.

More recently, there have been significant developments in terms of the shared management and governance of natural resources. In December 2009 Waikato-Tainui and the Crown entered into a Deed of Settlement in relation to the Waikato River.[6] The overarching purpose of the Waikato River Settlement was "to restore and protect the health and wellbeing of the Waikato River for future generations".[7] The settlement provides for multiple co-governance and co-management arrangements, including the establishment of the Waikato River Authority, and a statutory co-governance entity comprised of equal Crown and *iwi* representatives that oversees the vision and strategy for the improved health and well-being of the Waikato River.[8] It also provides an obligation for Waikato-Tainui and the local authorities to enter into a joint management agreement to work together in relation to the exercise functions and powers under the Resource Management Act 1991 (RMA); the recognition of the Waikato-Tainui environmental plan by local and consent authorities; and the exercise of authorised customary activities by Waikato-Tainui.[9] This was an innovative regime that required Māori and the Crown to share the exercise of public power as never before and firmly incorporated Waikato-Tainui participation and values into the legislative scheme governing the Waikato River.

Innovative relationship redress can also be seen in the Whanganui River and Ngāi Tūhoe Settlements. The Whanganui River settlement, effected by legislation in March 2017, declared the Whanganui River or "Te Awa Tupua" to be a "legal person" that has all the rights, powers, duties, and liabilities of a legal person.[10] Two people, one appointee from the Whanganui *iwi* and one appointee from the Crown, are to be appointed as 'Te Pou Tupua' to act on behalf of the river to protect its status and health and well-being.[11] In a similar vein is the Ngāi Tūhoe settlement where the Te Urewera Act 2015 deemed the Te Urewera national park to effectively be a legal person with the associated rights and obligations to be exercised and performed by the Te Urewera Board.[12] The membership composition of the Board, however is particularly notable as for the first three years, the make-up is an equal number of Ngāi Tūhoe and Crown appointed persons (four representatives each).[13] Thereafter, the membership composition changes to six Tūhoe appointees and three Crown appointees.[14] While a high decision-making threshold is required under the Te Urewera Act, the Board composition is symbolically significant as Ngāi Tūhoe have a voice that outnumbers the Crown at the decision-making table.[15]

These settlements show that although a settlement may be grounded in a historical claim, the settlement process has been leveraged to gain additional value in the form of ongoing relationship redress. This is piecemeal across the country as all Treaty settlements are different reflecting the fact that each group has a unique history, suffered different Treaty breaches, are different sizes, have distinct characteristics such as geographical location and settled at different points of time. However, legislative redress that establishes some form of an ongoing relationship between the settling group and the Crown is evident in most Treaty settlements. This relationship redress, particularly that where authority, power, and decision-making are shared and Māori incorporated into governance, has legislatively sewn Māori further into our constitution and the decision-making fabric of New Zealand. This represents a subtle and incremental shift in the Crown–Māori constitutional relationship.

Projecting out into the future, relationship redress can act as a foundation and foothold from which to further build upon the Crown–Māori, as well as the Māori–local authority relationship. In particular, the 'innovative' Treaty settlements that incorporated co-management or co-governance arrangements set a precedent and move the stake further in the ground for *iwi* in terms of their input into environmental decision-making. Because all *iwi* have close *hononga* (connections) with particular natural resources, the type of relationship that the *iwi* of Waikato-Tainui and Whanganui have to their rivers and Tūhoe to the Te Urewera forest is not unusual. Philosophically, it would be difficult for the Crown and local authorities to justify not providing for Māori input and engagement in respect of decision-making to other *iwi*.

By way of example, after settling their Treaty claim, Ngāi Tahu managed to make gains in respect of the management of Te Waihora, the largest lake in Canterbury. In November 2012, the Te Waihora Management Board,[16] Te Rūnanga o Ngāi Tahu and Canterbury Regional Council entered into a voluntary co-governance agreement to 'share responsibility' for the Te Waihora catchment.[17] This extended significantly beyond the scope of what was provided for in the Ngāi Tahu Treaty settlement and included the collaborative sharing of certain functions and powers that the Canterbury Regional Council was responsible for.[18] There are a number of factors that likely contributed to Ngāi Tahu post-settlement being able to work with local authorities to create and implement a co-governance framework outside of their Treaty settlement. This includes Ngāi Tahu being relatively large, being one of the few *iwi* based in the South Island (compared with the significantly higher concentration of *iwi* in the North Island) and having had 20 years since their Treaty settlement to develop their relationships, infrastructure, and capacity. However, importantly, political progress in the co-governance space had already been made in other Treaty settlements such as the Waikato River settlement that could be built upon.

Another example, is the Hauraki Gulf Marine and Spacial Plan (the Plan) released on 6 December 2016.[19] The Plan is a non-statutory document designed to safeguard and improve the Hauraki Gulf. Māori input, and interests are at the heart of the Plan. The Project Steering Group, comprised eight *mana whenua* (territorial rights) representatives and eight central and local agency representatives (from the Auckland Council, Waikato Regional Council, Ministry for Primary Industries, Department of Conservation, and the Hauraki Gulf Forum). One of the core initiatives proposed by the Plan are 'Ahu Moana', or areas that are to be co-managed by coastal *hapū/iwi* and local communities along the Hauraki Gulf and islands that will extend from the high tide mark generally out one kilometre.[20] While the Plan is not legally binding, it provides a framework to build upon. The Plan was developed outside of the Treaty settlement framework as when it was being written, most of the *iwi* of Hauraki were in the process of negotiating Treaty settlements and had not yet settled. It shows, however, that the political climate was such that it was natural and accepted that Māori would play a central role within the project and ongoing governance of the Hauraki Gulf.

Treaty settlements have acted as a means of infusing the Crown–Māori relationship into the machinery of government, and legislative relationship redress has provided a platform and precedent to build upon. This has already occurred in the environmental co-management and co-governance space where these settlement agreements have put *pou* (support posts) in the ground and have better articulated a language and precedent for Māori having an active role in environmental decision-making. Building upon progress made in Treaty settlements, recent amendments were made to the Resource Management Act 1991 to introduce 'Mana Whakahono ā Rohe' or 'Iwi Participation Agreements'.[21] These are a mechanism for councils and *iwi* to come to agreement on ways *iwi* can participate in resource management and decision-making under the Act. Although these agreements are yet to be tested, they align with the increasing involvement of Māori in environmental decision-making and are an opportunity for those *iwi* that may have not had mechanisms incorporated into their Treaty settlements to seek greater input into resource management and to allow those *iwi* that have not settled to engage in the environmental space under the RMA without having to push for such environmental concessions in their Treaty settlements.

On the one hand, Treaty settlements have resulted in relationship redress that has written Māori further into the decision-making fabric of New Zealand and going forward into the future may act as a base upon which the Crown–Māori relationship can be improved, particularly in respect of environmental issues. On the other hand, it cannot be said that the Crown has emerged from the Treaty settlement process a changed Treaty-abiding entity that is always willing to progress

Māori input into decision-making and governance. Even with *iwi* groups that have been settled for many years, the Crown still engages in Treaty breaching behaviour, as is reflected in the many contemporary claims that are still coming before the Waitangi Tribunal. Progress in recognising Māori rights and interests and the Crown–Māori relationship is largely dependent on the politics of the day, including who is in power and what votes are required to pass legislation. One of the primary reasons the Mana Whakahono ā Rohe agreements were incorporated into the RMA is because the National Party required the support of the Māori Party to make the RMA amendments.[22] Further, after settling, groups lose the leverage of 'settlement' to seek further recognition and establish new legislative relationships with the Crown. The Crown–Māori relationship in a post-Treaty settlement context therefore has to stand on its own. In a post-Treaty settlement context, one concern is that the relationship redress provided for in Treaty settlements may be seen as a primary expression of the Crown's ongoing Treaty obligations instead of Treaty obligations being considered relevant in all Crown policies and decisions. Therefore, while there is promise for Māori going forward on the back of the Treaty settlement process, major challenges remain.

Ultimately, Treaty settlement relationship redress does not accurately reflect broader Māori constitutional aspirations. However, it does represent change and incremental progress. Since Treaty settlements began over 20 years ago, the trend has been that the Treaty relationship is becoming more infused in the machinery of government and in enactments of Parliament. The question seems to have moved from whether to recognise Māori interests *at all*, to debates on *how* to recognise Māori interests. There will be major barriers to overcome and there will inevitably be resistance. However, the new evolving normal is likely to be one where Māori are further cemented into the heart of governance and decision-making into particular matters.

ii) Growing economic influence and capacity

One of the obvious impacts of Treaty settlements that will likely influence the contextual matrix in which the Treaty will be interpreted in the future is that Māori will be better resourced, both financially and in terms of capacity. A direct impact of Treaty settlements is that Māori receive commercial redress. The total value of settlements paid out by the Crown so far is in excess of $2 billion. Since Waikato-Tainui first settled their claim in 1995 and Ngāi Tahu in 1997, both *iwi* have gone on to increase their Treaty settlement asset base significantly. In their 2016 annual report, for example, Waikato-Tainui reported that their total assets were valued at $1.22 billion.[23] Ngāi Tahu, who also received $170 million in their Treaty settlement, in the same year reported assets valued at over $1.5 billion.[24] This high value is partly explained by Waikato-Tainui and Ngāi Tahu receiving the upper end of what the Crown has been willing to pay out to settling groups so far and they have also had over 20 years to grow their asset base. Not all settling groups have fared so well.[25] However, overall as a direct consequence of settlements, the Māori asset base has substantially increased and Māori organisations will be better resourced and are bigger powerhouses and players in the New Zealand economy. As articulated by Maria Bargh, "Ngāi Tahu and Tainui are prime examples of iwi that are significantly stronger economically, politically and culturally post-settlement. Ngāi Tahu have come to be seen as an unavoidable political force for any division of government operating in Te Waipounamu."[26] Crown agencies have similarly commented on the growing political and economic influence of Māori and how as a result of Treaty settlement redress Māori are now seen as key drivers in facilitating regional economic growth in their *rohe*.[27]

Capacity building at all levels is also an inevitable necessity in the post-Treaty settlement context. Relationship redress, where the Crown and Māori have to work together on particular issues, will require the Crown to be sufficiently culturally competent to deal with Māori and to have an increased understanding of *tikanga* (protocol), *kawa* (ceremony), *te reo Māori* (Māori language), and Māori cultural values. It will also require Māori to be able to effectively participate in these arrangements. Post-settlement governance organisations (PSGEs) more broadly, have to navigate multiple bottom lines and need people that cannot only operate in *te ao Māori* (the Māori world) and understand *tikanga* and culture, but also operate in a multitude of contexts including complex regulatory environments. The skills that are required include influence, strategy, finance, negotiations, and politics. While there are now unprecedented numbers of Māori graduating from universities, building and obtaining the right capacity is a major challenge for Māori and Māori organisations, and smart training and succession plans are required.

Coming in to the post-Treaty settlement era, there will be better resourced Māori groups that will have built internal capacity and emerge as strong economic and political forces in their regions. This is relevant, as how the Treaty is practically interpreted is now often worked out in negotiations between the Crown and various groups. In the post-Treaty settlement era, Māori may be in a stronger position to negotiate the Treaty relationship.

II. Collectivisation

Māori have always been effective at collectivising when it is productive to do so, while maintaining the autonomy to divide up and act autonomously on different issues. Traditionally, it was common for smaller *whānau* (family) and *hapū* groups to collectivise into an *iwi* when there was a common enemy. The signing of the Treaty of Waitangi itself, to which about 540 chiefs gave their agreement, is an example of collective action. At a grassroots level, Māori are also no strangers to unifying in protest to push political issues and advance common causes. Well-known examples include the 1975 Māori land march, where approximately 5,000 marchers arrived at Parliament and presented a petition signed by 60,000 people objecting to the ongoing alienation of Māori land. Similarly, in May 2004, a *hikoi* (march) resulted in over 20,000 gathering at parliament to protest the Foreshore and Seabed Bill and what was seen as a mass land confiscation by the Crown. After both of these major political actions, changes to the existing legislation were made.

Collectivising is therefore not new and comes naturally to Māori. However, there are trends in respect of relatively new collectives that may impact on the Treaty relationship and who the Crown engages with. In a 2015 report by Statistics New Zealand on Crown–Māori engagement, some of the key trends and changes observed by Crown agencies were that Māori entities are consolidating their interests into bigger and fewer entities; Māori entities are amalgamating their interests, particularly for Treaty settlements; and the Iwi Chairs Forum and Iwi Leaders Groups have increasing political influence and are emerging as a prevalent forum and point of engagement for the Crown.[28]

In the business sphere, we are finding that consolidation of Māori interests into bigger entities is occurring and Māori collectives are fast emerging as prominent and influential. The collectives adopt different forms, some coming together in formalised legal structures and others simply forming loose informal business clusters. They are comprised of *iwi*, *hapū*, Māori trusts, incorporations, companies, partnerships, and individuals. Limited partnership structures, established pursuant to the Limited Partnerships Act 2008, in particular, have recently become popular and the preferred vehicle for Māori organisations that wish to operate collectively for a common, usually commercial, purpose.[29] These collectives operate in a number of sectors, including having a particularly strong presence in the primary industries such as dairy, honey, kiwifruit, forestry and fish, as well as a lesser but growing presence in the food and beverage industry, health and social services, and the information technology space. The benefits of collectivisation in a commercial context are numerous. Some of the benefits cited by the Iwi Collective Partnership (ICP), a limited partnership established in 2010 made up of 15 *iwi* members that collectivised their commercial seafood interests and fisheries quota, include improved economic returns, opportunities to create economies of scale, building *iwi* capacity, capability and participation in the fisheries sector, and utilising cost savings.[30] Victor Goldsmith in discussing Ngāti Porou Miere Limited Partnership, a collective of Ngāti Porou land owning trusts and incorporations operating in the honey sector, stated that[31]

> Although each landowner would still retain the mana over their own whenua, as a Collective group they have the power to influence and achieve things they cannot do as individuals working alone in silos. Presently the honey companies play us all off each other – it's the divide and rule strategy. But if we worked together, we could negotiate better contracts, buy our own hives, control who comes in and out of the rohe, enforce our own bio-security regulations. The potential of what we could achieve is unlimited.

Overall, collectivisation of Māori within the business sphere is increasingly common and some of these collectives are becoming powerhouses in the New Zealand economy. As internal Māori capacity and resources increase, this is a trend that will likely continue.

Another trend that has emerged is for Māori entities to amalgamate into collectives, particularly for Treaty settlement claims. This, however, is largely as a result of the Crown's Treaty settlement policy, unilaterally adopted by the Crown in 1994, that has a strong preference to negotiate settlements with 'large natural groups' (LNGs).[32] Although there is no formal definition of a LNG, they tend to be *iwi* or collectives of *hapū* as opposed to individual *hapū*, *whānau*, or landowners.[33] Correspondingly, PSGEs that are established pursuant to settlements are generally centralised *iwi*-based entities that administer and hold settlement assets on behalf of the LNG. Although there has been some sympathy for the LNG policy, including from the Waitangi Tribunal that recognised that there are sound practical and policy reasons for settling at *iwi* or *hapū* aggregation level where that is at all possible,[34] the LNG has been criticised on the basis that it may prejudice smaller groups such as *hapū* and ultimately be a breach of the Treaty itself.[35] However, rightly or wrongly, centralised tribal governance entities are emerging as prominent entities from the Treaty settlement process.

Additionally, Crown agencies have pointed out the emerging role of the Iwi Chairs Forum (ICF) and Iwi Leaders Groups (ILG) as a forum and a point of engagement.[36] The ICF is an informal collective of *iwi* chairpersons from across the country. The ICF convene quarterly at different *marae* (meeting houses) across the country to discuss the advancement of Māori aspirations in terms of cultural, social, economic, environmental, and political development. All *iwi* chairpersons have an open invitation to participate in, and contribute the ICF, and there are currently 72 *iwi* that are members. The Forum regularly invites Crown representatives, Members of Parliament and stakeholder and community groups to present on projects and issues of concern to *iwi* and Māori.

Various ILGs have been established from the membership of the ICF in relation to particular *kaupapa* (discussion topics) including conservation; climate change; oil and minerals; *whānau ora* (family health); housing; constitutional reform; *mātauranga* (education); and fresh water. These ILG directly engage with the Crown on matters of mutual interest and concern. The membership, meeting schedules and agenda of each ILG depends on the nature of the *kaupapa*. For example, the Freshwater ILG is comprised of the leaders of Ngāti Tūwharetoa, Ngāi Tahu, Te Arawa, Whanganui, Waikato–Tainui, Ngāti Porou, Ngāti Kahungunu, Ngāti Raukawa, Ngāti Kuri, and Ngāti Tama ki Te Tau Ihu.[37] The Freshwater ILG, as endorsed by the ICF, engages directly with the senior Ministers of the Crown at a leadership and governance level and at a technical level with Crown officials to advance the interests of *iwi* and *hapū* in the Crown's review and reform of the framework for freshwater management in New Zealand.[38] Each ILG convenes national and regional *hui* (meetings) with *iwi* and *hapū* around the *motu* (land or island) and also reports to and seeks direction from the ICF at its quarterly hui.

In the Statistics New Zealand report, Crown agencies stated that, despite the growing prominence of the ICF and ILG, they do not purport to represent the interests of all Māori and that, accordingly, they are good for high-level engagement, but not a substitute for broader engagement with other groups.[39] However, much of the criticism that has been directed at the ICF and ILG's is that they do play a major role in shaping the direction of Crown policy and legislation.[40] It has been argued that this is problematic because, particularly in respect of the ILGs, they only represent certain *iwi* and more generally are made up of an undemocratic and self-selected small elite section of the Māori community that has little accountability to the *whānau* and *hapū* it serves.[41] Annette Sykes argues that forums such as the ICF "have sidelined traditional communities and their *tikanga Māori* processes of engagement".[42] The new Labour–led government has emphasised that, while the ICF and ILG's are important groups in the Crown–Māori relationship, they are not exclusively important and therefore they are unlikely to treat this forum as being a one-stop shop for engagement purposes.

While there are challenges, there are major opportunities and benefits for Māori to work together to collectively wield power and influence. At a global level, the utilisation of technology to collectively mobilise Indigenous peoples offers new possibilities. In early 2016 the Standing Rock Sioux tribe began protesting the construction of an oil pipeline (the Dakota Access Pipeline) that they saw as constituting a threat to their clean water and ancient burial grounds. Thousands of people from across the United States and around the world, including strong support from Indigenous peoples, joined the protest to halt the Dakota Access Pipeline. One of the features of the Dakota Access Pipeline protests was the utilisation of social media and social networks to expand support. In the New Zealand context, Native American protestors reached out to their Māori networks to effectively proliferate the cause among the broader Māori community.[43] Māori responded. A "Haka with Standing Rock" Facebook page was established (which quickly attracted over 46,000 members), *haka* in support of the protests were performed across New Zealand, contingents of Māori travelled to the Standing Rock Reservation to show their support, donations were made and the Standing Rock protests attracted extensive coverage in New Zealand's national news. While Indigenous peoples showing support for each other is not new, the power of collectivising on grand international scales by tapping into expanded social networks through technology such as social media offers much potential.

Working in community and collectively comes naturally to Māori. The way of the future will likely be one where Māori, and more broadly Indigenous peoples, will increasingly collectivise and find modern and sophisticated ways of working efficiently and effectively on common enterprise at a macro and micro levels. This will be across the spectrum including in the business realm, in the exercise of political influence and in addressing social needs.

Collectivisation in different forms does, however, raise challenging questions around who the Crown should be engaging with as the Māori Treaty partner and whether the governance structures adopted and available are sufficiently nuanced to reflect the complexities of Māori identity, voice, values, and representation. The reality of Crown–Māori engagement is that there are major limitations on what Māori can achieve within the current legal and political framework. Māori therefore tend to use any tools or forums that they can to influence Crown policy to achieve what might only be small gains. In doing this, however, it is important to regularly reflect on who engages with the Crown on behalf of Māori and their constituent *iwi* and *hapū* and whether there are appropriate governance models and accountability mechanisms in place.

III. Marking a time to look forward

Joe Williams in the Wai 262 "Ko Aotearoa Tēnei" Waitangi Tribunal Report states that[44]

> Over the next decade or so, the Crown-Māori relationship, still currently fixed on Māori grievances, must shift to a less negative and more future-focused relationship at all levels. This change is expected and intended. It will reflect growing Māori confidence, drive from continued demographic change and settlement-based tribal economic renewal. It will also provide a more positive platform for jointly addressing current Māori social problems.

There is no clear 'post-Treaty settlement' era, as settlements have been taking place for the last 20 years. However, in many ways, Māori have had over 20 years of looking back at the wrongs done by the Crown and how those wrong should be righted. The end of Treaty settlements will likely entail a transition from focusing on historical Treaty grievances to Māori turning their focus more sharply on the broader Crown–Māori relationship. This is not to say history will be forgotten. The impact of the colonial period on Māori and the Crown's actions in flagrantly breaching the Treaty of Waitangi during this period, will never end for Māori. It is also not to say that Māori have not been looking forward. Many *iwi* that have settled have long had strategic forward-looking plans that set out their aspirations for the future.[45] However, the post-Treaty settlement environment will likely entail a renewed forward-looking focus, including navigating the ways in which the Māori and Crown Treaty relationship should be reflected.

This re-navigation is reflected in the Prime Minister creating the new Crown–Māori relations portfolio held by Minister Kelvin Davies. The specific scope of this portfolio is still being worked out, in consultation with Māori. However, the initial priority areas for the Minister in the first three years include: taking the lead on resetting Crown/Māori relationships on hard issues; finding opportunities for active partnership; measuring how healthy the relationship is over time; helping government better engage with Māori; supporting Māori capability and capacity to deal with government; lifting public sector performance to better respond to Māori issues; and developing a way to deal with contemporary Treaty claims and other processes for restitution and reconciliation. Two areas that will challenge the new government and this portfolio, but that are particularly pertinent in the post-Treaty settlement Crown–Māori relationship, is addressing inequality and constitutional change.

i) Inequality and social issues

The disproportionate Māori representation in negative social and economic statistics is stark and getting worse. In health, Paparangi Reid and Bridget Robson state that[46]

> The story of Māori health is one of systematic disparities in health outcomes, in the determinants of health, of health system responsiveness and

> in representation in the health workforce. . . . In almost every major disease category, Māori bear a disproportionate burden of risk, morbidity, disability and mortality.

The statistics make for sobering reading. In 2013, Māori male life expectancy at birth was 7.3 years less than non-Māori males.[47] In 2010–2012 Māori suicide rates were almost twice as high than those of non-Māori.[48] Diabetes is almost three times more common in Māori than non-Māori.[49] More broadly, the Ministry of Health in 2013 reported that non-Māori were more advantaged than Māori across all negative socio-economic indicators investigated.[50] The Māori unemployment rate was more than double that of non-Māori, Māori adults had lower rates of school completion, were more likely to have a personal income of less than $10,000, and were more likely to receive income support. Māori were also more likely to live in households without any telecommunications (including internet access), without motor vehicle access, and were more likely to live in rented accommodation and crowded households.

Given this reality, in a post-Treaty settlement environment, there is likely to be a renavigation of focus towards issues of inequality, poverty, and disparity and what the Treaty requires of the Crown to substantively address these issues. The Waitangi Tribunal has dealt with disparity issues on a number of occasions and have found that the disproportionate socio-economic circumstance of Māori in some instances is a Treaty issue and that the Crown is obliged to take active measures to reduce these disparities. Where the Crown has not done so, it may constitute a Treaty breach. In particular, in their Napier Hospital and Health Services Report released in 2001, the Waitangi Tribunal found that[51]

> Where adverse disparities in health status between Māori and non-Māori are persistent and marked, the Crown is obliged to take appropriate measures on the basis of need so as to minimise them over the long run. Such measures may extend to the use of affirmative action for Māori as a population group in order to reduce structural or historical disadvantage.

Similarly, in the Tribunal's 2017 report "Tū Mai te Rangi! Report on the Crown and Disproportionate Reoffending Rates", the Waitangi Tribunal found that the Crown has a Treaty responsibility to reduce inequities between Māori and non-Māori reoffending rates to protect Māori interests.[52] The Crown had breached the principle of active protection by not appropriately resourcing and having a long-term strategic and targeted commitment to reducing the rate of Māori reoffending, as well as the principle of equity by not sufficiently prioritising the reduction of Māori reoffending rates.[53] The statistical context to this claim is that while Māori only comprise about 15 per cent of the national population, Māori make up more than 50 per cent of the prison population.

In the next phase of Treaty jurisprudence, there is likely to be an increased focus on the Crown's obligations to address these types of issues and how they can best be addressed. This ranges from better delivery and funding of mainstream services (that could disproportionately lift the welfare of Māori), targeted or special measures specifically for Māori and/or decentralisation and devolution of services to Māori.

In terms of the Treaty, an increased focus on inequality will likely bring to the fore jurisprudential arguments around what Article III of the Treaty might mean and whether it stands for formal equality or substantive equality are likely to come to the fore. Given the passions that can become inflamed in respect of substantive equality and differential and targeted treatment, the Waitangi Tribunal is a useful forum to use in this respect, as having an independent Court interpreting the Crown's Treaty obligations can assist in depoliticising the issue and removing it from direct Māori–Pākehā confrontation. However, this forum is only useful to the extent that the Crown is willing to pick up and implement these recommendations.

Another Treaty interpretation issue that is likely to arise is whether the guarantee of *tino rangatiratanga* (sovereignty or self-determination) under Article II of the Treaty requires a greater devolution of power to Māori to address issues of inequality and poverty. Māmari Stephens articulates the tension that can arise between Article II and Article III of the Treaty in this context:[54]

> On one hand Māori have sought to be included in mainstream New Zealand society without differentiation on the basis of race or culture. On the other hand, Māori have consistently sought recognition of rights accruing to all Māori by virtue of the Treaty of Waitangi. Such rights have included the rights (and duties) of common citizenship under Article III and the guarantee of tino rangatiratanga under Article II.
>
> In social policy, the tension between ideas of common citizenship and long-lived notions of *rangatiratanga* is particularly starkly observed because social laws and mechanisms are supposed to be universally applied, tribal and community affiliation notwithstanding. Yet, in line with the notion that Māori have the right to control their own destinies, Māori have been consistent in calling for greater control of resources and decision-making over Māori families and *whānau* development.

Māori are already active to an extent in the delivery of certain social services to Māori. Māori health providers operate through the Ministry of Health and District Health Boards, and there are also opportunities under the Whānau Ora initiative for community providers such as *iwi*, *marae*, education providers, church groups, land trusts, sports groups, and *whānau* to deliver services to *whānau*. Innovative relationship redress also emerged in the Tūhoe Treaty settlement that was aimed at transforming the Tūhoe–Crown relationship in respect of social services. This included a Social Services Management Plan (SMP) that is a 40-year agreement by the Ministries of Education, Social Development, and Business, Innovation and Employment to work with Tūhoe to improve the social circumstances of the Tūhoe people. The SMP acknowledges the goal of Tūhoe to manage their own affairs to the maximum autonomy possible in the circumstances. Christopher Finlayson, Minister for Treaty Settlement Negotiations, also stated that[55]

> One of the goals of the SMP is to assist Tūhoe to build their capability to manage their own affairs as much as possible, while assisting the Crown in improving delivery of services in Te Urewera.

Although the focus of the SMP is not specific, the language used around the SMP indicates that a move to devolve delivery of services, or at least to have Tūhoe heavily involved in the delivery of services, is anticipated.

With the shift away from historical grievances, the Crown–Māori Treaty relationship in respect of tackling some of the difficult realities for Māori is likely to come to the fore. State-funded devolution of services to Māori is likely to increasingly form part of that framework. If this occurs, one of the issues that will need to be confronted directly is that Māori should not have to spend Treaty settlement money on compensating for the failure of the State to adequately provide basic social services that they are funded by taxpayers to perform. The relationships established under the Tūhoe SMP will be watched carefully by other *iwi*, as they may provide a useful model and precedent to build on in the future.

ii) Constitutional change

The current place of the Treaty in New Zealand's constitutional legal framework is complex. Sir Geoffrey Palmer describes the Treaty as "half in and half out of the legal system".[56] The existing orthodox view is that, even though the Treaty of Waitangi may be a valid international Treaty binding at international law as a matter of honour, it is only enforceable by New Zealand courts when it has been incorporated into legislation.[57] There are numerous references to the Treaty of Waitangi in legislation, most of which refer to the 'principles' of the Treaty of Waitangi. The Courts and the Waitangi Tribunal have played a major role in Treaty jurisprudence including interpreting what the Treaty of Waitangi means and what it requires from the Crown in an array of different legislative contexts. However, because the Treaty has not been incorporated into legislation generally, Courts have been limited in their preparedness to refer to the Treaty in the absence of explicit statutory reference. The exception to this has been in the area of judicial review of legislative action and as an aid and context to statutory interpretation.[58]

For the most part, how the Treaty is practically interpreted and manifested on a day-to-day basis is a political question and decisions are ultimately made by the executive branch of government.[59] While Māori have recourse to the Waitangi Tribunal when they disagree with how the executive has interpreted the Treaty, the Waitangi Tribunal is largely limited to making recommendations on Crown Treaty breaches, which the Crown can choose to ignore. The manifestation of the Treaty relationship is therefore inherently constrained by politics. Matthew Palmer identifies the problem as[60]

> [H]owever loudly Māori voices are now heard in politics, it is still the majority who rules the sovereign Parliament. The Treaty of Waitangi, as an explicit written commitment to the rights of people who are now a minority, lies in deep and enduring tension with New Zealand's majoritarian constitutional culture.

Majoritarian sympathy for rights recognition can wax and wane. The infamous 2004 'Orewa Speech' delivered by Don Brash, the then leader of the New Zealand National Party, and the public reaction to this speech reflect a wane in public opinion on Māori rights recognition. Don Brash advocated for 'one rule for all' and ending what he saw as being special privileges for Māori. This position gained significant traction from the New Zealand population and resulted in a surge in the National Party poll rating, which was sustained through until the 2005 general election which Don Brash almost won. This backlash against the recognition of Māori Treaty rights and interests has since waned. However, groups such as Hobson's Pledge that campaign on the same basis of formal equality rhetoric intermittently emerge. Leading up to the 2017 elections, New Zealand First is polling high.[61] Although New Zealand First is not campaigning primarily on a Māori and Treaty platform, one of their policies is that the Treaty is not part of the New Zealand Constitution. If New Zealand First form part of the 2017 government, their policies may impact on the expression of the Crown–Māori Treaty relationship.

Although great progress has been made in the last 20 years, and the trend is that the Treaty of Waitangi is "a part of the fabric of New Zealand society"[62] and will continue to shape the constitutional and legal landscape of New Zealand, there is a fragility to our constitutional arrangements. Protection for minorities against the tyranny of the majority is not well developed as, technically, any progress made in respect of the recognition of Treaty rights can be wiped away with a stroke of the legislative pen. Accordingly, Māori have long been pushing for fundamental constitutional reform so that their rights and interests are better protected.

Constitutional reform could take a variety of forms. Some suggestions are based on incorporating the Treaty into the existing constitutional system. For example, entrenching the Treaty as supreme law that can be struck down by the Court or incorporating the Treaty into legislation in a manner akin to the Bill of Rights Act 1990 so that the Crown is required to act consistently with the Treaty but parliament is not prevented from enacting legislation to the contrary.[63] Matthew Palmer prefers a middle ground between these two options, whereby the Treaty is incorporated generally into legislation and if parliament legislates to the contrary, the judiciary can make a declaration of inconsistency that has the effect of offering a remedial order to amend the incompatibility which can then be adopted or not.[64] Matike Mai Aotearoa, the 'Independent Working Group for Constitutional Transformation' chaired by Margaret Mutu and convened by Moana Jackson, in their 2016 Report proposed six different indicative constitutional models.[65] These models, however, were based not on incorporating the Treaty into the existing constitutional system but New Zealand's constitutional arrangements themselves reflecting Te Tiriti in a manner that allows for the both the independent exercise of Māori *rangatiratanga* and Crown *kāwanatanga* (governorship). The suggested models indicate a range of possibilities "for those who really want a good faith honouring of Te Tiriti" and are based on the interpretation of Te Tiriti that provides that Māori and the Crown were to have different "spheres of influence".[66] An example of one of the models proposed is a tricameral model consisting of an *iwi/hapū* assembly (the *rangatiratanga* sphere), the Crown in Parliament (the *kāwanatanga* sphere) and a joint deliberative body (the relational sphere where joint decisions are made). The ultimate recommendation from the Working Group was a process to work towards constitutional transformation in 2040 that involved internal discussions among Māori and the initiating of a dialogue with the Crown.

In many ways, Māori have a veto on constitutional change. On one hand, any constitutional reform that does not address the Treaty would likely result in significant civil unrest and concern. As the Rt Hon Chief Justice Sian Elias has stated, "If constitutional reform is ever in prospect in New Zealand, it is certain that the Treaty cannot be ignored."[67] On the other hand, Māori constitutional aspirations may not be acceptable by the Pākehā majority. In 2007, Sir Geoffrey Palmer noted he was "struck by the impression that while we cannot go back, there is no widespread will to go forward either".[68] In response to this constitutional stalemate, Sir Geoffrey Palmer suggested that a pause is necessary and that, once historical grievances are out of the way and there has been a period of consultation and reflection, New Zealand will be in a better position to decide upon next steps in relation to the position of the Treaty.

In 2017, ten years after Sir Geoffrey Palmer made these comments, historical Treaty settlements and grievances are still outstanding for some *iwi*, and the political climate is such that radical constitutional change would be difficult to achieve. An opportunity may arise to push constitutional reform if New Zealand makes a move towards becoming a republic.[69] The two flag referendums held in 2015 and 2016 on whether to change the New Zealand flag sparked new discussions on whether New Zealand should become a republic. The then Prime Minister John Key in 2014 described republicanism as an "inevitability", and there are polls that suggest there is growing support for republicanism.[70] However it appears that if there is a move towards republicanism, that it is still a long way off.

In the meantime, before New Zealand is in a place where major constitutional reform in relation to the Treaty might be possible, there is much to be done. This includes internal reflection and discussions in Māori communities about our constitutional aspirations and what constitutional transformation may look like. It includes building on the progress achieved in Treaty settlements and pushing for further incremental constitutional change where possible. It also includes a process of socialising reform and change. In the Courts, there is a role for lawyers to undertake coordinated strategic litigation to work towards a more plural legal system. This includes pushing the role and place of *tikanga* in the law, advancing the notion of the fiduciary duty of the Crown and questioning the orthodox position adopted in *Te HeuHeu Tukino v Aotea District Māori Land Board* [1941] NZLR 590 that a claim could not be rested on the Treaty without some statutory recognition of the Treaty.

Conclusion

This chapter is not proposing anything revolutionary. It is a small stocktake from an academic/practitioner perspective of some of the developments and trends that we are seeing now in respect of the Crown–Māori Treaty relationship and how they may project into the hazy destination that is our future. In particular, I focus on some of the legacies of the Treaty settlement process. The settlement process is a landmark development in New Zealand history and from it flows particular impacts: some good, some bad, and some unintended.

The resolution of Treaty settlements has been a time-consuming and extremely challenging process for Māori. However, even bigger challenges lie ahead. The task is daunting, as it requires us to take a hard look at where the Māori nation is currently at and ask big questions about where we are heading as a nation. What is our vision for New Zealand? What role and place should the Treaty play in that vision? What is the current Treaty relationship between the Crown and Māori and what should it be? And, how do we practically achieve change? It is time to move forward from historical grievance mode, and there is much work to be done.

Notes

1 Nō Ngāti Awa, Ngāti Hine, Ngāti Tuwharetoa, Tūhoe, Te Arawa hoki ahau. I am a senior associate at Kahui Legal.
2 Note that all references to Te Tiriti o Waitangi, the Treaty of Waitangi, or the Treaty are a reference to the full document comprising both language texts.
3 Each settlement has its own individual definition of the claims that it is settling. However, it is usually comprehensive and captures all claims of the settling group arising from actions of omissions on behalf of the Crown before 21 September 1992 that may be founded on rights arising from Te Tiriti of Waitangi/the Treaty of Waitangi or its principles; legislation, the common law (including aboriginal title or customary law), or fiduciary duties.
4 This number includes all of those groups that have either had settlement legislation passed, signed a Deed of Settlement, or initialled a Deed of Settlement before 31 March 2017.
5 Office of Treaty Settlements "Year-to-Date Progress Report 1 July 2016–31 March 2017" <www.govt.nz/assets/Documents/OTS/Quarterly-report-to-31-Mar-2017.pdf>.
6 This was given effect, as far as legislation was required, by the Waikato-Tainui Raupatu Claims (Waikato River) Settlement Act 2010. I note that this was a revised Deed of Settlement, as the first Deed of Settlement in relation to the Waikato River was entered into by Waikato-Tainui and the Crown on 22 August 2008.
7 See Clause 2.110 of the 17 December 2009 Deed of Settlement in Relation to the Waikato River.
8 See Clause 7 of the 17 December 2009 Deed of Settlement in Relation to the Waikato River.
9 See Clauses 8.4, Clauses 8.3.3–8.3.6 and Clause 10 of the 17 December 2009 Deed of Settlement in Relation to the Waikato River.
10 See section 14 of the Te Awa Tupua (Whanganui River Claims Settlement) Act 2017.

11 See section 20 of the Te Awa Tupua (Whanganui River Claims Settlement) Act 2017.
12 See sections 11(1), 11(2) and 17(a) of the Te Urewera Act 2014.
13 See section 21(1) of the Te Urewera Act 2014.
14 See section 21(2) of the Te Urewera Act 2014.
15 Section 33 of the Te Urewera Act 2014 sets out those decisions that the Board must make unanimously, such as the approval of the Te Urewera management plan, and section 34 sets out those decisions that are to be made by consensus.
16 This is a Committee established by Te Rūnanga o Ngāi Tahu to represent the Papatipu Rūnanga holding mana within the Waihora Catchment to exercise Te Rūnanga o Ngāi Tahu's responsibilities pertaining to the lakebed of Te Waihora.
17 Te Waihora Management Board, Te Rūnanga o Ngāi Tahu and Canterbury Regional Council "Te Waihora Co-Governance Agreement" (23 November 2012) <http://tewaihora.org/wp-content/uploads/2014/07/te-waihora-co-governance-agreement.pdf>.
18 The Ngāi Tahu Settlement provided for the ownership of the lakebed of Te Waihora to be vested in Ngāi Tahu and for a joint management plan to be created between Ngāi Tahu and the Department of Conservation in relation to the lakebed and surrounding land (see section 168 and 177 of the Ngāi Tahu Claims Settlement Act 1998). The collaborative functions and powers to be shared under the Voluntary Co-Governance Agreement included preparation, review, or change of RMA planning and policy instruments; resource consenting; compliance, monitoring, and enforcement; annual and long-term planning; operational works within the catchment; biodiversity and biosecurity programmes; by-law making; and relationship management (see Clause 5.1).
19 "Tai Timu Tai Pari, Seachange, Hauraki Gulf Marine Spacial Plan" (April 2017) <www.seachange.org>.
20 At 48–51.
21 See section 58L to 58U of the Resource Management Act 1991.
22 Māori Party "Māori Party Held to Make History With Mana Whakahono-ā-rohe Agreements" (2017) <www.maoriparty.org/m_ori_party_help_to_make_history_with_mana_whakahono_rohe_agreements>.
23 Waikato-Tainui "Puurong-aa-Tau o Waikato-Tainui 2016" (2016) <www.versite.co.nz/~2016/19210/files/assets/basic-html/page-1.html> at 8.
24 Te Rūnanga o Ngāi Tahu "Annual Report" (2016) <http://ngaitahu.iwi.nz/investment/ngai-tahu-annual-reports/2016-annual-report/>.
25 For example, Ngāti Tama lost almost all of the $14.5 Treaty of Waitangi payment it received in an investment that went wrong; see Rob Maetzig "Iwi Loses Almost $20 Million" (16 April 2012) <www.stuff.co.nz/taranaki-daily-news/news/6753868/Iwi-loses-almost-20-million>.
26 Maria Bargh "The Post-Settlement World (So Far): Impacts for Māori" in Nichola Wheen and Janine Hayward (eds) *Treaty of Waitangi Settlements* (Bridget Williams Books, Wellington, 2012) 166 at 174.
27 Statistics New Zealand *Crown-Māori Engagement and Statistical Information Needs* (Statistics New Zealand, Wellington, 2015) at 18–19.
28 Statistics New Zealand, above n 27, at 17–19.
29 One of the benefits of this model are that each of the partners are only liable for the debts and liabilities of the limited partnership to the extent of its contribution to the limited partnership, which can safeguard Māori assets.
30 The ICP is the largest collective of *iwi* in New Zealand and the partnership currently manages 16,000 tonne of fish on behalf of the *iwi* members; see Dr Robert Joseph and others *Te Pai Tawhiti: Exploring the Horizons of Māori Economic*

Performance Through Effective Collaboration (prepared for Nga Pae o Te Maramatanga, 2016) at 95.

31 Te Runanganui o Ngati Porou "Take the Honey, Not the Money" (2015) <www.ngatiporou.com/article/take-honey-not-money>.

32 Office of Treaty Settlements *Ka Tika a Muri, Ka Tika a Mua: Healing the Past, Building a Future* (Office of Treaty Settlements, Wellington, 2002) at 39.

33 An exception to this is the Maraeroa A & B Blocks Deed of Settlement entered into by the Crown and the descendants of the original owners of the Maraeroa A and B blocks on 12 July 2012 for the settlement of historical claims. This settlement was with the owners of the land blocks and not an *iwi/hapū*.

34 Waitangi Tribunal *The Pakakohi and Tangahoe Settlement Claims Report* (Legislation Direct, Wellington, 2000) at 57.

35 Malcolm Birdling "Healing the Past or Harming the Future? Large Natural Groupings and the Treaty Settlement Process" (2004) 2 *New Zealand Journal of Public and International Law* 261.

36 Statistics New Zealand, above n 27, at 18.

37 Joint Brief of Evidence of Mark Wiremu Solomon and Donna Liarne Arihia Flavell on Behalf of the Freshwater Iwi Leaders Groups (7 October 2016) presented in the Waitangi Tribunal in the National Freshwater and Geothermal Resources Inquiry at [13].

38 At [12].

39 Statistics New Zealand, above n 27, at 18.

40 Annette Sykes "Politics of the Brown Table" (Bruce Jesson Memorial Lecture, 2010) <www.brucejesson.com/annette-sykes-2010-bruce-jesson-memorial-lecture/> at 20–27.

41 At 18.

42 At 8.

43 On 26 October 2016, Myron Dewey, a Native American filmmaker, posted a video on Facebook calling upon Māori to perform *haka* and join the Standing Rock protest. In the video he drew upon the relationship he had with Māori through the sister organisations AIO (Americans for Indian Opportunity) and AMO (The Advancement of Māori Opportunity), and more broadly the need to show "The Power and Strength of Indigenous International Unity" <www.facebook.com/myron.dewey1/videos/vb.16811406/10104028319088219/?type=2&theater>.

44 Waitangi Tribunal *Ko Aotearoa Tenei: Te Taumata Tuatahi* (Legislation Direct, Wellington, 2010) at 16.

45 For example, "Whakatupuranga Waikato-Tainui 2050" is Waikato-Tainui's blueprint for the "cultural, social and economic advancement". It focuses on three pillars: upholding tribal identity and integrity, succeeding in education and beyond, and self-determination for socio-economic independence. "Ngai Tahu 2025" sets out Ngāi Tahu's tribal vision orientated around trusted tribal governance; cultural and whānau development; educational opportunities; having tribal members participating in tribal affairs and strengthening marae communities; being part of the decision-making in Aotearoa and in their tribal territory; and managing and growing their cash yield to support their journey.

46 Paparangi Reid and Bridget Robson "The State of the Māori Health" in M. Mulholland and others (eds) *The State of the Māori Nation* (Reed Publishing (NZ) Ltd, Auckland, 2016) at 17.

47 Statistics New Zealand "New Zealand Period Life Tables 2010–2012 Media Release" (2013) <www.stats.govt.nz/browse_for_stats/health/life_expectancy/NZLifeTables_MR10-12.aspx>.

48 Ministry of Health "Suicide and Intentional Harm" <www.health.govt.nz/our-work/populations/maori-health/tatau-kahukura-maori-health-statistics/nga-mana-hauora-tutohu-health-status-indicators/suicide-and-intentional-self-harm>.

49 Matire Harwood and David Tipene-Leach "Diabetes" in B. Robson and R. Harris (eds) *Hauora: Māori Standards of Health IV: 2000–2005* (Te Roopu Rangahau a Hauora a Eru Pomare, Wellington, 2007).

50 Ministry of Health "Socioeconomic Indicators" <www.health.govt.nz/our-work/populations/maori-health/tatau-kahukura-maori-health-statistics/nga-awe-o-te-hauora-socioeconomic-determinants-health/socioeconomic-indicators>.

51 Waitangi Tribunal *The Napier Hospital and Health Services Report* (Legislation Direct, Wellington, 2001) at 54.

52 Waitangi Tribunal *Tu Mai te Rangi! Report on the Crown and Disproportionate Reoffending Rates Report* (Legislation Direct, Wellington, 2017) at 34.

53 At XI.

54 Māmari Stephens "Tūhoe-Crown Settlement – A Transforming Dawn? The Service Management Plan" *Māori Law Review* (October 2014) <http://maorilawreview.co.nz/2014/10/tuhoe-crown-settlement-a-transforming-dawn-the-service-management-plan/>.

55 Christopher Finlayson "Social Services Management Plan With Ngāi Tuhoe Agreed" (2012) <www.beehive.govt.nz/release/social-service-management-plan-ng%C4%81i-tuhoe-agreed>.

56 Geoffrey Palmer "The Treaty of Waitangi – Where to From Here?" (2007) 11 *Otago Law Review* 381.

57 Matthew Palmer *The Treaty of Waitangi in New Zealand's Law and Constitution* (Victoria University Press, Wellington, 2008) at 167.

58 *Radio Assets* [1996] 3 NZLR 140 (CA) at pp 183, 184–185 and 189; *Takamore* [2011] NZCA 587 at [107], [255] and [259]; *Radio Frequencies* [1991] 2 NZLR 129 (CA) at pp 135, 139, 140, 142 and 144; and *Barton-Prescott* [1997] 3 NZLR 179 (Full HC) at p 184.

59 Palmer, above n 57, at 316.

60 At 26.

61 Patrick Gower "Newshub Poll: Record Surge for New Zealand First" (2017) <www.newshub.co.nz/home/politics/2017/06/newshub-poll-record-surge-for-new-zealand-first.html>.

62 *Huakina Development Trust* [1987] 2 NZLR 188 (HC) at 210 per Chilwell J.

63 Palmer, above n 57, at 338–340.

64 At 340–342.

65 Constitutional Advisory Panel *New Zealand's Constitution: A Report on a Conversation: He Kōtuinga Kōrero mō Te Kaupapa Ture o Aotearoa* (Ministry of Justice, Wellington, November 2013) <www.ourconstitution.org.nz/store/doc/FR_Full_Report.pdf p104-105> at 104–112.

66 At 104–112.

67 Rt Hon Dame Sian Elias "The Meaning and Purpose of the Treaty of Waitangi" *Māori Law Review* (October 2015) <http://maorilawreview.co.nz/2015/10/the-meaning-and-purpose-of-the-treaty-of-waitangi-dame-sian-elias/>.

68 Palmer, above n 56, 381.

69 Nicholas Jones "Bill English: Flag Vote Shows Republic a Ways Off" (2016) <www.nzherald.co.nz/nz/news/article.cfm?c_id=1&objectid=11613203>.

70 See Richard Bedford "Republicanism and the Treaty of Waitangi: Cutting the Colonial Ties that Bind" in Robert Patman and Chris Rudd (eds) *Sovereignty Under Siege: Globalization and New Zealand* (Routledge, Oxford, 2005); also see Stacey Kirk "Nearly 60 Per Cent of Kiwis Want the British Monarchy Out – Poll" (2016) <www.stuff.co.nz/national/politics/83864989/nearly-60-per-cent-of-kiwis-want-the-british-monarchy-out-poll>.

10 'He rangi tā Matawhāiti, he rangi tā Matawhānui'

Looking towards 2040[1]

Māmari Stephens

As we look forward to 2040 and the bicentenary of the signing of te Tiriti o Waitangi[2] it is tempting to frame the discussion of '*quo vadis*, Aotearoa?' (Whither goest thou, Aotearoa?) as one giving rise to an instrumental question: just which constitutional or political mechanism, or approach, or plan, or model will best deal with 'the Treaty issue' and give rise to the best result, the most harmonious society, the best protection of rights, and the best and most inclusive overall cultural template?

I. An uncertain place

Such framing may simply not deliver the desired pathway. One particular set of problems arises from the well-known fact that te Tiriti o Waitangi continues to inhabit a position of uncertainty. We are not yet, as peoples and as a nation, at ease with, or reconciled to, our divided history. Consequently, the place of the Treaty is not broadly understood, or defined in New Zealand's social, political, and legal fabric.

As has been well explained by commentators and experts, the Treaty is perhaps most commonly understood, in the context of the general legal framework in New Zealand, to have comprised an international agreement between polities, recognisable within the domestic system to the extent that Parliament has expressly incorporated it within legislation.[3] Consistent with this recognition is its use as an extrinsic aid to statutory interpretation[4] on the courts' presumption that Parliament intends to behave in accordance with Treaty principles.[5] The Treaty is also accorded status as a 'foundational' document. This position is often called legal 'orthodoxy', but despite this assertion, debate continues as to the true nature of what the Treaty *actually* does, as both a matter of Western law and as a matter of Māori law.

Over the past 175 years judges, scholars, politicians, and commentators have variously asserted the Treaty did effect cession of sovereignty to the Crown by *hapū* (tribes), as Māori were capable of ceding sovereignty;[6] or that it did not because Māori were not capable of doing so;[7] or that Māori would never have ceded sovereignty and did not,[8] thus the Treaty legitimised an (illegitimate) constitutional revolution;[9] or that the Treaty become obsolete over the passage of time, like other international treaties;[10] or that the Treaty is a contract,[11] a grand, even sacred compact[12] or covenant, that ought to be *tapu* (sacred), or set aside, from the machinery of law and government;[13] or that it is a supreme law document that upholds and protects Māori power and authority.[14] Each of these positions has been, or is, correct, at least, for some. None of these positions explains at all the real importance of this agreement, one of many, and their contested meanings that have shaped political discourse and revealed what Mark Hickford refers to as the "plurality of powers", legal and political, that jostle for attention in this country.[15]

This ambivalence is hardly new. Regardless, more than 33 pieces of legislation incorporate mentions of the Treaty or Treaty principles, and such references establish the Treaty as a mandatory relevant consideration for a significant amount of State activity. Thus, the Treaty has a very practical effect, despite its ambivalent status. In the context of Crown–Māori relationships, some limited steps have also been taken towards what Carwyn Jones describes as two key objectives of the entire Treaty settlement process, and a central concern of much of Māori legal history: self-determination and reconciliation, although these steps are fraught with tension.[16]

II. A careful debate

Much of the debate about the legal effects and dominant conceptions of the Treaty has been highly sophisticated, in specific contexts. As we have seen in this very book, current Treaty scholarship coalesces a set of richly nuanced accounts of the role, function, and importance of te Tiriti o Waitangi, and its parties, in New Zealand law, society, and cultures. Such scholarship eschews easy foundational narratives that seek to locate te Tiriti o Waitangi as the complete moment that somehow created nationhood, or that ascribe to the Treaty texts any kind of unbalanced exceptionalism. Such scholarship carefully avoids characterising Māori or Crown parties as homogenous entities, as in this scholarly realm uncomplicated dualism is rightly dismissed as an inadequate tool of analysis.

Some degree of this careful nuance has also made its way into the various public platforms established in recent years to pursue and interrogate the roles of the Treaty, particularly within the context of what we conceive to be the New Zealand constitution. For example, as a result of the 2008 Relationship Accord and Confidence and Supply Agreement between the National and Māori parties, the government established the Constitutional Advisory Panel, to stimulate public debate and awareness of the current constitutional arrangements, including the role of te Tiriti o Waitangi. The panel was also to provide Ministers with an understanding of New Zealanders' perspectives on those arrangements.[17]

Further, there was the separate establishment in 2010 of Matike Mai Aotearoa, the Independent Working Group for Constitutional Transformation, at a meeting of the Iwi Chairs' Forum. This establishment arose out of perceptions of Māori constitutional powerlessness in the face of the ongoing persistent exercise by the Crown of constitutional power without apparent Māori input. The working group, convened by Moana Jackson, was charged, in its terms of reference, to develop[18]

> a model for a constitution for our country based on our tikanga and fundamental values, He Whakaputanga o te Rangatiratanga o Niu Tireni (the 1835 Declaration of Independence) and Te Tiriti o Waitangi.

Both consultative processes ran across a broadly similar time period. Both processes provided in-depth information to the public, often by way of public meetings as well as web-based resources. Te Tiriti o Waitangi was a critical component for both processes, and it proved to be the subject of substantial numbers of public submissions. Both processes asked participants to imagine what role the Treaty plays and ought to play, and how it ought to govern how Māori, Pākehā, and other New Zealanders live and share power in this land. Both reports arising from both processes *declined* to recommend a definitive pathway, recommending instead further long-term conversation, further substantive public engagement, further sheer hard work to articulate a shared vision that should be at the base of, or a component of, this country's power-sharing, social, and political future.

While acknowledging that submissions revealed that "many New Zealanders remain sceptical that the Treaty can be a constructive element of our constitution and so may be reluctant to participate in a conversation about its future,"[19] the report of the Constitutional Conversation in 2015 recommended that gradual, inclusive, evolution of the Treaty's place in the New Zealand constitution continue, and recommended that the Government:[20]

- continues to affirm the importance of the Treaty as a foundational document;
- ensures a Treaty education strategy is developed that includes the current role and status of the Treaty and the Treaty settlement process so people can inform themselves about the rights and obligations under the Treaty;
- supports the continued development of the role and status of the Treaty under the current arrangements as has occurred over the past decades;
- sets up a process to develop a range of options for the future role of Treaty, including options within existing constitutional arrangements and arrangements in which the Treaty is the foundation; and
- invites and supports the people of Aotearoa New Zealand to continue the conversation about the place of the Treaty in our constitution.

Matike Mai Aotearoa, by comparison, proffered six possible models for constitutional reform to uphold Māori authority and Māori sovereignty. Most submitters appear to have identified the Treaty as integral to any reform, but even so, Matike Mai Aotearoa refrained from identifying a specific model or code. Instead, the Working Group recommended the following long-term plan:[21]

1 That during the next five years Iwi [tribal federations], Hapū, and other lead Māori organisations promote ongoing formal and informal

discussions among Māori about the need for and possibilities of constitutional transformation.

2 That such discussions also be included as an annual agenda item at national hui [gathering] of lead Māori organisations such as the Waitangi hui of the Iwi Chairs' Forum.

3 That a Māori Constitutional Convention be called in 2021 to further the discussion and develop a comprehensive engagement strategy across the country.

4 That at an appropriate time during the next five years a further Working Group be appointed to begin consideration of relevant structural and procedural issues as they pertain to Māori.

5 That at an appropriate time during the next five years Iwi, Hapū, and lead Māori organisations initiate dialogue with other communities in their rohe [regions] about the need for and possibilities of constitutional transformation.

6 That at an appropriate time during the next five years Iwi, Hapū, and lead Māori organisations initiate formal dialogue with the Crown and local authorities about the need for and possibilities of constitutional transformation.

7 That in 2021 Iwi, Hapū, and lead Māori organisations initiate dialogue with the Crown to organise a Tiriti Convention to further discussions about the need for and possibilities of constitutional transformation.

At the end of perhaps a few years of public consultation processes for these two projects, not to mention other processes in earlier years, it could be said that we are no further along in defining what the Treaty 'truly means' as the basis of any kind of commonly accepted future power-sharing arrangement. So, perhaps, in the context of the future, it does not much matter what the Treaty is supposed to be or do; rather, what matters is what people actually do in their daily lives as a result of its existence. Individuals, interest groups, *hapū*, conglomerates, alliances, will all project on to the Treaty their hopes and fears for the future, regardless of the labels and functions attributed to it.

III. A practical partnership?

In 2011, Justice Joseph Williams made the following observation about the future of the Treaty of Waitangi and the New Zealand constitution: "So, the real question here is not what we should do with the Treaty of Waitangi, but – . . . 'how do we perfect our partnership?' "[22]

Leaving aside those to whom the very idea of a Treaty partnership is anathema (across all cultural and political divides), I choose to interpret these words to refer to the idea of partnership as extending well beyond legislated settlements, political accommodations, regulatory checks and balances, policy documents, and corporate vision statements to the relationships we experience in our everyday reality. The problem is, as we gaze around our current social and political landscape, that true partnership 'on the ground' might well be an elusive thing.

For one thing, exceptionalism, uncomplicated dualism, foundationalism, unvarnished bigotry, and self-interest can be pretty common in ordinary unmediated public discourse about the Treaty in the wake of the Māori resurgence of the 1970s and beyond. These elements of discourse may not advance the bicultural awareness or agenda necessary to implement practical partnership. This is not to ignore the fact that so much more high-quality information is now available to all or most New Zealanders about our history and the role of the Treaty in it.[23] Significant longitudinal research now suggests that one particular roadblock to effective partnership can be simple self-interest in regards to the allocation and preservation of material resources. Research carried out as a part of the University of Auckland's School of Psychology's New Zealand Attitudes and Values Study[24] suggests that the New Zealand Pākehā population is perhaps more likely to be comfortable with a symbolic form of biculturalism, founded upon the idea of the Treaty, but this tolerance is less likely to be sustained if the practical implementation of redistribution is required, threatening economic self-interest. In short, where biculturalism (arguably a necessary condition for partnership) requires sharing of economic resources by Pākehā, it is more difficult to achieve.[25] The authors of this study suggest that this result suggests a reframing of public discourse is needed, away from entrenched ideological contests to address realistic concerns about the threats to self-interest.[26]

Justice Williams has also asserted that we are currently mired in the 'original sin' phase of partnership.[27] In this phase, Māori and Pākehā are often defined in relationship to each other, in terms of fault and blame for hara, or wrongs done, avenged and renewed, that are yet to be expiated, as well as perhaps fear of betrayal.

Indeed, there is a definite tendency for different camps to regard the other in moral and ideological absolutes. At least some of those who believe the Treaty has an important role in the future of New Zealand's constitution appear to regard those who do not as unmitigated racists. By the same token, those who would deny a prominent place for the Treaty in New Zealand's constitution also resent those who think differently, characterising them as 'reverse racists' or bigots, liberal or tribal elites, lacking a connection to the 'real world'. Both broad camps use facts or perceptions of facts to shore up their positions, and the positions are entrenched. In fact, Justice William's notion of our relationships being mired in the 'original sin' phase is consistent with other recent research from the New Zealand Attitudes and Values Study.

In one study, published in 2012, roughly 4,600 Pākehā and 1,600 Māori were surveyed from the 2009 electoral rolls about both Pākehā and Māori cognitions of rejection by each other, ethnic identification, intergroup anxiety, negativity towards each other, and political support for Māori.[28] The study found that members of the majority group (Pākehā) and minority group (Māori) fear rejection from the other group ('outgroup'), and they themselves respond by disparaging that outgroup. The authors of the study conclude this fear of mutual rejection and resulting mutual disparagement at the intergroup level has "tremendous capacity to thwart intergroup relations".[29] But in the case of Māori, such fear of rejection also proves a highly effective motivator for political actions.

In the wake of the year of Trump and Brexit, this demonstrable intergroup tension does not bode well for a measured and a truly bilateral approach to a new era of bottom-up partnership at the level of ordinary lives that reflects or matches some of the more positive partnership developments in regards to regulation, governance, and in some political contexts, as will shortly be discussed. Nor does this tension bode well for moving towards actual constitutional change with broad consent for the role, place, and effect of te Tiriti o Waitangi.

IV. A written constitution for uncertain times?

Perhaps the apotheosis of a top-down approach to constitution-building, albeit with strong and principled regard for a very specific conception of te Tiriti o Waitangi, has recently emerged. September 2016 saw the unveiling of Sir Geoffrey Palmer and Andrew Butler's Constitution Aotearoa project.[30] Unlike its cautious antecedents, the Constitutional Conversation and Matike Mai Aotearoa, this project cuts straight to what its framers hope is a usable outcome by creating a draft constitutional code. This document sets out the rules, principles, and processes about government in one document so that they are accessible, available, and clear to all. This draft code is intended also to eliminate the need for significant unwritten constitutional conventions and customs. Importantly, the document will "remove the mystery and provide an accurate map about how we govern ourselves".[31]

The framers of Constitution Aotearoa view the place and role of te Tiriti o Waitangi as a significant contributor to such mystery. A written constitution could also address the 'problem' of the Treaty's uncertainty. It could be argued that seeking to eradicate constitutional uncertainty ignores the critical role that uncertainty has played in New Zealand political constitutionalism.[32] Te Tiriti o Waitangi was but *one* agreement between the Crown and Māori among hundreds in our multi-textual legal history.[33] Each such agreement opened up new relationships between the signatories (and their descendants), new portals for negotiation, new sites of political uncertainty. These phenomena continue regardless of the state of legal constitutionalism.

To some degree, the minimalist text of the Treaty has provided a degree of potential freedom to the Treaty parties to forge and build such negotiated relationships and *ad hoc* solutions to identifiable problems, these relationships being inherently uncertain. Such relationships, be they co-governance arrangements, political alliances, negotiation-focused, or otherwise, ideally require a focus on which actions and principles would best uphold the relationship between those parties. That also cannot be known in advance. This kind of uncertainty requires constant communication between parties, because there must be an acceptance that no party to the relationship has the privilege of perfect information. Indeed, all perspectives and presumptions are mutable; they are in a state of positive uncertainty.

However, there is a significant danger in over-simplifying the virtue of uncertainty, particularly when that uncertainty results, not from the interpretation of the text of an agreement and the positive dynamic of maintaining a functional relationship, but from lack of transparency or from obfuscation, or from caprice exercised in the context of relationships where a high degree of trust is demanded. If uncertainty results from these things or from lack of access of parties to sufficient information to be able to make decisions, then uncertainty is not positive at all; it creates the potential for abuse and the perpetration of disadvantage.

Thus, the creation of a codified constitution incorporating the texts of the Treaty will, the authors of Constitution Aotearoa expect, eradicate the potential for abuse that may be caused by sterile uncertainty.[34]

Accordingly, the draft constitution seeks to re-visit the 1985 White Paper Proposal that would have seen te Tiriti o Waitangi incorporated in legislation (in that case an entrenched Bill of Rights for New Zealand, which eventually did not come to pass as envisaged).[35] Many Māori at the time opposed the 1985 proposal on the basis that the texts of the Treaty could to be too easily amended.[36] Constitution Aotearoa proposes to include a provision to prevent amendment of the Treaty texts. The relevant draft articles will recognise and affirm existing rights, duties, and obligations held by Māori, and to which the Crown (to become the State) are subject. In addition, the document will affirm that the Treaty is 'always speaking' and that it applies to new circumstances as they arise. The Waitangi Tribunal will remain, and the Waitangi Tribunal and 'established experts' can be consulted on issues involving the Treaty and *tikanga Māori*.[37] Constitution Aotearoa also appears to be a work driven by urgency. Demographic and social change is gathering pace, without the protections the authors view as necessary for retaining a secure and coherent place for the Treaty and Māori rights within our constitutional framework.

It is also important to note that by embarking on this particular journey towards a written constitution, and in providing a draft (republished with a bilingual Māori/English text in April 2018),[38] Sir Geoffrey and Andrew Butler seem to eschew an approach based on constitutional realism, and in particular the notion that constitutional practice (including culture) comes before constitutional form.[39] On the other hand, both authors identify the importance of consultation with Māori,[40] yet downplay the fears of 1986 (assuming that it is just not clear those fears still exist).[41] The authors acknowledge the consultative recommendations of the "long and thoughtful report" of Matike Mai Aotearoa mentioned above, advocating instead the implementation of the much more generic 30 year-old recommendation of the 1986 Royal Commission on the Electoral System, for Parliament and the government to[42]

> enter into consultation and discussion with a wide range of representatives of the Māori people about the definition and protection of the rights of the rights of the Māori people and recognition of their constitutional position under the Treaty of Waitangi.

It remains important, however, to pay heed to the notion of Māori as constitutional agents in their own right: with a constitutional culture worthy of enactment, upon which the Matike Mai report was based. Māori ought not merely be presumed to be a specific subset of citizens, or special interest group, petitioning for the protection of their rights and position. Such an approach, even by default, would restrict any constitutional conversation with Māori to the limits imposed by what Moana Jackson sees as the Crown monologue, of course without the Crown, but with no appreciable change in effect.[43]

Certainly, Constitution Aotearoa does aim to engage in more concrete attempts to allay Māori fears, by way of more substantive, less pigeonholed, engagement. Whether this process as a whole will help us move towards a broader and more practical notion of partnership remains to be seen. The worrisome alternative is that this process achieves little more than further entrenchment of existing and opposed positions. Perhaps the even more worrisome alternative is that nothing comes of these efforts at all.

V. Towards *whanaungatanga*

In addition to legal constitutional change as sought by the authors of the Matike Mai report and Constitution Aoteroa, we must also move to a new and practical era of partnership. Such a partnership reaches beyond (but without jettisoning) elite relationships, legal forms, regulation, policy, and symbolism. We cannot wait until 2040 to do so. We must move to understanding each other (and each other's practical needs) as *whanaunga*, relations, being deeply connected to one another, regardless of ethnic kinship, although, in the changing demographics of this country, such kinship will also inevitably retain importance. In 2017 New Zealand reached the dubious milestone of a prison muster of 10,000 inmates strong, more than half of whom are Māori.[44] We have a long way to go.

So, what to do? For one thing, in our everyday lives, and not just the lives we put on show, we have to resist the temptation to heap scorn and contempt on those we fear or resent. For another, engage with those self-same people. Talk to the people we loathe the most, within reasonable limits. *Whanaungatanga* might be defined as the art of creating connection, perhaps even when we may not want to connect with certain kinds of people. Perhaps those kinds of actions can be counted as part of the enduring legacy of the existence of te Tiriti o Waitangi. Only once that civic form of *whanaungatanga* truly exists for most New Zealanders will substantial formal and legal constitutional change and true power-sharing by broad consensus become possible.

Notes

1 To the person of narrow vision – a narrow horizon, to the person of broad vision – a broad horizon.

2 In this chapter I refer to the proper name of te Tiriti o Waitangi to refer to the full name of the document comprising both language texts, and 'the Treaty' is used as the shorthand label.
3 *Hoani Te Heuheu Tukino v Aotea District Māori Land Board* [1941] AC 308.
4 *Huakina Development Trust v Waikato Valley River Authority* [1987] 2 NZLR 188 (HC).
5 *Attorney-General v New Zealand Māori Council* [1991] 2 NZLR.
6 Grant Morris *Law Alive: The New Zealand Legal System in Context* (3rd ed, Oxford University Press, Melbourne, 2015) at 69.
7 Phillip Joseph *Constitutional and Administrative Law in New Zealand* (4th ed, Thomson Reuters, Wellington, 2014) at 51–52.
8 Waitangi Tribunal *He Whakaputanga me te Tiriti The Declaration and the Treaty: The Report on Stage 1 of the Te Paparahi o Te Raki Inquiry* (Legislation Direct, Wellington, 2014). The Tribunal determined that the Treaty was not a treaty of cession, that is, it was not an agreement, whereby *Rangatira* ceded authority to the Crown to make decisions for *iwi* and *hapū*.
9 F. M. Brookfield *Waitangi and Indigenous Rights: Revolution Law and Legitimation* (Auckland University Press, Auckland, 1999) at 85–107.
10 Jeremy Waldron "FW Guest Memorial Lecture 2005: The Half Life of Treaties: Waitangi, Rebus Sic Stantibus" (2006) 11(2) *Otago LR* 161.
11 K. J. Keith "International Law and New Zealand Municipal Law" in J.F. Northey (ed) *The AG Davies Essays in Law* (Butterworths and Co, London, 1965) 130 at 146; Meredith Gibbs "Justice as reconciliation and restoring mana in New Zealand's Treaty of Waitangi settlement process" (2006) 58(2) *Political Science* 15.
12 Geoffrey Palmer and Andrew Butler *A Constitution for Aotearoa New Zealand* (Victoria University Press, Wellington, 2016) at 148; R. Cooke "Introduction" (1990) 14 *NZULR* 1 at 8.
13 See for example, C. J. Elias "The Meaning and Purpose of the Treaty of Waitangi" (2015) *Māori Law Review* <http://maorilawreview.co.nz/2015/10/the-meaning-and-purpose-of-the-treaty-of-waitangi-dame-sian-elias/>.
14 Moana Jackson "The Treaty and the Word: The Colonization of Māori Philosophy" in Graham Oddie and Roy Perrett (eds) *Justice, Ethics, and New Zealand Society* (Oxford University Press, Auckland, 1992) at 1. Cited in J. Orsman "The Treaty of Waitangi as an Exercise of Māori Constitutent Power" (2012) 43 *Victoria University of Wellington Law Review* 345.
15 Mark Hickford "Interpreting the Treaty – Questions of Native Title, Territorial Government and Searching for Constitutional Histories" in B. Patterson, Richard Hill and Kathryn Patterson (eds) *After the Treaty: The Settler State, Race Relations and Power in Colonial New Zealand* (Steel Roberts, Wellington, 2016) at 101.
16 Carwyn Jones *New Treaty, New Tradition: Reconciling New Zealand and Māori Law* (University of British Columbia Press, Toronto, 2016) at 142–143.
17 Constitutional Advisory Panel "New Zealand's Constitution: A Report on a Conversation: He Kōtuinga Kōrero mō Te Kaupapa Ture o Aotearoa" (2013) *Ministry of Justice* <www.ourconstitution.org.nz/store/doc/FR_Full_Report.pdf> at 9.
18 Moana Jackson and Margaret Mutu "The Working Group for Constitutional Transformation: Primer Number 1" (April 2012) <www.converge.org.nz/pma/iwi-primer1.pdf> at 2.
19 Constitutional Advisory Panel, above n 17, at 22.
20 Constitutional Advisory Panel, above n 17, at 16.
21 Moana Jackson and Margaret Mutu "He Whakaaro Here Whakaumu Mō Aotearoa: The Report of Matike Mai Aotearoa – The Independent Working Group on Constitutional Transformation" (2016) <www.converge.org.nz/pma/MatikeMaiAotearoaReport.pdf> at 11.

22 Justice Joseph Williams "The Status and Nature of the Treaty of Waitangi" in C. Morris, J. Boston and P. Butler (eds) *Reconstituting the Constitution* (Springer, Berlin/Heidelberg, 2011) 185–190 at 186.

23 Particularly in view of the extraordinary popularity of publications such as Claudia Orange's 1987 book *The Treaty of Waitangi*, which has sold over 40,000 copies. Claudia Orange *The Treaty of Waitangi* (rev ed, Bridget Williams Books, Wellington, 2011).

24 In regard to the broader study, see <www.psych.auckland.ac.nz/en/about/our-research/research-groups/new-zealand-attitudes-and-values-study.html>.

25 See Chris G. Sibley and James H. Liu "Attitudes Towards Biculturalism in New Zealand: Social Dominance and Pakeha Attitudes Towards the General Principles and Resource-specific Aspects of Bicultural Policy" (2004) 33(2) *New Zealand Journal of Psychology* 88 at 95. This study identified that biculturalism and the core place of the Treaty of Waitangi was more positively viewed by Pākehā subjects where those subjects did not face direct competition (for example, for access to scholarships in affirmative action programmes).

26 See Sibley and Liu, above n 25, at 96.

27 Williams, above n 22, at 187.

28 Fiona Kate Barlow, Chris G. Sibley, and Matthew J. Hornsey "Rejection as a Call to Arms: Inter-racial Hostility and Support for Political Action as Outcomes of Race-based Rejection in Majority and Minority Groups" (2012) 51(1) *British Journal of Social Psychology* 167.

29 At 175.

30 Palmer and Butler, above n 12, at 148.

31 At 25.

32 Mark Hickford *Lords of the Land: Indigenous Property Rights and the Jurisprudence of Empire* (Oxford University Press, Oxford, 2012) at 9.

33 See generally R. Boast "Rethinking Multi-textualism: Rethinking New Zealand's Legal History" (2006) 37 *VUWLR* 547 at 555–558; R. Boast "Treaties Nobody Counted On" (2011) 42 *VUWLR* 653–670. See also Mark Hickford *Lords of the Land: Indigenous Property Rights and the Jurisprudence of Empire* (Oxford University Press, Oxford, 2012) 101–102.

34 Palmer and Butler, above n 12, at 25.

35 See Geoffrey Palmer "A Bill of Rights for New Zealand: A White Paper" [1984–1985] I *AJHR* A6.

36 Perhaps aptly demonstrating what the researchers in the New Zealand Attitudes and Values Study research from 2012 pointed out above: demonstrable fear of presumed rejection from the minority group (Māori) by the majority group (Pākehā).

37 Draft Articles 72, 73, 74 and Appendix, in Palmer and Butler, above n 12, at 25.

38 In Geoffrey Palmer and Andrew Butler *Towards Democratic Renewal: Ideas for constitutional change in New Zealand* (Victoria University Press, 2018).

39 Matthew Palmer "New Zealand Constitutional Culture" (2007) 22 *NZULR* 565 at 567.

40 At 567.

41 Palmer and Butler, above n 12, 156.

42 Royal Commission on the Electoral System "Towards a Better Democracy" [1986–1987] IX *AJHR* H3 at 112, cited in Palmer and Butler, above n 12, 159.

43 Moana Jackson "Where Does Sovereignty Lie?" in Colin James (ed) *Building the constitution* (Institute of Policy Studies, Wellington, 2000) at 196–200. See also Richard Dawson *The Treaty of Waitangi and the Control of Language* (Institute of Policy Studies, Victoria University of Wellington, 2001).

44 Department of Corrections "Prison Statistics" <www.corrections.govt.nz/resources/research_and_statistics/quarterly_prison_statistics.html>.

Appendix

THE TREATY OF WAITANGI

(The Text in English)

HER MAJESTY VICTORIA Queen of the United Kingdom of Great Britain and Ireland regarding with Her Royal favour the Native Chiefs and Tribes of New Zealand and anxious to protect their just Rights and Property and to secure to them the enjoyment of Peace and Good Order has deemed it necessary in consequence of the great number of Her Majesty's Subjects who have already settled in New Zealand and the rapid extension of Emigration both from Europe and Australia which is still in progress to constitute and appoint a functionary properly authorized to treat with the Aborigines of New Zealand for the recognition of Her Majesty's Sovereign authority over the whole or any part of those islands—Her Majesty therefore being desirous to establish a settled form of Civil Government with a view to avert the evil consequences which must result from the absence of the necessary Laws and Institutions alike to the native population and to Her subjects has been graciously pleased to empower and to authorize me William Hobson a Captain in Her Majesty's Royal Navy Consul and Lieutenant Governor of such parts of New Zealand as may be or hereafter shall be ceded to her Majesty to invite the confederated and independent Chiefs of New Zealand to concur in the following Articles and Conditions.

Article the First

The Chiefs of the Confederation of the United Tribes of New Zealand and the separate and independent Chiefs who have not become members of the Confederation cede to Her Majesty the Queen of England absolutely and without reservation all the rights and powers of Sovereignty which the said Confederation or Individual Chiefs respectively exercise or possess, or may be supposed to exercise or to possess over their respective Territories as the sole Sovereigns thereof.

Article the Second

Her Majesty the Queen of England confirms and guarantees to the Chiefs and Tribes of New Zealand and to the respective families and individuals thereof the full exclusive and undisturbed possession of their Lands and Estates Forests Fisheries and other properties which they may collectively or individually possess so long as it is their wish and desire to retain the same in their possession; but the Chiefs of the United Tribes and the individual Chiefs yield to Her Majesty the exclusive right of Preemption over such lands as the proprietors thereof may be disposed to alienate at such prices as may be agreed upon between the respective Proprietors and persons appointed by Her Majesty to treat with them in that behalf.

Article the Third

In consideration thereof Her Majesty the Queen of England extends to the Natives of New Zealand Her royal protection and imparts to them all the Rights and Privileges of British Subjects.

(Signed)
William Hobson, Consul and Lieutenant-Governor

Now therefore We the Chiefs of the Confederation of the United Tribes of New Zealand being assembled in Congress at Victoria in Waitangi and We the Separate and Independent Chiefs of New Zealand claiming authority over the Tribes and Territories which are specified after our respective names, having been made fully to understand the Provisions of the foregoing Treaty, accept and enter into the same in the full spirit and meaning thereof: in witness of which we have attached our signatures or marks at the places and the dates respectively specified.

Done at Waitangi this Sixth day of February in the year of Our Lord One thousand eight hundred and forty.

[*Here follow signatures, dates, etc.*]

(The Text in Māori)

Ko Wikitoria, te Kuini o Ingarani, i tana mahara atawai ki nga Rangatira me nga Hapu o Nu Tirani i tana hiahia hoki kia tohungia ki a ratou o ratou rangatiratanga, me to ratou wenua, a kia mau tonu hoki te Rongo ki a ratou me te Atanoho hoki kua wakaaro ia he mea tika kia tukua mai tetahi Rangatira hei kai wakarite ki nga Tangata māori o Nu Tirani-kia wakaaetia e nga Rangatira māori te Kawanatanga o te Kuini ki nga wahikatoa o te Wenua nei me nga Motu-na te mea hoki he tokomaha ke nga tangata o tona Iwi Kua noho ki tenei wenua, a e haere mai nei.

Na ko te Kuini e hiahia ana kia wakaritea te Kawanatanga kia kaua ai nga kino e puta mai ki te tangata Māori ki te Pakeha e noho ture kore ana.

Na, kua pai te Kuini kia tukua a hau a Wiremu Hopihona he Kapitana i te Roiara Nawi hei Kawana mo nga wahi katoa o Nu Tirani e tukua aianei, amua atu ki te Kuini e mea atu ana ia ki nga Rangatira o te wakaminenga o nga hapu o Nu Tirani me era Rangatira atu enei ture ka korerotia nei.

Ko te Tuatahi

Ko nga Rangatira o te Wakaminenga me nga Rangatira katoa hoki ki hai i uru ki taua wakaminenga ka tuku rawa atu ki te Kuini o Ingarani ake tonu atu-te Kawanatanga katoa o o ratou wenua.

Ko te Tuarua

Ko te Kuini o Ingarani ka wakarite ka wakaae ki nga Rangatira ki nga hapu-ki nga tangata katoa o Nu Tirani te tino rangatiratanga o o ratou wenua o ratou kainga me o ratou taonga katoa. Otiia ko nga Rangatira o te Wakaminenga me nga Rangatira katoa atu ka tuku ki te Kuini te hokonga o era wahi wenua e pai ai te tangata nona te Wenua-ki te ritenga o te utu e wakaritea ai e ratou ko te kai hoko e meatia nei e te Kuini hei kai hoko mona.

Ko te Tuatoru

Hei wakaritenga mai hoki tenei mo te wakaaetanga ki te Kawanatanga o te Kuini-Ka tiakina e te Kuini o Ingarani nga tangata māori katoa o Nu Tirani ka tukua ki a ratou nga tikanga katoa rite tahi ki ana mea ki nga tangata o Ingarani.

(Signed)
William Hobson, Consul and Lieutenant-Governor

Na ko matou ko nga Rangatira o te Wakaminenga o nga hapu o Nu Tirani ka huihui nei ki Waitangi ko matou hoki ko nga Rangatira o Nu Tirani ka kite nei i te ritenga o enei kupu, ka tangohia ka wakaaetia katoatia e matou, koia ka tohungia ai o matou ingoa o matou tohu.

Ka meatia tenei ki Waitangi i te ono o nga ra o Pepueri i te tau kotahi mano, e waru rau e wa te kau o to tatou Ariki.

Ko nga Rangatira o te wakaminenga.

Glossary

Atua god or gods
Hapū tribe
Hononga connections
Hui meeting; gathering
Iwi tribal federation
Kaitiakitanga guardianship
Kaupapa discussion topics
Kawa ceremony
Kāwanatanga governorship; government
Kawenata covenant
Kōrero speech
Mana motuhake self-determination; self-government
Mana whenua territorial rights
Mana prestige or status; spiritually sanctioned authority
Marae meeting house; courtyard or spiritual and symbolic centre of community affairs
Mātauranga education
Mauri life force
Moko facial tattoo
Mokopuna descendants
Motu land or island
Paepae orator's bench
Pou support posts
Pōwhiri welcome ceremony
Rangatira chief or person of high rank
Rangatiratanga chieftainship
Rohe region
Tangata whenua indigenous people of the land
Taniwha water spirit/monster
Taonga treasure; those things which are highly valued
Tapu sacred
Te ao Māori the Māori world
Te reo Māori Māori language

Te tiriti o Waitangi the Treaty of Waitangi
Tikanga Māori law; protocol; a customary system of values and norms, embedded in social contexts; the right or correct way of doing things
Tino rangatiratanga sovereignty or self-determination; chiefly authority
Tipuna ancestor
Tohunga skilled spiritual leaders or experts
Utu reciprocity
Wai water
Waiata song
Whakapapa genealogy
Whakataukī proverb
Whānau ora family health
Whānau family or extended family
Whanaungatanga the centrality of relationships
Whenua land

Index